# PORTRAIT OF
# NORTH YORKSHIRE

*By the same author*
Walking in the Yorkshire Dales
Yorkshire Dales Anthology

*Portrait of*
# NORTH YORKSHIRE

by

## Colin Speakman

ROBERT HALE · LONDON

© *Colin Speakman 1986*
*First published in Great Britain 1986*

Robert Hale Limited
Clerkenwell House
Clerkenwell Green
London EC1R 0HT


British Library Cataloguing in Publication Data

Speakman, Colin
  Portrait of North Yorkshire.
  1. North Yorkshire—Description and travel
  I. Title
  914.28′404858        DA670.N68

  ISBN 0-7090-2580-7

To the memory of Dr Frederick Michael Penford,
traveller extraordinary, who would have enjoyed
a journey through these pages.

Photoset in North Wales by
Derek Doyle & Associates, Mold, Clwyd.
Printed in Great Britain by
St Edmundsbury Press, Bury St Edmunds, Suffolk.
Bound by Hunter & Foulis Limited.

# Contents

# Illustrations

*Between pages 176 and 177*

## CREDITS

The following photographs are reproduced by kind permission of: John Fawcett, 1, 26; Geoffrey N. Wright, 2, 3, 4, 5, 8, 9, 11, 12, 13, 14, 15, 17, 20, 21, 23, 25, 32, 35, 36; Howard Beck, 6, 7, 16, 28, 29, 34; Lydia Speakman, 24, 33; Simon Warner, 27; and the author, 10, 18, 19, 22, 30, 31, 37, 38, 39, 40

# Introduction

A portrait is a somewhat personal thing.

It can do no more, in the space of a small canvas, with a few brush strokes, than capture a few chosen aspects of its subject.

That's as true if you work in words as if you handle paint.

And if it so happens that the subject is as complex, rich and diverse as North Yorkshire, the task might seem a hopeless one.

Better by far, therefore, to produce a series of sketches, outlines, themes which the reader can for him or herself transform into a fuller picture, filling in detail, adding colour, depth.

So I have taken eight related themes and in eight chapters – following a brief chapter to put North Yorkshire into some kind of context – chosen to present each of these different aspects.

Now the intention is, let us say this from the outset, to persuade the reader to go and see for him or herself what it's all about. Wherever possible we'll descend from the general to the particular, to name a particular place where there's something to see and do.

Though the armchair reader, whether a total stranger to North Yorkshire or someone who knows the county well, should have enough to enjoy, the emphasis is on seeing, looking, sharing.

'Heritage' is a somewhat over-used word, but it does at least imply something worth sharing with both present and future generations. North Yorkshire has got quite a lot of things that fall into that category, much of it of national importance. Almost everything that appears in this book can be easily and readily seen, though you might have to leave car or coach and make some modest physical effort to get there.

There's a look at the physical evolution of the landscape, then something of the human influence. The monastic communities who made such a profound impact on landscape and culture come into focus, followed by a brief glance at the rise of the great country houses and estates that are still one of North Yorkshire's chief glories. Then the story of North Yorkshire's most famous spa town and seaside resort, Harrogate and Scarborough, before a change of mood to see how communications across those broad acres have also left a considerable impact on town and countryside. Finally, there's something of the twin contributions of agriculture and industry, forces very much at work in the creation of North Yorkshire of the twenty-first century.

Now *Portrait of North Yorkshire* forms part of a famous series of *Portrait* guides and as such needs to avoid undue overlap with three other recent books which also deal with North Yorkshire – Ronald Willis' *Portrait of York,* Frank Duerden's *Portrait of the Dales* and Peter N. Walker's *Portrait of the North Yorkshire Moors.*

But if you try to take out the great city of York from the centre of North Yorkshire, then lop off the Dales and Moors from the west and east respectively, you're left with a very odd-shaped county indeed, an author's nightmare.

The solution has been largely to ignore York itself, a very self-contained city so admirably dealt with in Ronald Willis' excellent guide, and only very selectively to trespass into the two major National Park areas, focusing, wherever possible, on areas outside the Dales and Moors. It doesn't always follow. You can't talk about industry in North Yorkshire and ignore Dales lead-mining and Cleveland iron-mining for instance. But where possible the aim has been to dovetail with my illustrious predecessors, concentrating on what is essential to the North Yorkshire story rather than the particular local region.

So much for Part I of *Portrait of North Yorkshire*

Part II is a brief guide to seventeen North Yorkshire towns. These have all been chosen because they are well worth a trip out to see and enjoy, and although York again has been excepted (and why not – the other towns of North Yorkshire are often unjustly overlooked), a few within the Dales and Moors are included for completeness' sake.

Each town enjoys a brief introduction and then, on the principle of it's nice to have a stroll around in between shops, cafés and museum, there's a suggested walk, looking at some of the more impressive buildings and viewpoints. Towns always have a lot of interest in their own right.

Sadly there hasn't been space to include several larger villages or towns with much to offer, towns such as Hawes, Leyburn, Northallerton, Harrogate, Scarborough or Whitby. In some cases this is because they are included elsewhere in the text, or, like Whitby, are described so well in Peter Walker's *Portrait of the North York Moors*. But they should not be neglected for that reason.

# Acknowledgements

Every author is something of a magpie; this author particularly so. There isn't space to list all the very many sources or all the people who have given help and advice, but here is a brief list of some of the most valuable sources which helped get this book into being: Sir Nikolaus Pevsner's *Buildings of England,* especially *North Riding* and *West Riding,* Professor Jennings and his WEA Group on Harrogate and Knaresborough, and local guides by Arnold Kellett (Knaresborough, Harrogate), Barbara Blakeson (Harrogate), Ted Gower (Filey, Whitby, Grassington), J.M.Melhuish (Middleham), Muriel Humphries (Ingleton), Ted Pearson (Ripon), Susan Cunliffe-Lister (Masham), Patricia Brady (Masham) Malcolm Boyes (Richmond), Geoffrey Rowley (Skipton), Joan and Bill Spence (North Yorkshire Monasteries), the Middleham Publicity Association, A.J.Pollard (Middleham), the North Craven Heritage Trust (Settle), the Richmond Civic Society, Raymond Fieldhouse and the Scarborough and District Civic Society, Thirsk Museum, the Rotunda Museum of Scarborough, whose 1985 exhibition of three hundred years of Scarborough entertainment was an inspiration, and Ralph Robinson, Public Relations Officer of North Yorkshire County Council, whose help has been particularly appreciated.

And finally to my wife, Fleur, who has typed, edited, indexed and deciphered much of the manuscript and who has provided help and support in so many ways.

# Part I

*The Evolution of a County*

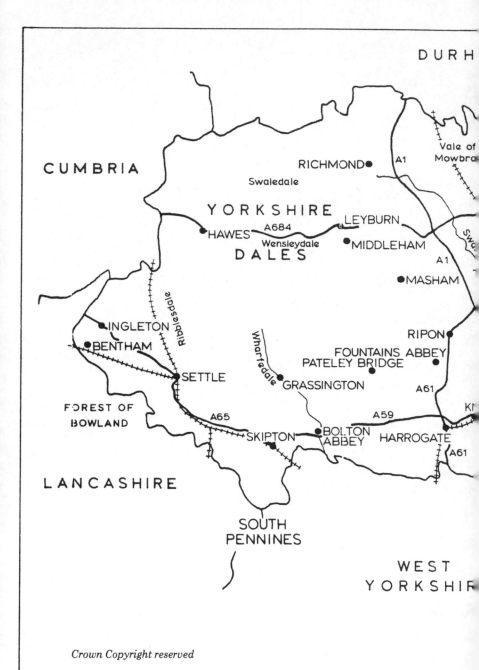

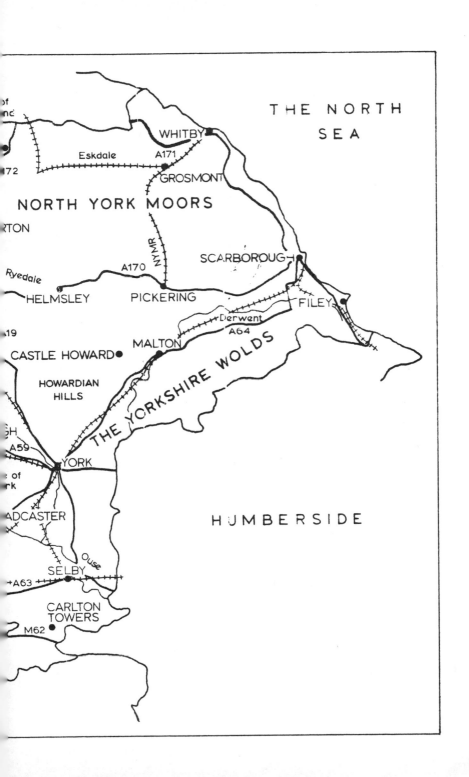

# 1

## Why North Yorkshire?

North Yorkshire, England's largest county, is immense. Its 3,200 square miles, or 2 million acres, make it as big as many a small country or province. It's approximately the same size, for example, as Cyprus and Puerto Rico. It's three times the size of Luxembourg. It's almost a quarter the size of both Holland and Belgium.

Stretching from the dizzily high cliffs against which the North Sea pounds in the east, to within sight (from hilltops) of the glittering Irish Sea in Morecambe Bay in the west, from the edge of the South Yorkshire coalfield a few miles north of Doncaster in the south, to County Durham and Teesdale in the north, it dominates northern England. Once out of North Yorkshire to the north, you're in the Border Country. To the south of North Yorkshire you're in the Midlands.

Look at a map of North Yorkshire. It's an odd shape, rather like a gigantic oak tree, the branches extending across the North York Moors to the east, and across the high Pennines and Yorkshire Dales to the west, the great trunk of the tree going down through the Vale of York, past Selby, until it squeezes its narrow way between the great bulk of West Yorkshire and Humberside, actually reaching a point south of both Pontefract and Goole.

It's not a shape that makes any sense in terms of physical geography. True, there's the coast in the north-east, the Pennine watersheds in the north-west, the odd length of river like the Wharfe, the Derwent and the Went upon which to inscribe a convenient boundary. But these things together no way explain that odd shape.

17

It's only when you realize that the total population of North Yorkshire is a mere 680,000 that you begin to understand why. What is missing from North Yorkshire is any major, industrial conurbation on the scale of those in West Yorkshire, Cleveland or even Humberside. More people live in Leeds Metropolitan District alone than in the whole of North Yorkshire, and West Yorkshire's population of just over two million live in an area barely a fifth the size.

North Yorkshire was created at the time of local government reorganization in England and Wales in 1974. Many people at that time held the view that the new local government boundaries should, as the Redcliffe-Maud Report had proposed, reflect the influence of the major towns and cities on the rural hinterland. You can trace this 'hinterland' influence in how and where people commute to for work, business or major shopping trip, where buses and trains run to and from and, above all, an excellent test, by what evening papers they read.

On this basis, much of North Yorkshire might, in the north, have gone into either Cleveland or Durham; towns to the west such as Ingleton and Bentham would have gone into Lancashire, whilst Bradford's influence would have extended as far as Ribblesdale and the top of Wharfedale, with Leeds taking in Harrogate, Knaresborough and perhaps even Ripon. York might well have found itself the focal point of a new county covering much of the Vale of York and taking in part of the Moors, the Howardian Hills, Scarborough and the coast, and part of the northern Wolds.

Such proposals, logical though they might have seemed in many ways, were received with almost universal dismay by people living in the outlying areas who didn't want in any way to consider themselves city folk or to be dominated by city authorities. The 1972 Local Government Act in effect rejected the Redcliffe-Maude proposals and created, in North Yorkshire, that huge new predominantly rural county that communities living even quite close to the major conurbations were anxious to join, wishing to be identified with the rolling acres to the north or south rather than with industry and urban life.

Now in many ways this isn't at all surprising. English people are essentially country people at heart, even if they've lived in cities for many generations. If they dislike towns, they positively hate

cities and are glad to escape from them at every opportunity;
where they have to live in city suburbs, they quickly create round
themselves an image of rural seclusion in the form of an
attractive suburban garden. A rural area, however, is somewhere
to escape to. A village is somewhere to belong in. If the village is
also in attractive countryside, what better place to live in (even if
you've to travel some considerable distance, by car, every day
into that dreaded city to work) or to retire to?

In a nutshell, therefore, North Yorkshire is Yorkshire with all
the major centres of population taken out – the Leeds, Bradfords,
Sheffields, Hulls, Middlesbroughs – like great bites taken out of
a slice of bread, leaving that curious shape.

Only York remains as a city of some importance, with a
population of over 100,000. Only Harrogate and Scarborough
have a claim to be something more than country towns, and they
too are linked, historically, as we shall see, to the old West
Riding cities by an umbilical cord of road and rail.

The irony is, of course, that all the way around the edge of the
conurbations, in the bigger villages, the population is increasing,
as people move out of West Yorkshire and Cleveland into North
Yorkshire, converting country cottages and farmhouses, buying
property on new executive housing estates, requiring schools,
shops and transport facilities with them, extending the cities
into the new county and in so doing making nonsense of political
boundaries.

Nevertheless, North Yorkshire is still vast enough to absorb
such changes. The heartland remains a true rural county.

This isn't to say it lacks industry. Far from it. Even forgetting
agriculture and tourism, major industries in their own right,
there's some fairly heavy industry in North Yorkshire. 'Rural' is
something different.

'Rural' is really a way of looking and thinking about things.
It's to do with country ways and country values, traditional ways
of thinking about things and doing things. It's about networks of
friendships and relationships, an attitude of mind which can also
be parochial in outlook, suspicious of strangers, slow to accept
change.

So, in a sense, that serpentine boundary of North Yorkshire is
more ideological than geographical, bringing together rural
communities as vastly different as Bentham, only a few miles

from Lancaster, Thixendale in the chalk Wolds, Castleton in the
North York Moors, Robin Hood's Bay on the coast, and Hensall,
in the shadow of Eggborough Power Station in the south, and
administrating them from a small market town, Northallerton,
in the far north.

It's wrong to make too much of boundaries. Old allegiances,
old loyalties cling. The old West Riding, carved up between
West, South and North Yorkshire, and even between Cumbria
and Lancashire, in 1974, is still alive in the hearts and minds of
people of the older generation. The name Yorkshire is more
potent a sense of place than any initial epithet, and this is
entirely as it should be.

And whether politicians, planners or bureaucrats appreciate
the point or not, the old relationships between town and
countryside exist and are very much alive in Yorkshire – for
example, between the cities of what is now West Yorkshire and
the countryside and country towns of North Yorkshire, and
between the industrial towns of Cleveland and the North York
Moors.

If you live in the towns or cities, North Yorkshire is the
countryside into which you go for a drive or a ramble, for a
pleasant shopping trip or seaside visit, for an educational outing
or merely to escape urban drabness.

Escapism isn't necessarily a bad thing. Wherever or however
you spend your leisure time, whether it's bird-watching,
archaeology, botany, photography or simply absorbing the
beauty of the landscape, this time may well be the most
important, the most significant, in your life, far more important
than the routine tasks you have to perform to earn a living or
keep yourself alive. As the century progresses towards its close, it
seems that leisure pursuits will be of ever greater significance,
and a county like North Yorkshire, relatively unspoiled, rich in
history and beauty, will be of increasing importance to people
not only from the conurbations of West Yorkshire and Teesside
but from many other parts of Britain including the Midlands and
the South East and, increasingly, for visitors from overseas.

The other side of the coin shows the inhabitants of North
Yorkshire vitally dependent on the cities – not merely on the
relatively tangible things like shopping trips and services but on
their market for produce and their own services. Farming, in

particular, would have a lean time of it in North Yorkshire but for the existence of large, insatiable appetites for beef, cereals, wool and dairy produce in the wholesale markets of the conurbations.

Anyone who fails to understand this complex and constant interaction between town and countryside in North Yorkshire fails to appreciate some important truths about the nature of both urban and rural communities.

How is this vast area administered ?

The highest tier of local government is a directly elected assembly, the County Council, elected every four years and meeting at the majestic County Hall in Northallerton, former headquarters of the old North Riding County Council. Like all local authorities, the county council divides into several major sub-committees to handle responsibilities which include highways, transportation, planning, education, libraries, police, National Parks. Each committee controls its own staff and budgets, raising revenue from rates and from a government rate-support grant.

The sheer size and complexity of North Yorkshire pose special problems of scale and logistics. County Councillors must travel often considerable distance to vital council and council committee meetings. Officers must likewise cover enormous mileages on official duties, simply to get around the county. The County Surveyor, for example, has no fewer than six thousand miles of road to look after, enough to stretch half way around the world. There are more than fourteen hundred bridges to maintain, some of them old and historic structures dating back several centuries. More than two hundred lorries have to be kept available for conversion to snowploughs to keep roads open during the long North Yorkshire winter, supplemented when necessary by another three hundred vehicles belonging to local farmers and hauliers. The budget for gritting and snowploughing alone for an average winter comes to around £2 million, and very much more in a bad winter. The total highways budget is £23 million per annum.

Education is another country service where distance and isolation can cause problems. North Yorkshire has more than twice the national average of small primary schools (i.e. fewer than fifty-one pupils) and small secondary schools (fewer than

401). This simply reflects the nature of scattered rural communities but means higher than average maintenance and administrative costs than in more centralized counties. Country schools are, however, vital focal points of rural communities, and the County Council's policy is to keep schools open wherever humanly possible.

Libraries, social services, police, fire services, planning, consumer protection and museum services are all County Council functions, and all have to cope with the problems of distance. It is a tribute to the quality of officers and management within North Yorkshire County Council that, even at a time of severe expenditure restraint, standards are in fact so high.

Two of North Yorkshire County Council's major committees differ in fundamental ways from other committees. These are the two National Park Committees – the North York Moors National Park Committee and the Yorkshire Dales National Park Committee.

Although North Yorkshire's two National Parks do not enjoy the same degree of autonomy as the Peak District and the Lake District, which have Special Planning Boards that precept the relevant local authorities for funds, membership of these committees is split between the constituent County Councils (the Moors and Dales have members from Cleveland and Cumbria respectively) with representative members of District Councils. A third of their members however, are appointed directly by the Secretary of State for the Environment. These are people with specialist interest and knowledge of farming, wildlife conservation, archaeology and outdoor recreational pursuits; they bring to the relevant park committees a national perspective to balance more parochial interests. Given the importance, to the nation, of these, the region's finest heritage landscapes, and the fact that the nation foots the equivalent of eighty-five per cent of the bill for their administration and activity, this is entirely as it should be. Whether or not arrangements have worked as well as they should in either National Park is open to some debate, but there has nevertheless been major progress in conservation and recreational management in both National Parks since 1974.

The second, more local tier of government in North Yorkshire consists of the District Councils. There are five purely rural District Councils in North Yorkshire – Craven (based in Skipton),

Hambleton (based in Northallerton), Richmondshire, Ryedale (based at Malton) and Selby, together with two incorporated boroughs, Harrogate and Scarborough, and, of course, the City of York. In effect the two boroughs and York City Council exercise the same powers as the Districts, though they have other historic powers and responsibilities. They are all responsible for local planning matters, housing and refuse collection and share certain other functions such as local transport and tourism with the county council.

The third, and lowest, tier, but a vital part of local democracy, are parish councils or parish meetings, which in a rural community are a focal point of local opinion and have powers to achieve useful environmental improvement within villages, as well as being the owners and managers of such useful facilities as village halls.

No account of local democracy in an area like North Yorkshire would be complete without some reference to local voluntary groups and organizations, from parochial church councils to Women's Institutes, voluntary amenity groups and charitable organizations which form part of that important but unseen network within the rural community. The Yorkshire Rural Community Council, based in York, acts, with local authority assistance and support, as a valuable link between various groups in North Yorkshire villages. The voluntary network, organizing transport, meals, care and concern, is one way in which local communities in North Yorkshire compensate for the disadvantages of distance.

Enough of bureaucracy and country institutions. To the countryside itself.

# 2

# A Matter of Rock

Let's begin with the bedrock.

Rock, more than anything else, determines the shape and, through its effect on soil and vegetation, the colour of a landscape. The beauty and astonishing variety of North Yorkshire's contrasting landscapes reflect an equally contrasting underlying rock structure.

If you take an imaginary line from Ingleton in the west to Scarborough in the east and plot along that line the rocks that underlie, and in many places intrude upon, the landscape, you would produce a geological time-chart covering well over a million years of the Earth's history. In shape the line would look like the silhouette of a gigantic, broad-rimmed dish, the western rim, sloping into the central bowl, formed from the ancient Carboniferous rocks that constitute the Pennines. To the east the upreared rim is formed from newer Jurassic rocks that rise to the broad summits of the North York Moors and continue to the sea cliffs of the coast. The centre of our bowl contains the richly fertile Vale of York and Vale of Mowbray, whose intermediate Triassic rocks lie buried deep underneath the clays of alluvium.

Little wonder that North Yorkshire, throughout the last century and well into the present one, attracted many of the great names of British – and that meant world – geology. Geology is, in many ways, a supremely nineteenth-century science, reflecting the Victorian passion for observation and endless classification. But for the early Victorians in particular, geology was the great scientific, and even religious, frontier, the work of many gifted professional and amateur geologists helping to piece together our own understanding of the planet Earth and its inhabitants, the equivalent to the twentieth-century imagination of nuclear physics and radio astronomy exploring the outer limit of the known universe. So they came, the great men, to unravel Yorkshire's geology. Men like William 'Strata' Smith, called 'the Father of Modern Geology', who produced the first scientifically reliable geological maps of England and Wales in 1815 and who lived for many years in Scarborough. Men like Adam Sedgwick, born in Dent (which used to be part of Yorkshire until 1974) and now recognized as one of the world's greatest field geologists, who first understood and explained the complex faulting system of the Pennines. Men like John Phillips, curator of the Yorkshire Museum at York, who first described the Yoredale limestones and whose book *The Geology of Yorkshire* is one of the great classics of geology. Or even figures like the Reverend William Buckland who excavated Kirkdale Cave, near Kirkby Moorside, and saw evidence, albeit mistakenly, of Noah's flood. These remarkable figures, and many who literally followed in their footsteps, have provided a treasure-house of information to help later generations understand how Yorkshire came to be.

So, to share that understanding of what makes North Yorkshire, let's start in the west, where the dramatic landscape of the Yorkshire Dales is a paradise even for the most amateur geologist. There isn't space here to attempt to unravel the incessant process of subterranean pressure, contortion and upthrust that created mountainous ranges, such as the Pennines, nor to detail the long periods of weathering and erosion which took place until mountain summits lay under great seas, to be subsequently covered by sediment, sand, clay and skeletons of long extinct creatures, before being once again thrust upwards in some cataclysmic mountain-creating upheaval.

An image geologists use is that of a vast layer cake, each layer with its different kind of rock and remains of fossilized creatures, representing a different era of the Earth's history. The layers do not remain level for long but are compressed and squeezed, fractured and shattered, perhaps worn away competely by the rivers, seas, wind and rain of later ages. Often enough clues remain in the rock, to be identified by their texture, colour or particular fossil creatures, for geologists to piece together part of the puzzle.

The Pennines were formed from just such a folding, with the Carboniferous rocks (that is, rocks of coal-bearing age which indeed include some Coal Measures), laid down some 340–280 million years ago, pushing upwards into the surface, their covering of new rocks long eroded away to leave their limestones and gritstones exposed – and forming the landscape we enjoy today.

What makes the Yorkshire Dales rather special, differing in appearance from the gritstone of the South Pennines, south of the Aire Gap, is limestone.

Limestone is a sedimentary rock, laid down in shallow tropical seas (Britain was, in mid-Carboniferous times, close to the Equator). You have to imagine millions of sea creatures, such as corals and molluscs, whose skeletons and shells sank slowly to form a white, hard sediment, many hundreds of feet thick which, after countless ages of compression, has turned into grey-white rock which gleams white in the sun, its fossils extruding so perfectly that early geologists were convinced that to find such sea shells on a mountaintop proved, indeed, the truth of Genesis and Noah's flood.

In the Dales, the limestones have been particularly and spectacularly exposed. It is as if a great fist had, between the Aire and the Tees, pushed upwards against the earth's surface so fiercely that great cracks or faults have appeared, tipping the countryside eastwards as huge sections, in places many thousands of feet thick, were lifted upwards to reveal those underlying layers in the west and south, creating in the Craven district of North Yorkshire in particular some of the finest limestone features in England, the very name Craven being derived from the Celtic 'Craeg wan', 'land of crags'. This upthrust, on a bed of ancient granite, created what is known as the Askrigg Bock. In some places, the upheaval was so great that the most ancient rocks of the Pennines, underneath even the Carboniferous Limestone and gritstones, are exposed.

The best place to see such rocks from a footpath is in the Ingleton Glens, that 4½-mile walk round the waterfalls in Ingleton, where the Rivers Twiss and Doe have carved deeply into the living rock, exposing ancient bluish Silurian and Ordovician slates and mudstones, rocks that pre-date the Carboniferous System by between 65 and 120 million years, a timescale almost impossible to grasp in its sheer immensity. If you follow the path along the Twiss as far as the beautiful Thornton Force, you can actually see where the Carboniferous Limestone overlies the ancient Ordovician rocks, and span with the fingers of your hand a geological period of well over 100 million years. This is what geologists describe as an unconformity, the intervening layers of Devonian and Silurian rocks, representing vast ages of geological time, having been totally eroded away.

It is on or near the cracks or fault lines in the earth's surface in the south and west of the Dales that many of the most spectacular features appear – Kilnsey Crag in Wharfedale, Gordale Scar near Malham where the beck has cut its way into a deep gorge, Malham Cove itself, relic of a gigantic, prehistoric waterfall, Attermire Scar above Settle, and Giggleswick Scar, such an obvious feature to motorists driving along the A65 across Buckhaw Brow between Settle and Ingleton.

This thick bed of limestone, many hundreds of feet thick, is for self-evident reasons called Great Scar or Mountain Limestone; not only is it rock of great beauty but it has considerable economic importance as quarries at Giggleswick, at Horton in Ribblesdale, in Wharfedale and at Embsay near Skipton bear witness, being an essential material for use in the steel, chemical and construction industries. This can lead to conflict between conservation and industrial interests as, almost by definition, limestone quarries and all the noise, dust and traffic they produce lie in areas of great natural beauty.

Not only does limestone outcrop along the fault lines in Craven, and along various escarpments, but, being water-soluble along its many joints, it quickly weathers into remarkable natural features. Limestone pavements, for example, are created where acid rainwater dissolves along the joint lines to produce the characteristic 'clints' (rock) between the 'grykes' (fissures). There is more limestone pavement in North Yorkshire than anywhere else in British Isles except for southern Ireland.

The action of water on limestone also creates the famous pot-holes of North Yorkshire as surface streams find their way underground, in many cases into complex underground cave systems, none more spectacular than Gaping Gill on the shoulder of Ingleborough, where a slender cataract of water tumbles into a space big enough to contain St Paul's Cathedral, and at Alum Pot, close to the B6479 at Selside in Ribblesdale, where foam from the thundering waterfall disappearing into a tree-lined hole was believed, by early travellers, to be smoke from the fires of Hell. Little wonder that the Yorkshire Dales almost became known as 'the Cave District' and the region remains the best caving and pot-holing region in Britain.

If you don't want to risk life and limb, three dry, well-lit show caves welcome visitors. These are White Scar Cave near Ingleton on the Ingleton-Hawes road, Ingleborough Cave, a mile and a half along the path through the Ingleborough estate road from Clapham village on the A65, and Stump Cross Cavern on the B6160 road between Grassington and Pateley Bridge, the latter with a splendid exhibition of recent finds of fossil mammals in the cave, which include remains of hyena and wolverine.

A particularly impressive little limestone gorge, which gives insight into the power of fast-flowing Pennine streams to cut deeply into the limestone, can be discovered if you find your way up to How Stean, at the top of Nidderdale, where carefully constructed paths round the edge of the gorge offer splendid viewpoints. There's even a short length of cave to wander down, Tom Taylor's Cave. But limestone country offers much to charm even the least energetic, a lightness, a softness. The pastures are sweet and fertile, ash trees twist out of the miles of drystone walls, small farmsteads and scattered barns seem to have grown organically out of the landscape. Limestone country is superb walking country, always with interesting features to observe from footpath or bridleway.

As you climb from the more fertile valley floor, where the rich soils brought down by ancient glaciers or flooding rivers yield to the thin soils of the valleysides where the white rock juts out like bone, you will be aware of the scent of wild thyme, the flash of colour of wild flowers, and then further changes of vegetation as you move towards the more acid gritstones of the hilltops.

Above the Great Scar limestones lies the Yoredale Series – so named by John Phillips after those very characteristic Wensleydale mountains that seem to have a series of gigantic steps, jutting rims, where the harder limestones have eroded more slowly than the softer shales. There are even little outcrops of coal to be found, often close to old pit workings where Dalesfolk, for generations, worked the thin seams of coal.

The hard, protective summits of the western fells – and all the eastern moorlands of the Dales above Swaledale, Wensleydale, Coverdale, Nidderdale, Washburndale and mid-Wharfedale and that beautiful under-rated stretch of countryside forming the southern edge of North Yorkshire stretching from the fells of Bowland and the South Pennines below the Aire Gap – are dominated by another very characteristic rock, Millstone Grit.

Gritstone, a coarse sandstone, is synonymous with most people's image of Yorkshire. It's an acid, impervious rock, as its name implies, just the thing for millstones, hard, tough, ideal for grinding. But it's also excellent for building-work of all kinds. Just as Dalesmen in the limestone country use the pale limestone for walls and farmsteads, so in the gritstone country that darker, more dour stone gives so much to the character and feel of the landscape – even, strangers have observed, to the character of the people of the Pennines themselves.

Millstone Grit is another sedimentary rock, the remains of a vast granite mountain range of Alpine proportions, situated approximately where modern Scandinavia is now, eroded away through millions of years by a fierce-flowing mountain river system that finally deposited its sand and detritus in a vast delta, more than 2,500 square miles in area, and in places more than half a mile thick. Compressed and in turn covered by swamp – the fossilized trees of which are modern coal seams, it has produced a hard, golden, sandy-coloured rock that quickly weathers to that characteristic grey-cream, soon to soak any atmospheric pollution like fossilized blotting paper and turn to sooty black.

Less spectacular than limestone, gritstone has nevertheless its moments of drama, most obviously where it outcrops on summit boulders and crags, and best of all where an exposed ridge produces these fantastic, wind-carved shapes – what are called in the south-west 'tors'. The finest example in North Yorkshire is undoubtedly at Brimham Rocks, near Pateley Bridge. Now owned and managed by the National Trust, Brimham Rocks consist of a series of spectacular gritstone crags, split and eroded by wind, rain and frost, given inevitably such fanciful names as 'the Dancing Bear' and 'the Idol' by Victorian topographers.

These natural sculptures, set in the midst of beautiful heather moorland and offering superb views across the Vale of York to York Minster and the North York Moors, can be explored by the least energetic, with a network of winding footpaths from the main car-park through the rocks and an excellent visitor centre.

More energy is perhaps required to scramble up Almscliffe Crag, just off the A658 Bradford-Harrogate road, another splendid viewpoint but easy and safe enough for most energetic children to manage, whilst Plumpton Rocks, set in woodlands and by a lake, in private grounds (open weekends in the summer months), just off the Harrogate-Wetherby road, is another example of gritstone eroded to dramatically shaped forms.

More typical, away from the edges and the tors, gritstone produces mile after mile of wild, uncultivatable, acid moorland and bleak fellside, with only the poorest moorland grass and, on the summits, not even that, with stunted, tundra-like vegetation struggling for existence in a hostile environment; or miles of cotton grass, vividly white in early summer but dull most of the year; or featureless peat bog, drear and uninviting. But in the drier areas, where the moorlands are managed for grouse, ling and heather dominate, magnificent purples and crimson from August until October that delight painter and photographer alike. There are lots of places in the east and southern Dales to enjoy the glories of the heather moorland at its best. For example, the summit of Pinhaw Beacon, above Carleton, west of Skipton) and Halton Heights between Embsay and Burnsall, looking across an expanse of Barden Moor which is the northern equivalent of Thomas Hardy's Egdon Heath – wild, beautiful, yet menacing in its vastness; or Washburndale, perhaps from the Skipton-Blubberhouses road, cutting across to Timble. Or, best of all, the head of Nidderdale, above Lofthouse, and over the moorland eastwards to Kirkby Malzeard; or, into the real Herriot country, almost anywhere above Wensleydale and Swaledale.

Both the Mountain Limestone and the Millstone Grit landscapes of the west are dominated by water – water in the form of ice which, some 70,000 years ago, last covered northern Britain, smoothing the hill summits, deepening the valleys into the characteristic U-shaped ravines. You can even see, at Kilnsey, in Upper Wharfedale, how the ice has undercut the limestone crag, leaving a gigantic lip or overhang beloved of daredevil climbers. You see the effects too, in numerous gills that tumble their streams down the steeply carved valleysides. Nothing is lovelier in the Pennines than these gills, often overhung with birch and rowan, sometimes with primroses clinging to the rocky shelves. You see evidence of the ice too, in the great glacial moraines where the retreating glaciers left crescent-shaped mounds or small hillocks of boulders, clay, gravel, debris, forming lakes, causing rivers to switch their courses. Or higher up the valleys, such as the head of Ribblesdale, or around Long Preston and Gargrave between the Aire and the Ribble where the glaciers have left drumlins, low, dumpy hills, which give the landscape shape and interest, with often a little copse or shelterbelt crowning the hilltop.

If water in the form of slow-moving ice has shaped the North Yorkshire Pennines, so too have the fast-flowing waters of the mountain rivers, cutting, carving their way through the bedrock itself, deepening the ravines made by the ice. Almost wherever you are in the Dales you are aware of water, moving water in rivers, streams and becks, and above all in waterfalls.

Nowhere in Britain has a greater delight and variety of waterfalls than the Yorkshire Dales. In Wensleydale, for example, there are obvious show-stoppers – at Aysgarth Force, where the River Ure is thrust through a narrow gorge over gigantic steps in the great Scar Limestone, the peaty brown waters at time of spate turning to foaming white torrents that have delighted the famous – Turner, Wordsworth, Ruskin, as well as generations of ordinary visitors with camera or easel to record the experience or simply to have memories to take away. Or, on a more intimate scale, Mill Gill Force, reached by taking a footpath from Askrigg church which lies in a wooded ravine with its cataract hidden from sight until you are almost on top of it. Or where all the tourists go, Hardraw, near Hawes, where, beyond that great natural amphitheatre where brass band concerts are held, you can stand behind slender columns of water and see delicate rainbows evaporate into light. Yet little waterfalls, some even without a name, that you come across by chance on a moorland path or quiet lane, are in some ways even more enchanting. Particularly in late winter or early spring, if there's been a mild spell of weather, perhaps a westerly depression with a couple of days of rain, streams which are little

more than seeps in summer become angry cascades, often dropping great heights of hillsides; at such times you look along a dale
and see the steep fellsides quick and alive with the shiver and
glitter of water; at such times, when the bottom meadows flood,
you have a sudden vision of what the Dales must have been like in
late glacial times, before the tarns and lakes had been drained.

Little wonder that they decided in 1954 to designate the most
spectacular parts of the Yorkshire Dales a National Park. But the
problem with any designation is that it tends to devalue that
which lies outside the arbitrary line. So it is in the North Yorkshire
Pennines, with much wonderful countryside, such as the whole of
Nidderdale, Colsterdale, Washburndale, lacking formal
designation. But there are other fine areas of North Yorkshire,
particularly of gritstone country which offer a different kind of
countryside.

Take for instance the Forest of Bowland. This area of austerely
beautiful moorland, forest and reservoir catchment is quite different in character from the Dales to the north – an Area of Outstanding Natural Beauty, it is predominantly in Lancashire. But its
northern fringe, including the massive bulk of Burn Moor and the
characteristic gritstone crags on Bowland Knotts, together with
several of these little known, secluded side valleys of great interest
and individuality that lead from the Ribble or Wenning, are in
fact North Yorkshire.

Even the Brontë country around Haworth, so firmly in spirit a
part of West Yorkshire, comes within North Yorkshire's all-
embracing boundaries. Just above the Brontë villages Stanbury
and Ponden, where the Pennine Way climbs to the peaty summit
of Wolf Stones, North Yorkshire begins, taking in Ickornshaw and
the mill villages of Cowling, Crosshills and Glusburn, all set
within a typically South Pennine landscape. It isn't until Lothersdale, with the first sighting of Mountain Limestone, Cononley
with its lead-mines and the old town of Skipton itself that the
more characteristic Yorkshire Dales landscape begins to make its
presence felt.

But let's leave the North Yorkshire Pennines and move eastwards, picking up the theme of the geological time-chart from
west to east.

It's suddenly quite a different countryside once the gritstones
have vanished. To the east of the Dales is a narrow belt of a

particularly lovely, undervalued countryside, low, rolling hills, fertile, rich farmland, well wooded. The mellow stone of the cottages, farmhouses, villages, churches, walls, gives the clue. This is limestone country again, not the grey or white Carboniferous Limestone of the Dales, but a yellowy cream Magnesian Limestone that runs in a long, narrow strip through the north-eastern side of England, from Nottingham to Northumberland.

It's a newer rock, in many cases overlying the older coal-bearing Carboniferous rocks as the many coal-mining villages on the south strip of North Yorkshire demonstrate – and indeed as the great Selby coalfield also proves. It dates from the Permian era which began some 280 million years ago and was formed mainly from an intensely salt inland sea, from the shells and skeletons of creatures that somehow managed to survive in this soupy liquid and helped to form, with the many mineral salts, a limy ooze which became one of the most interesting and unusual of Yorkshire's rocks. In some places the rock is in thin, crumbly beds, mixed with clay and marl; in other places, as in Ripon Parks, there are exposures of thick beds. You can see it splendidly exposed on the River Nidd downstream from Knaresborough, a yellowy, crumbly rock, full of holes of martins' nests, or little caves, a warm, comfortable rock.

It's a rock beloved of brewers and builders – brewers because the mineral content of the spring water is excellent for brewing ale – hence the celebrated Tadcaster breweries, John Smith and Samuel Smith's, which continue a tradition from medieval times, and the old brewery at Masham close to the magnesian springs, which has a national reputation for its strong, old ale. As far as builders are concerned, there can be no finer advertisement for Magnesian Limestone than York Minster itself, built of stone mainly from Huddleston Quarry near Sherburn-in-Elmet and from Hazlewood, near Tadcaster, and carried in barges along the River Wharfe. Evidence for the stone's enduring qualities is to be found in the Roman multiangular tower which continues to defy the elements in the gardens of the Yorkshire Museum at York, and of course the walls and gates of York itself, and many fine churches.

You don't have to look far to enjoy that lovely, mellow stone in almost every village along the Magnesian Limestone belt – Monk

Fryston, Sherburn, Womersley, Tadcaster itself, Healaugh, Saxton, Bilton, Tockwith, Hammerton, Knaresborough, Farnham, Staveley, Boroughbridge, Ripon, Tanfield, Masham. It produces fertile soils, excellent farmland, mainly arable land, quite different from the thin pastures of the upland limestone pastures or hostile gritstone moorlands. This is a rich, well-wooded landscape of comfortable farms, country houses, villages close enough to the big towns to be highly desirable to live in (even if modern neo-Georgian doesn't quite match the faded elegance of the past) and splendid old churches, such as those of Womersley and Sherburn-in-Elmet. If Magnesian Limestone has a fault, it's that there's too little of it, though that lovely stone turns up in all kinds of places in the fabric of houses, churches and public buildings.

Continuing eastwards, the time-chart leads into the Vale of York, that great central trough, barely twenty or thirty miles wide, that runs between the Pennines and the Moors.

This is the land of the hidden rocks – the Triassic rocks, laid down about 225 million years ago and virtually invisible in North Yorkshire to all but the most persistent, trained eye which can spot the odd outcrop in a streambed. Astonishingly enough, these are Alpine rocks – forming the Dolomites, parts of Switzerland, Austria, the Black Forest. But in Yorkshire as softer sandstones they have been eroded away, lost under thick beds of boulder clay, glacial moraine and alluvial deposits that Pennine glaciers and rivers have laid over the Vale of York.

This is the route almost all Yorkshire's rivers have taken, bringing with them sand, silt, clay, alluvium, filling the trough so that rivers have to wind their way through their own deposits, sometimes flooding the plain: the Swale, the Ure, the Nidd, the Ouse, the Wharfe, the Aire, the Calder, the Rye and even the Derwent, which begins life only a few miles from the coast behind Scarborough but, finding its way blocked by moraine out of the Vale of Pickering, forces its way through the Howardian Hills, east of York into the great Vale. Finally all the rivers converge into the mighty Humber, pushing eastwards past Hull and Holderness into the North Sea. The only North Yorkshire river apart from the Ribble and the Wenning in the far west not to find its way into the Vale of York and the Humber, but which curves north-east, through the Moors to Whitby, is the little River Esk.

To someone who loves the wild fell and mountain country, the Vale of York might appear dull. After all, it's flat – though not as flat as it might at first seem, because a number of broad glacial moraines spread themselves across the valley floor giving it shape and feature.

You are no longer aware of stone in the landscape. No stone walls, no stone cottages. Brick and tile have replaced the Pennine stone, and drystone walls are replaced by hedge and fence. But as you travel east, the vivid red pantiles of cottages and barn give new colour to the landscape.

Yet wherever you are in the flat land, north of York, you are aware of the presence of the hills at each side – the Pennines to the west, the imposing bulk of the Moors to the east. Horizons end in hills that rear up dramatically, purposefully. The Vale of York, and to a degree the Vale of Mowbray which continues the plain northwards into County Durham, provides that essential contrast to the hills, giving them the sense of scale and proportion. Without that intervening gap provided by those softer Triassic rocks there wouldn't have been those steep river valleys that form the Dales, there wouldn't be that magnificent headland bluff of the Cleveland Hills, there wouldn't be those magnificent views from west to east, from east to west – all would have been a rather dull plateau.

It's only when you get south of York, towards Selby, that you really begin to think of yourself in lowland Britain, those long, empty horizons punctuated as you go south by power station, pylons, railways, motorways.

Of course, these rich, heavy soils are superb for agriculture. This is arable land, splendid for cereals, root crops, huge new fields stretching as far as the eye can see. Not so good for walking, perhaps, though lowland footpaths do have a charm and attraction of their own, because grubbed-up hedgerows leave the rambler having to cross huge, open fields, ploughed or with growing crops – barley, potatoes, peas, turnips. But this is excellent cycling country, with networks of quiet lanes between villages, and for the motorist with time to linger, picking a route from an Ordnance Survey map, opportunity to find villages in quiet cul-de-sacs that seem never to have known a tourist, work-a-day communities with perhaps a couple of farms, half a dozen pebble-dashed local authority houses originally for farm

workers but now occupied by pensioners, perhaps a telephone
kiosk, a postbox. It's probably a mile down the lane to the
nearest bus stop on the main road, three miles to the nearest
shop, though a van probably comes on a Wednesday. Dull,
ordinary places perhaps, but the real North Yorkshire,
nonetheless, rural England away from that picture postcard
England of the Dales and the Moors.

But let's continue our time journey eastwards to the sudden,
almost startling uplift of the hills which rise out of the Vale of
York to form the great headlands of the North York Moors, the
Cleveland Hills to the north, curving round into the Vale of
Mowbray and Cleveland, the Hambleton and Tabular Hills to
the south. Unlike the Pennines, which have extensive foothills,
gently building up to the climax of the fell tops, these hills form
an abrupt line of steep hillside and escarpment, familiar to any
traveller up the Great North Road or the East Coast Main Line
railway between York and Durham.

A notable landmark from as far away as Harrogate, and many
of the eastern ridges of the Pennines, is the great White Horse of
Kilburn, on Roulston Scar in the Hambleton Hills. This figure,
314 long and 228 feet high, was carved out in 1857 by a local
village schoolmaster, with thirty people helping him, in
imitation of the ancient White Horses to be seen on the southern
chalk downs. In a sense it is a *trompe l'oeil* in that it has to be
whitewashed to enable it to stand out clearly across the Vale.

The North York Moors National Park (to give it its full and
correct title) is perhaps one of the least known and most
undervalued of Britain's ten National Parks. Unlike the
Yorkshire Dales, which are constantly on everyone's television
screen, the Moors remain elusive, their especial magic kept to
the enjoyment of a relative few.

It is the geology of the Moors which gives this National Park its
unique and distinctive character. Our time-chart has moved to
between 190 and 135 million years ago, relatively recent times in
geological terms, when the complex Jurassic rocks which form
the Moors were laid down.

Unlike the Carboniferous sandstones, gritstones and limestones of the Dales, which are omnipresent, dramatic in their
effect on the landscape, the Cleveland Hills, forming the
north-east corner of the North York Moors, contain the highest

hills, rising to 1,489 feet at Urra Moor. More than one writer has suggested that the name is derived from 'cliff', and the cliffs and scars above Ingilby, Arncliffe and Carlton support that thesis. These western summits, too, have been likened to the cantle of a gigantic saddle, dipping in the central moorland area, to rise again to the saddle's peak at Fylingdale Moor and the cliffs above Robin Hood's Bay. At Boulby, north of Whitby, the coastal cliffs rise to 660 feet, the highest in England.

To the south-east of the River Rye, the hills are known as 'the Tabular Hills' because of their plain-like summits. They descend rapidly to the Vale of Pickering, where there was once a great inlet of the sea and in later ages a vast lake.

The area as a whole, some forty miles across and twenty miles deep, is in shape not unlike an old-fashioned cottage loaf, with the 'bun' extending into the edge of County Cleveland. The Moors, like the Dales, present an astonishing variety of scenery, most especially where the river valleys – the Esk and its tributaries in the north, the Rye and the Derwent and their tributaries in the south, form the enclosed dales, so very different from the Dales of the west, yet as richly green and fertile, contrasting their gentleness against the brown and purple moorland ridges of 'riggs' which extend like the fingers of a giant hand out from the central moorland areas.

The oldest of the rocks which form the Moors are the Lias (a name derived from quarrymen in the West Country who so described the thin, shaly beds in quarries as 'layers'), sedimentary rocks, mainly shales and mudstones, but rich in fossils, most notably that impressive curled shell of the ammonite, used in its many forms to date the Jurassic rocks and inevitably closely associated with the Yorkshire Moors. These oldest Jurassic rocks are impressively displayed at Robin Hood's Bay, along the shoreline. The next series of rocks, Middle Lias, can also be seen at North Cheel, near Robin's Hood's Bay, and at Staithes. These rocks are particularly important because their strata contain the ironstone which resulted in the formation of the Cleveland iron industry. The Upper Lias contain shales which include jet Rock, the source of jewellers' jet, a form of fossilized conifer, and the alum shales, which for many years were worked around Sandsend and Kettleness on the coast.

In Middle Jurassic times a vast river delta covered the whole of what is now the eastern side of North Yorkshire, depositing thick beds of sand, silts and mud. These in turn were covered by shallow seas in which further limestones were laid down. These Mid-Jurassic or Deltaic rocks are sometimes referred to as Oolitic Series because of the herring-rock-like 'oolites' in the limestones which produced the main bedrocks of the Moors as we now know them. They form the cliffs from Scalby to Ravenscar, continuing above the Liassic cliffs to form the massive cliffs at Boulby, and inland to form the major moorland areas across to the Cleveland Hills. On the moorland summit they support only a thin, acid soil and contain much of the characteristic heather landscape.

Further south, across the Tabular Hills and the Hambleton Hills, lie newer Upper Jurassic Rocks, the evocatively named Cornbrash, a sandy limestone, than the sandy red sandstone known as Kellaway Rock, and the Oxford Clays. Above these are the Corallian Series, fine-grained sandstone and limestone, producing the rich, fertile soils and fine building-stone that characterize the villages and valleys to the south of the Moors, yielding to the softer Kimmeridge Clays in the Vale of Pickering.

Such a brief and simplified outline can do little to convey the richness and complexity of landforms that make the North York Moors such a fascinating area. The Ice Age has, in many ways, made an even greater impact on the Moors than in the Pennines. There are former glacial lakebeds in Eskdale and in the Vale of Pickering, connected by an astonishing glacial overflow channel which is now Newtondale, carrying the trackbed of the North York Moors Railway. Several smaller lakes existed in the Goathland-Wheeldale area, and glacially created features, such as Mullion Spout waterfall, abound. A curious feature of these lakes is that their outflow rivers and streams went not eastwards into the North Sea but southwards, via Lake Pickering, as it was then, and the Derwent to the Humber. This was owing to the existence of the Great Scandinavian Glacier covering the North Sea, pressing the Scottish and Cheviot Glaciers into the Yorkshire coast, blocking river exits with ice and later glacial debris, forcing the pent-up meltwaters to seek an exit southwards and westwards, eroding such valleys as Newtondale, or by the Kirkham gap through the Howardian Hills into the Vale of York.

The most spectacular of these glacial overflow channels to explore on foot is in the Forge Valley, south of Hackness, where the Derwent swings south through a narrow, wooded valley of great botanic interest and beauty, carving its way through the soft Corallian rocks, a superb piece of natural engineering. Ironically, it was left to the hand of twentieth-century man, concerned at the constant threat of flooding when the Derwent was in spate, to create a four-mile 'Sea Cut' or overflow channel to link the river with the sea near Scarborough.

At Sutton Bank, where the main A170 Thirsk-Scarborough road climbs the murderously steep Hambleton Hills escarpment, you can still see a surviving moorland lake, Lake Gormire, captured behind a landslip. Unlike the solid rock architecture of the Pennines, the Jurassic rocks are relatively unstable, with hard sandstones or limestones overlying soft shales or sticky clay and causing frequent landslips, particularly along the western slope faces. The Hole of Horcum, for example, north of Pickering, is a huge natural amphitheatre produced by the action of a spring eroding away clays which underlie harder Corallian rocks until the rock collapsed.

The real glories of the Moors, as their name implies, are those vast tracts of heather and ling which in late summer are one of England's treasures. The road from Pickering to Whitby, for example, crosses the moorland summits and offers superb views; the great early warning domes of Fylingdales, hideous reminder as they are of the nuclear age in which we live, nevertheless give an epic scale to the landscape, whilst the first view of Whitby Abbey on the coastal horizon across that expanse of open moorland never fails to thrill. Almost as fine is the journey along the A171 from Whitby to Guisborough, again with superb views, or over the unclassified Castleton-Kirkbymoorside road, the heartland of the Moors.

The relatively flat summit of the Moors, with easy road access, prevents the Moors from enjoying quite the feeling of mountain isolation to be found in the Pennines, though certain areas, crossed by ancient tracks and footpaths marked by prehistoric burial mounds and those evocative medieval crosses, come as close to the true wilderness as anywhere in England. But often the walker will climb a valley ridge, an empty, lonely place, to be greeted by a busy tarmac road, car-park and parked cars. More worrying in the Moors, man's economic activity constantly impinges upon the surviving wilderness. A recent survey of the heather moorland of the North Yorkshire Moors National Park revealed that about a third of all the heather had vanished since the Second World War – turned into dull, fenced, if productive grassland or covered with dense sitka spruce plantations. For those who argue that the moors are the precious jewel in the crown of the National Park, every acre of fine moorland converted is a loss of something beyond price.

Away from the tops, the Dales – little side valleys off the Rye, the Esk and the Derwent – offer a beauty which is similar to that of the more famous Dales of the west but in other ways distinctly different. Many of them are on a much smaller scale, with not even a hamlet to grace them, just a farm or two and outlying barns. There are stone walls but they are a less dominant feature of the landscape, and lower in the valleys, and in the larger valleys, hedgerows dominate. The southern valleys, those that drain the Tabular Hills and open out from Ryedale, are often richly wooded, fertile, splendid places for wild flowers – bluebells, wood anemones, orchids. Most famous of all in this respect is Farndale, whose wild daffodils attract such numbers that during the key spring weekends the traffic flows one way nose-to-tail along the narrow lanes, and wardens positioned at strategic points prevent picking of the precious blooms.

But many of the smaller dales remain little known, sometimes with only a track or footpath along them, quiet, secret places to discover from a large-scale map, to explore by foot, to treasure.

The villages of the Moors are another glory. Some, such as Goathland, Rievaulx, Hutton-le-Hole and Coxwold, are justly famous. The soft brown stone, harmonized with red pantiles, against a green backcloth of hills, forms part of a classic English landscape which deserves to be treasured, even if, as in the Dales, the owners of weekend cottages and second and retirement homes are becoming more numerous than natives in the settlements.

The third element of the North York Moors which makes it outstandingly fine is the coast. You can walk along the edge of almost all of it in North Yorkshire, from Humberside to Cleveland, and if 'heritage' is an over-used word, this magnificent series of cliffs and bays, punctuated only by resorts and old ports, deserves that epithet. It isn't the kindest of coasts, the north-east, where the North Sea pounds away against the cliffs. The sea, usually grey, is cold, often covered by a chill sea fret, and even where there are fine beaches you need a certain willpower to plunge into the water. But its beauty and those magnificent clifftop views are ample compensation, especially on those glorious days of late summer and early autumn of calm sea and clear sky.

The Vale of Pickering divides from the Vale of York by a range of low, mainly Jurassic hills, dominated by the artificially created splendours of Castle Howard and its great estate. Named the Howardian Hills by geologist John Phillips, the hills extend from Malton to the Coxwold-Gilling gap, including such attractive villages as Hovingham, Terrington, Sheriff Hutton, Welburn and Kirkham with its priory. This area is now proposed for designation as one of Britain's Areas of Outstanding Natural Beauty, a classification which recognizes its superb landscape qualities: a rich, mature, eighteenth-century landscape set in low, rolling hills, with a sense of a timeless English countryside. This is a particularly rich, gentle countryside and deserves to be better known.

With such glories North Yorkshire has riches enough. But our time-chart is not yet exhausted. Motorists along the A64 between York and Scarborough and rail travellers to Scarborough see more pale hills rise to the right, not as steep or as dramatic as the Cleveland Hills but impressive enough. These are the Yorkshire Wolds, whose northern section comes into North Yorkshire, including that impressive ridge line overlooking the Vale of Pickering.

These, the newest of North Yorkshire's hills, are of chalk, an exceptionally pure form of limestone, laid down as marine deposits over an extended period of about 60 million years, from 135 to 64 million years ago. They form part of that great belt of chalk downland which extends from Devon and Dorset to Wiltshire and Berkshire, across to Kent and Sussex, northwards through Oxford and East Anglia, underneath the Wash to form the Lincolnshire and Yorkshire Wolds, ending on these North Yorkshire escarpments.

So when this seems like a little bit of southern English landscape which has escaped to the North, in effect this is exactly what it is, a very distinctive countryside of smoothly formed Wolds, curious 'dry' valleys, beautiful green pasture, large arable fields, old trackways, scattered woodlands.

Unlike the Dales and the Moors, the Wolds are no wilderness landscape but carefully husbanded, with fields of rape, root crops, cereal. It's an area intertwined with lanes, many of them going along the top of the Wolds, others following the dry valley bottom, between steep pastures, superb for cycling along, with such villages as Thixendale, Birdsall, Settington and Wintringham to explore, places were few tourists go. It is also fine walking country, particularly along the Wolds Way, the 79-mile Long Distance Footpath from Hessle on the Humber to Filey Brigg on the coast, taking in its progress much of the finest Wolds scenery, including this North Yorkshire section. The motorist who doesn't mind coping with narrow lanes, sharp turns and steep inclines will find much to enjoy in the Wolds, once more a quite different kind of landscape, reflecting a different bedrock.

Such is the variety of landscapes of North Yorkshire, an astonishing cross-section of rock structures and with them kinds of countryside. It has been correctly suggested that one of the greatest qualities of the English landscape is its variety. If England lacks the epic grandeur of the Central European Alps or the Scandinavian Forests, it contains, a microcosm, an impressive range of landscape types. Nowhere is this better illustrated than in North Yorkshire, where you can move, over a few miles and in a few hours, from the bare semi-tundra vegetation of the Pennine summits, through the spectacular karst limestone and sombre gritstones of the Dales and South Pennines, to the softer Magnesian Limestone country and a fertile plain; then to change mood again through the massive cliff and moorland country of the Moors ending in one of the grandest coastlines in all Britain, before moving south to the fertile valleys of the Tabular Hills, the exquisite Howardian Hills and finally the intimate beauty of the chalk Wolds.

It's difficult to imagine that so much could be in one county.

# 3

## The Shaping of a Landscape

When, over twelve thousand years ago, the ice finally retreated to high gullies and north-facing slopes in the Pennines, North Yorkshire would have been very different in appearance from the present time. The hilltops, scoured by ice to the bedrock, would have been bare of vegetation, the valleys, the Vale of York in particular, filled with mud, clay, boulders. Much would have been under water – great lakes filling the valleys, held back by moraines, their waters forcing their way across the rim in great cataracts which were to carve gorges in the clay and even bedrock. Tarns and ponds fill every hollow. Much was shallow, impenetrable swamp. Gradually over the centuries, it all began to dry out and warm up. Lichens, sedges and tough grasses began to colonize the higher slopes – and birch trees. This tundra-like landscape was occupied by wild horses, reindeer, bear, hare.

At this time Britain was attached to the continental European landmass, and before long small groups of palaeolithic huntsmen were to find their way as far north and west as the Pennines. A fish lance found in Victoria Cave, Settle, and a crudely decorated rod of reindeer horn are evidence of their presence, probably on summer hunting parties, seeking their prey on the higher, better-drained slopes.

By about 7500 BC the climate had warmed until it was very much warmer than the present day, closer to Mediterranean conditions. The sinking and flooding of the great area of lowland between the European continent and what is now the British Isles to form the North Sea and the English Channel was also occurring. The improved climate improved the vegetation too. Tree cover now included birch, hazel, alder, oak and other deciduous trees. The valleys would be filled with luxuriant scrub. New generations of more sophisticated mesolithic huntsmen now made their way across the hills – the Wolds, the Moors and, most notably, the Pennines, their skills including the manufacture of tools, axe-heads and arrowheads from flints. Many of their weapons and tools have been found, a fine reindeer harpoon head in Victoria Cave, a remarkable reindeer bone and boar's tooth scraping-implement from Elbolton Cave, in Wharfedale, and countless arrowheads, harpoon points, scrapers, small implements. They are often most abundant near surviving or former lakes, such as around Malham Tarn, Semerwater and the former Giggleswick Tarn, where the lake fish provided excellent food supplies.

Some years ago Mr John Moore, a keen local archaeologist, noted what he thought were bone and antler fragments protruding from a deep drainage ditch at the edge of a field at Star Carr, about half a mile off the main A64, three miles south of Seamer, near Scarborough. Further investigation, led by Professor Clark of Cambridge University, discovered a temporary summer camp, situated at the edge of a shallow lake and marshland – remnants of the glacial Lake Pickering. The camp had been constructed on a platform of birchwood and would have provided a rough landing-stage for fishing canoes and a base for a camp, of which no traces remain. What has remained, however, are bone fragments of the hunters' prey – mainly red deer but also wild ox, elk, roe deer and wild pig, as well as tools from antler and bone. Particularly intriguing were stag antlers adapted to be worn as a helmet for stalking or ritual purposes, and rolls of birch bark used to produce a primitive but effective glue to attach flint arrowheads to spears. Carbon-dating of the birchwood has established the date of the site to around 7500 BC. Axes of a similar type have been found as far inland as Nova, near Pickering, Glaisdale and Blubberhouses in the Pennines, suggesting quite considerable hunting trips from such bases as Star Carr. Nevertheless, the evidence confirms that these were still primarily a nomadic people, hunting in small groups in a vast, otherwise uninhabited landscape.

Around 3000 BC fresh waves of immigrants from the Continent brought with them new skills and customs. These neolithic peoples used the land they came to occupy in a fundamentally different way: they were food-producers not food-gatherers, Yorkshire's first farmers. They avoided the forest and bleak uplands and chose the softer and sweeter lands of the Wolds, the limestone hills on the southern edge of the Moors, parts of the Howardian Hills, the limestone terraces of Craven, as settlement places where the well-drained soil could be cleared to make enclosures for grazing animals and where wooden huts could be erected. They buried their dead in graves piled over with stone to form the long barrows familiar in the eastern side of the county – though rare in the Pennines. They had axes and hammers to clear the scrub and to make shelters. They knew how to make crude pottery, rough textiles. They began to make, through their scattered settlements, an impact upon the virgin landscape.

By 2500 BC new waves of immigrants from the Rhine estuary brought with them new technology – the ability to work metal, alloys of tin and copper, bronze, to make better tools, better weapons. They buried their dead in round barrows and could make functional and decorative beakers so successfully that modern archaeologists dub them 'the Beaker People'.

These people and their successors over the next two thousand years undoubtedly began the major clearances of the primeval forests which helped to create our modern landscape. Their lines of communication and major trade routes, in some cases crossing northern England from Ireland in the west to the Continent, can still be traced, sometimes as modern tarmac roads or lanes but often as evocative stony tracks or green ways along moorland edges, or as sunken ways between clusters of barrows, particularly on the great riggs of the North York Moors, many of them close to the moorland tracks, acting as primitive waymarks. They left monuments in the form of stone circles whose purpose is far from clear; they may well have been linked to important religious rituals. Examples are to be found above Bordley, near Malham and close to the roadside near Yockenthwaite, in Langstrothdale in the Yorkshire Dales, on Danby Rigg, Eskdale, on the Moors, close to an impressive large settlement, and at High Bride Stones on Sleights Moor near Grosmont, where six large stones survive from a major circle. There are many standing stones or henge monuments, again undoubtedly having a religious significance, perhaps as fertility symbols – sometimes they are single stones, sometimes triangles. The most impressive of such monuments in North Yorkshire are the Devil's Arrows, to be seen at either side of the Rosecliffe road, immediately to the west of Boroughbridge, between the town and the A1. These consist of three huge gritstone pillars – the most northerly is 18 feet high and 22 feet in circumference; the second, 22½ feet high and 18 feet in perimeter, stands some 200 feet away, across the field; the third, a further 370 feet away, lies immediately to the other side of the road, in a small thicket. According to earlier historians, there were other, smaller stones standing in the group in Elizabethan times, removed by villagers in the vain hope of finding money underneath! What is truly remarkable about these monuments is that the stone they are made of came from Abbey Plain, Knaresborough, seven miles away, and their extraction, transportation and erection, with only the most primitive tools, suggest a sophisticated social organization in Bronze Age times. This is borne out by the mysterious 'circles' at Thornborough, about a mile east of West Tanfield. These are not the usual kind of henge monuments but a series of three circles, 550 to 600 feet in diameter, high banks of earth and stone, surrounded by a small ditch, close to the road. They still have the feeling of being some kind of amphitheatre, where a great population was gathered to witness a ceremony, a rite, a piece of theatre. The fact that these sites are not, as most Bronze Age sites are, on the high moorland or limestone pastures, suggests that much of the wildwood and even scrub was being cleared from the lowland, and the more fertile soils drained and cultivated.

We know tantalizingly little about Bronze Age civilization; archaeological evidence suggests constant improvements were taking place in technical skills in tool-making and pottery, in textiles and weaponry, and the creation of sufficient income to create real disposable wealth – splendid gold rings and ornaments have been unearthed, such as a superb gold dress-fastener found in Swinton Park, near Masham, and a gold girdle, found in 1843 at Scalby, near Scarborough – unfortunately this is now lost. Such gold jewellery and finery were imported via trade routes from Ireland, again evidence of the sophistication of Bronze Age culture.

Archaeologists now agree that firm dividing lines cannot be

drawn between 'Bronze Age' and 'Iron Age' culture, or even people, because, as the North Yorkshire archaeologist and historian Frank Elgee has suggested, Bronze Age peoples probably continued to practise a centuries-old way of life in areas like the North York Moors long after the land had been settled by later waves of Continental invaders, the Celtic peoples with the ability to forge that most useful of minerals, iron, into long swords. Through trade and improved communications, new cultures merged. Material wealth increased, and with it population. Taking a Malthusian view of Bronze Age man being limited in numbers to the available food supplies to sustain him through the winters, which were now becoming cooler, the invaders who came westwards into North Yorkshire from the Continent from around 500 BC had more efficient tools for that most important of all skills, cultivation of the land. It was not that Bronze Age man was unaware of the value of cultivating, rather than collecting, useful cereal grain; it was just that by Iron Age times he had the techniques to do it rather better. Winter stores of food for man and beast made a cold climate habitable, as did the ability to weave the fleeces of domestic animals, notably of sheep, to make effective clothing.

These people sought the limestone and chalk uplands, clearing and cultivating the thin soils for crops of barley, corn and peas in the short summer, looking after herds of goats, sheep and probably poultry, and hunting deer and wild pigs. They also lived in communities – villages. Many of the settlements have long vanished under the plough or later development, but at Lea Green and High Close, above Grassington, Wharfedale, the outlines can clearly be seen, especially in late afternoon and after light snow – ridges of what were little field enclosures around huts, and what almost amounts to a village street. Such patterns are decipherable in hillsides above Malham, also on the limestone terraces in Littondale and Upper Wharfedale.

Archaeologists are constantly revising their view of Celtic Britain away from the child's schoolbook notion of woad-painted savages to an understanding of a complex, sophisticated civilization sustaining quite a large population in village communities, again their agriculture and weaving and meta-lwork skills able to create wealth and with it art, including magnificent, carefully wrought enamelled brooches, their manufacture and crafting requiring a 'leisure economy' rich and stable enough to sustain it. Two major federations of tribes occupied what is now North Yorkshire – the Brigantes in the Pennines and north-east (though it is likely that Bronze Age peoples continued to occupy much of the North York Moors) and the Parisii in the Wolds.

What is certain is that, for the first time in North Yorkshire, the demands of this much larger population were beginning to make significant changes on the landscape. Vast tracts of forest would now be cleared for settlement, for agriculture, for food, for building. There is even evidence to suggest that Iron Age man knew the value of managing woodland – coppicing rather then clear-felling trees, so that he could return again for stakes and staves.

The Romans would have been well aware of the riches of Brigantia before preparing their long series of campaigns to extend the Empire northwards. Evidence of the bitter military struggle survives in numerous defensive earthworks where Iron Age people sought to defend their homeland against the military might of Rome, or possibly to wage effective guerrilla warfare. In the Yorkshire Dales massive earth dykes at Tor Dyke, on Park Rash between Kettlewell and Coverdale suggest a defensive fortification, whilst Fort Gregory, at the summit of Grass Wood, Wharfedale, was undoubtedly a look-out point in the defence of the Brigantian villages; other impressive examples survive at Castle Steads, just south of Dalton between Richmond and Barnard Castle, and across the dale at Framlington in Swaledale.

It was at Stanwick St. John, just off the B6274 between Richmond and Winston, that the last decisive battle took place between the Romans and the Brigantians. Excavations by the late Sir Mortimer Wheeler have revealed the extent of the earthworks, though the modern visitor sees no more than a few grassy mounds. It was here that the Brigantians, betrayed by their Queen, the notorious Cartimandua, made their last stand under the leadership of the Brigantian former consort, Venutius.

But the most remarkable hill fort of all in North Yorkshire is the actual summit of Ingleborough, where, on the flat summit plateau, hut circles confirm an Iron Age settlement, surrounded by a massive stone wall along the perimeter of the summit – a fortification without parallel in the British Isles, though little remains of the fortification but rubble. Exactly who fortified the mountain summit and how long they survived, in a place where the climate could be crueller than any Roman sword, must remain a mystery.

It is reasonable to suppose that the Romans' main concern with the Brigantians was to have access to their mineral wealth, namely the lead-mines in the Pennines which must have been discovered by the Brigantes. Successive military leaders worked to ensure, by a highly efficient system of interlinked military roads and forts, that any trouble the hill people were to create was to be dealt with by the legions quickly and sharply. Sporadic incidents there must have been, but it is likely that ordinary life continued in the Iron Age communities into Romano-British times, very much as before. Few Roman villas were erected outside the military settlements of York and Malton, the one exception being the capital of Romanized Brigantia, close to the strategic Roman highway, the Great North Road. This was Isurium Brigantium, modern Aldborough. It is a moving experience to visit the little Roman Museum in Aldborough, the fragments of red Samian ware, pottery, glassware, the Altar in the museum, then to walk through the gardens past sections of partially concealed wall, outlines of villas, to reach the splendid mosaic pavements, worn thin and bare in places by generations of feet. Aldborough's finest example of many mosaic pavements is in Leeds Museum, but those still *in situ* give a vivid impression of a community of people taking upon themselves a veneer of Mediterranean culture in the midst of a cold and hostile land, a way of life which continued long after the fall of the Roman Empire itself.

An altar found in Bordeaux in 1921 refers to a *colonia* at Eboracum in the province of 'Lower Britain' which existed in AD 237. This 'colony' consisted of lands granted to ex-servicemen, who were liable to be called up in time of emergency, and was situated outside the fortress city – a community of farmer-soldiers. A similar colony existed at Malton, occupying the area now covered by the village of Norton. Other fortress towns such as Caractonium (Catterick) and Bainbridge would also have their attendant settlements.

If there were long periods of peace and prosperity, there were also times of horrifying strife, in AD 117, when the IX Legion was wiped out by the Scots and Brigantes, in AD 205, when the Caledonians broke through the protective barrier of Hadrian's Wall to murder and plunder, and from the late third century onwards, when invaders from across the North Sea – the Saxons – began to prove a major threat to Romano-British culture.

Clearly the imperial army needed feeding and, whether from farmers or colonists, native grain had to be provided in vast quantities from the land. Supplies had to be brought considerable distances – Yorkshire was then, as now, too cold for vineyards, and given the cost and difficulty of transport and despite use of rivers and waterways, there would be tremendous economic incentive to produce goods locally. Hence the potteries at places such as Castle Howard and Norton, iron-smithies near Catterick, lead-mines above Greenhow. Two famous pigs of lead imprinted wih the inscription 'IMP. CAES. DOMITIANO. AVG. COS VII BRIG EX ARG' were found in 1735 near a track across Hayshaw Bank, Greenhow, Nidderdale; the inscription indicates they came from local 'silver mines' around Pateley; one of these pigs is now kept, on show to the public, at Ripley Castle, near Harrogate.

For any Roman prepared to face the spasmodic risk of violent attacks from the north or east there was a prosperous living to be made in Roman Brigantium, good enough to earn the wealth to build a fine villa.

At Castle Dykes, just off the A6108 between Ripon and West Tanfield, are the foundations of a large villa, two rooms of which were fitted with a hypocaust. Several of the other rooms had baths, indicating a large and luxurious country residence. But it was twice destroyed. After the first destruction it was rebuilt, but the second time it was burnt to the ground and its unfortunate occupants were slain. Coins and pottery date the disaster to the close of the third century.

A line of cliff forts all the way along the Yorkshire coast was designed to provide the Roman Army with early warning of barbarian raids. These, the last military works constructed by the Romans in Britain, under the authority of Emperor Valentinian I (364–78), suffered burnings and sackings as wave after wave of Germanic invaders attacked the colony. When the Romans finally left in AD 407 to defend their homeland, the forts at Goldsborough, near Kettleness, at Ravenscar near Scarborough, on Scarborough Castle Hill and at Carr Naze, north of Filey, were the first military installations to suffer, their watchtowers fired, their occupants put to the sword and their corpses flung into the wells.

Most historians accept the view of Anglian invaders in Yorkshire pressing westwards in large numbers, forcing the Romano-British communities to retreat towards the hills of the west, where an occasional Celtic name (Pen-y-Ghent, Craven) implies a British presence, and finally to the fastnesses of Cumbria and Wales. The truth, as always, was perhaps a little more complex and reflected an ebb and flow of informal treaties and accommodation, with even an entire Celtic kingdom – Elmete – surviving into and beyond the seventh century in an area north-east of Leeds, recalled to this day in the name of such North Yorkshire villages as Sherburn-in-Elmet.

What seems undeniable is that the new invaders shunned the old Romanized township and hill-terrace settlements and worked with a will to develop settlements on the valley floor, clearing the forest, draining the marshes, working the richer, more sheltered soils, building up their nucleated settlements, leaving their uncouth Germanic names and dialect – the 'leys' of their clearances, the 'tuns' of their villages, to mark their progress to modern historians of human settlement as clearly as the primeval fossils had helped geologist William Smith to decipher the layers of bedrock.

Hardly had the Anglian invaders organized themselves into a kingdom – Northumbria – and adopted that revolutionary new philosophy, Christianity, than other invaders were threatening their own ownership of the land – the Danes in the east and the Vikings in the west, plundering, burning, looting, grasping land, coming to dominate and populate what is now North Yorkshire to a point that the old Roman city of Eboracum was to become Yorvik, their northern capital.

Again the picture is a complex one, struggles and enmity over the decades softening through intermarriage and interdependence; the dominant language of the Anglians, Old English, becoming modified in vocabulary, intonations and even speech

patterns with that of the Norsemen, to become a recognizable
northern form of English, Yorkshire dialect in its several forms.

It is remarkable how many villages in North Yorkshire can be
traced to their Anglian or Norse origins, scattered farmsteads
and hamlets that go back to the times when those early settlers
in what was still largely a primeval wilderness or small Celtic
settlement erected a shelter. As well as their 'leys', 'tuns' and
'bys', the Anglians frequently built their townships in
clearances – 'royds' or 'riddings', by the crossing-point of a
river – 'forth' or 'wath', in a stony place – 'stan', and by a
homestead – 'ham' or 'stead', in that North Country word
which has never quite been stolen by Standard English – 'dale'
(*c.f.* modern German *Tal*). Norsemen, on the other hand, called
their clearances of the forest 'thwaites', their farmsteads
'wicks' or 'bys', their barns 'laithes', their watermeadows
'ings' or 'holms', their wells or springs 'kelda'. A few minutes
with any large-scale Ordnance Survey map of North Yorkshire
reveals a fascinating picture of interwoven communities, certain
areas – for example, the area to the east of York having a very
strong Norse influence, others predominantly Anglian, most
areas being interestingly mixed. The Vikings penetrating the
western Dales from their Irish colonies often occupied the
daleheads, their 'scales' or little huts for use by shepherds in the
summer months often surviving as place-names. Most of North
Yorkshire's towns and villages were already settlements of a kind
before the Norman Conquest.

Though huge areas of wild, open country, of forest and swamp
remained, the landscape of North Yorkshire now began to take a
recognizable shape as villages spread out their open, common
fields, careful husbandry beginning to be practised to keep soil
fertility.

Again, recent archaeological discoveries are beginning to
change the views held of Anglian and Viking culture. It was a
period of expansion and growth in trade, in knowledge, a
flowering of art and learning, most spectacularly demonstrated
in the production of the Lindisfarne Gospels by a tiny monastic
community to the north, but, as always, under constant threat of
military invasion and disturbance until Eric Bloodaxe, the last
Viking King of York, was deposed in 952 by Eadred, King of
Wessex, which had the effect of uniting England but reducing

once mighty Northumbria to a vassal state.

Much has survived from Anglo-Viking days in North Yorkshire, most notably a number of intricately carved crosses and many sections of churches, gravestones and inscriptions. At Kirk Hammerton church, between York and Knaresborough, part of the nave, chancel and tower of an Anglo-Viking church has been incorporated into a nineteenth-century church, while at Kirby Hill, north of Richmond, much of the nave and chancel and the south nave door are pre-Conquest. Ripon Cathedral has a fine Anglo-Saxon crypt, now the cathedral treasury, where it is possible to imagine St Wilfred's little stone church on the banks of the River Ure as it would have been in the eighth century. Burnsall church, in Wharfedale, possesses fine Viking hog-back gravestones, while at Hackness, near Scarborough, there are an Anglo-Saxon chancel arch and two important early Anglo-Saxon crosses which refer to Abbess Oedilburga of Hackness nunnery.

Most moving of all, however, is the little St Gregory Minster, in secluded Kirkdale, close to Kirkby Moorside town. This church dates from the mid eleventh century and is famous for a remarkable sundial with one of the longest carved inscriptions in Old English to have survived. It reads: 'Orm, son of Gamal, bought St Gregorius Minster when it was all broken and fallen and he had let it make new from the ground ... in Edward's days the King, and Tosti's days the Earl' (i.e. 1060). It is signed: 'Hawarth wrought me and Brand Priests.' A vivid picture comes to mind of the little ruined chapel in the woods being restored by Orm, presumably a pious Anglian nobleman, and the two priests, Hawarth and Brand, gratefully carving the sundial and fitting it into place, little knowing that, in the era of the nuclear bomb and flights to the moon, men would come and wonder at their industry and their patron's generosity.

The Norman Conquest was a disaster for Anglo-Viking civilization and a particular disaster for Yorkshire, from which, some people would argue, the region has never fully recovered. Rebellion and trouble in the north prompted William to put into action the appalling 'Harrowing of the North' which, if history and the evidence of Domesday are to be believed, meant an army of thugs, murdering, burning, destroying, leaving Yorkshire a bleak and burned wasteland; a crime against humanity on a scale with the single-minded atrocities of the twentieth century.

It is difficult to imagine that William's butchery could have been as complete as the chronicles claim. Forests, moorland, swamp lands enough existed for those who could to find retreat and shelter. Even in modern warfare, troops equipped with long-range weapons, searchlight and helicopters are ineffective against determined insurgents and those fighting for their lives, and terrible though the slaughter must have been, many must have lived rough in the wild wood to escape the slaughter, then returned to find the devastation and worked to put it right.

Not even the nostalgic glow of history can conceal the fact that the Norman Conquest was a military occupation, the imposition upon a subject peoples of an iron dictatorship, and with it a ruthless bureaucratic structure. Its impact on the Yorkshire landscape had its most obvious manifestation in those massive castles, symbols of military power and oppression that even the erosive effects of time have not softened – that massive keep at Richmond built by Alan the Red, Bolton's great towers, the jagged outlines of Helmsley, Skipton's foreboding gateway, Scarborough's strategic position, York's Castle Hill, all speak of the power of the mighty Norman barons, given land and authority to quell a subservient population. Even where mere jagged fragments have survived, such as at Ravensworth, their massive scale dominates the cottages of the neighbouring village, and the contrast must have been even greater when the local peasantry occupied little more than thatched hovels.

Many of the Norman castle towns – the townships growing up as important administrative and trading centres around the protective walls of the castles, providing essential services – have remained important administrative centres to the present day: Skipton, Helmsley, Richmond, Scarborough, Pickering. Others, not having that strategic importance, have dwindled to mere villages: Castle Bolton in Wensleydale, Sherriff Hutton in the Howardian Hills, Ravensworth.

A crucial factor in the development of a town from a mere village was the granting of a charter for a weekly market and an annual fair. Such a boon had the immediate effect of developing the service trades – tavern-keepers, farriers, wheelwrights, chandlers, tanners, coopers – to a point where the village would become a town. Given the difficulty of travel along roads that were little more than muddy tracks, local market centres serving a handful of villages and outlying farms were all that was necessary for largely self-sufficient communities, and a network of tracks and roads into market centres developed to become motor roads leading to the important, bustling towns of modern North Yorkshire; others have lost their importance to become mere lanes, tracks or footpaths in the era of the motor car. As we shall see in Chapter 6, communications continue to be a major factor in the evolution of the towns and villages of North Yorkshire.

Whatever was happening in the outside world in medieval times (and York, let alone London might well have been on another planet for all the difference it made to the lives of people living in rural Yorkshire who rarely strayed more than five miles from their home village), life for most inhabitants of what is now North Yorkshire had a continuity dominated by birth, death and the seasons it is now difficult for us to imagine now. If the Middle Ages were devoutly Christian with the flames of Hell fire never very far away, the Old Religion – paganism – had never been quite obliterated, with superstition and folk lore having a vivid reality to match that of the Christian faith. Even in the noble priory church at Bolton Abbey there is the face of the Green Man – pagan fertility god – wreathed in leaves from the carved roof boss, and the wood-carvers of the choir stalls in Ripon Cathedral brought rich, pagan symbolism into the misericords under the choir seats.

What was the medieval landscape of North Yorkshire? Even by the start of the thirteenth century, before monasticism had made its major impact, many changes would have occurred compared with the landscape of Iron Age times. By now, vast tracts of the wildwood would have vanished to accommodate the new villages, the growing towns. Most villages in North Yorkshire were settled on their present sites by this time. The villages would have perhaps only one stone building, the church, which in many communities was the only place of refuge from raids by the Scots. The only other building of substance would be the manor house, perhaps built of stone, in many cases on the same site as the Anglian or Viking headman's hall. Other houses would be single-room 'toft and croft' cottages with tiny windows. Smoke from fires would have to escape through the roof, which, in the lowland areas, would be straw-thatched, in the uplands covered with ling. Houses would be made of rough-hewn timbers, many of them built on the cruck principle, using two substantial tree trunks to form a steep roof. Farmhouses would follow the traditional Anglian and Viking 'lang house' style, with beasts and men sharing the same roof, feed for the animals being kept above the stalls to act as a natural insulation.

Animals would be grazed in common on the vast tracts of open common or moor which still survive as such in many areas of Yorkshire where the land is too poor or steep to have been enclosed and improved. Small fields or intakes would surround villages, hedged in the lowland areas, enclosed with drystone walls in the uplands. Most of the fields would, however, be open fields farmed on the strip principle. In the hillier areas this was done by a series of terraces ('lynchets') which can still be seen centuries after the ox-ploughs have vanished, green shelves running in parallel lines along the hillside, easily distinguished in late afternoon sunshine. Arable crops would be grown at quite high altitudes, particularly oats, which, in the form of oatcake, haverbread or bannock, provided the staple fare for the majority of the population. Even as late as early last century an old Littondale farmer is reported to have confessed that he ate meat only once a year, at Christmastime. In hill areas in particular, crop yields were poor by modern standards, only the toughest species surviving the altitude, poor climate and short seasons. Poverty was endemic, the population kept down by the brutal effects of starvation and relieved, in later medieval times, only by the growth of trade, by specialization in agriculture and by the coming of cottage and other industries.

Nevertheless, there was pressure on the land, and the Norman princes and barons needed land for their most cherished leisure activity – hunting. Huge areas of North Yorkshire were reserved, from an early date, for sport; their inhabitants moved away, keepers or wardens were employed, hunting lodges were erected, moorland and heather for the convenience of noble huntsmen and the landscape of wildlife conserved. In some ways the creation of forests paralleled the growth of grouse-shooting in the nineteenth century, with conservation as a means of creating a pleasure reserve. A huge area of Upper Wharfedale – Langstrothdale Chase – was a game reserve in which the noble northern family of Percy, no less, set up Buckden as their main headquarters for the hunting of the red deer and the wolf, with hunting lodges at Cray, Hubberholme, Kirkgill, Raisgill, Yockenthwaite, Middlemore, Beckermonds, Oughtershaw and Greenfield, names still on the map as farms and scattered settlements. The Earls of Cumberland had their own deer park and hunting reserves behind Skipton Castle and extending over the fells to Barden Tower, a massive hunting lodge which still survives, while the Forest of Knaresborough, extending from Haveragh Park, west of Harrogate, was the hunting reserve of John of Gaunt. In the east the Forest of Pickering extended from the coast as far as Rievaulx and northwards onto the Moors, while the ancient Forest of Galtres occupied much land to the north and east of York. Middleham, in Wensleydale, with its great castle, was the administrative centre for the old Forest of Wensleydale.

The old term 'forest' causes some confusion. A forest was in effect a game reserve, with strict penalties for anyone found stealing the game or felling trees and enclosing the land without permission. Woodland there would have been, but it would certainly have not been a 'forest' in the modern sense of dense, continuous woodland. Not that there would not be some development in the forests; villages did exist, like islands in the sea of the forest, and demands were always being made to enclose and plough stretches of forest lands to feed a growing population. At times when the authority of the king was strong, the process was difficult or even impossible. When the throne was controlled less securely, local landowners enjoyed greater success.

These were recreational lands in a profound sense, and those who express surprise, in the late twentieth century, that areas of landscape should be set aside for conservation and recreation really don't know much about the history of our northern landscape. Even as early as Norman times, man was using the landscape of North Yorkshire for pleasure rather than for utilitarian purposes. The principle of maintaining large areas of countryside primarily for recreation and conservation has, in North Yorkshire, a long history.

# 4

## Black Monks, White Monks

When St Benedict, at the end of the fifth century, appalled at the corruption and decadence of the last days of the Roman Empire, chose to seek a new, simple life devoted to God, he could have had little conception of the influence his ideas would have on the evolution and history of modern Europe, or, to be more specific, how a remote, cold little province in the North would, more than a millennium and a half in the future, still be littered with a glorious architectural inheritance resulting from an idealism made manifest.

North Yorkshire has such an inheritance, of international importance. But the influence of monasticism on North Yorkshire is more than mere stones. It has helped to shape even the present-day way of life of people in the county.

Benedict settled at Monte Cassino, some eighty miles south of Rome, and in rural quietude evolved a philosophy and a code of conduct known, to later generations, as the Rule of St Benedict. It stressed communal living, a life of industry and devotion, curbing all physical excesses. It became the inspiration for all future monastic orders – offered a discipline, a structure, organization. Therein lay its success. It was soon to become a crucial mechanism in the spreading of Christianity throughout Europe, and particularly to Britain as Irish monks came to England via the islands of Iona and Lindisfarne to establish a northern mission, whilst St Augustine's monks were active in the south.

The two threads of Christianity in England were firmly woven together at Whitby, in North Yorkshire, in AD 664, at that crucial synod where representatives of Irish and southern monastic communities agreed to adopt common procedures and accept a common authority. Whitby, therefore, has a claim to be a site of major importance in the history of Christianity in England.

But it is significant in other ways. In 657 Hilda, Abbess of the first convent of nuns in England, at Hartlepool, on the Durham coast, was given land by Oswy, newly victorious Christian king of Northumbria, high above the little Anglian fishing port of Whitby, to establish a monastery. This monastery was a dual establishment, separate houses for monks and nuns, a not uncommon arrangement in Anglo-Saxon times.

Under the inspiration and direction of Hilda, herself an Anglian princess, the abbey soon enjoyed a European reputation for scholarship. It was to Whitby Abbey that Caedmon, an illiterate local herdsman, came and told of a dream in which a man asked him to sing. Hilda saw it as a sign from God and took Caedmon into the abbey community. His alliterative verse in the infant English language justifies the claim that he is the first identifiable English poet, sharing a common linguistic inheritance that in later centuries was to produce Shakespeare and Milton.

How splendid it would have been to be able to identify that Anglo-Saxon abbey, overlooking the sea from those wild clifftops, where St Hilda let the passionate spark of Christianity blaze into light and where Caedmon first struggled to shape an English poem. The Danes denied us that pleasure, burning and looting, destroying the abbey and the community in 866. Only the outline of the foundations has been traced by archaeologists, an Irish-style monastery whose inmates lived in separate houses, having only the church and possibly the refectory in common. No trace of the burial place of Caedmon, of St Hilda or of King Oswy himself has been recorded.

The revival of Whitby's fortunes came after the Conquest, when in 1078 Elfwy and Reinfrid from Evesham Abbey in Gloucestershire made a pilgrimage to the holy places of the North. Reinfrid, reputed to have been one of William's soldiers who took part in the Harrowing of the North, was so moved by the holy site that he determined to stay in Whitby and found a new monastery of Benedictine monks. Such developments were encouraged by the King, who saw advantage in a loose liaison of Church and State, the Church providing badly needed stability to an unsettled kingdom, a means of deflecting the otherwise rebellious energies of young Anglo-Saxon noblemen. Thus began that enormous flowering of monasticism throughout England, especially strong in the North, where, encouraged by the King, the new Norman owners of vast tracts of land, anxious for the welfare of their immortal souls, were ready and willing to give land to monastic settlers, often endowing the monasteries with other lands and properties to give the struggling communities income on which to survive.

At Whitby, the ruins of the Benedictine abbey, which have been described as amongst the most emotionally stirring in England, date essentially from the thirteenth century, the superb Gothic arches, buttresses and transepts, in weathered sandstone, enjoying a dramatic site, visible for many miles from the surrounding moorlands, dominating the little town to which they are linked by a 199-step stone staircase. The decay of the fabric of the abbey after the Dissolution has been well documented. Though the monastery itself suffered much demolition and rebuilding in the sixteenth and seventeenth centuries to create the present Abbey House, the church itself remained virtually intact till 1711, when damage became apparent. The nave collapsed in 1762, the south transept soon afterwards, whilst some thirty years later the west front fell and on 25 January 1830 the great central tower crashed to the ground. But not only did Whitby Abbey suffer the erosive effects of weather and time. On 16 December 1914 a German battle-cruiser, shelling Whitby in a pointless act of attrition, lobbed an explosive shell that hit the abbey wall and the west wall of the nave. Now enjoying the care of English Heritage, the ruins survive as a noble and impressive monument, crowning an already impressive coastline.

It is difficult for us who live in the safety and comfort of the twentieth century to imagine the utter hardship and deprivation faced by the pioneers of monasticism, struggling to survive in the harsh wilderness of North Yorkshire, or the organizational brilliance and acumen which created the wealth, the energy to produce those magnificent, soaring, soul-searching arches, which we can now enjoy for aesthetic, if not spiritual, experience.

Take Lastingham, a village in the south of the Moors just five miles from Kirkby Moorside, tucked into a fold of the hills below Spaunton Moor.

Cedd, one of St Aidan's monks from Lindisfarne, was sent to found a monastery at Lastingham in 654. For ten years the little band of men struggled to establish a community in the forest. In 664 plague struck, and several of the monks, including St Cedd himself, perished. Other monks from other parts of England, hearing of the plight of Lastingham, came to join the struggling community, but plague and pestilence struck again, all but one of the monks dying. Finally came Chad, Cedd's brother, later to be Bishop of both Lindisfarne and York, and he succeeded in establishing a community which survived for two centuries before being utterly destroyed by Danish invaders. It is thought that two mysterious massive gravestones at nearby St Gregory's Minster might have marked the last resting places of St Cedd and King Ethelwald, brought there by monks fleeing as the Danish raiders appeared.

In 1078 Stephen, a monk at Whitby, having quarrelled with his abbot, came to Lastingham to re-found the monastery and began work on a splendid church of which the crypt survives, four ornamental columns, carved with leaves, supporting massive arches. But constant disturbance and conflict with robbers – an interesting reflection of the lawlessness and civil disturbance of Norman England – forced the monks to abandon Lastingham yet again and to seek the relative safety of York, where they founded the great Benedictine monastery of St Mary's, immediately outside the city walls, whose ruins give such distinction and splendour to the Museum Gardens and where, fittingly enough, the great cycle of medieval mystery plays is performed during the York Festival.

In spite of such setbacks, the wild landscapes of North Yorkshire proved an enormous attraction to monastic communities. Great landowners, too, were more likely to give open wilderness, fell and moorland to the monks, rather than rich valley land. A recent estimate has suggested that by the end of the Middle Ages there were no fewer than sixty-nine separate monastic sites in North Yorkshire, some of them merely temporary establishments for groups of monks before they created a permanent base, others the focal point of enormous activity lasting many centuries.

One such was at Selby. The story is a curiously moving one. Benedict, not the Roman saint but a monk from Auxerre in France, had a vision, as a result of which he left his parent monastery in 1069 for England and took a ship bound for the port of York from King's Lynn. At Selby, on the way up the Ouse, he took the sight of three swans alighting on the river as a sign of the Holy Trinity – three swans bedeck Selby's coat of arms to the present day. Here he established his religious community, close to the small river settlement of Anglian tradesman and farmers. This settlement came to the notice of Hugh, Sheriff of York, following the Harrowing of the North. The King granted the brethren land in Selby and permission to build a monastery, with Benedict as its first abbot.

Work began on the great church in 1100, with stone – Magnesian Limestone – being brought from nearby Monk Fryston by specially constructed canal to the Ouse. Work on the church continued over the next 120 years, the early massive Norman style giving way to the more delicate Transitional and Early English work. The fourteenth century saw further extensions and development, with elegantly traceried windows, and the fifteenth century, among other additions, saw the building of a chapel.

The church suffered severe damage by Parliamentarian troops during the Civil War, with many statues and much fine glass being destroyed. It was allowed to fall into disrepair, with, in the eighteenth century, a wall being built across the chancel so that the nave could be used as a warehouse, whilst the choir remained in use as a church. This was removed during nineteenth century restoration, but a major fire in 1906 gutted the building. Mercifully, the excellent limestones chosen by the original builders withstood the holocaust well, making accurate and sympathetic restoration possible, and the great church of Selby Abbey still dominates the old town, making it one of the glories of North Yorkshire.

The original Order of St Benedict – called 'black monks' from their black robes – was inevitably subject to many variations as reforming groups modified the original Order, in many cases going back to what they saw as first principles, in other cases happy to accept minor but important changes. One such important variation came from groups of canons or clerks within the Church who, following the rule of St Augustine of Hippo, North Africa, were urged to form themselves into communities. Though they were basically Benedictines in philosophy and outlook, their disciplines were a little less strict.

A group of such Augustinian (Austin) Canons from Huntingdon were given lands at Embsay, near Skipton, by William de Meschines and Cecilia de Romille, local Norman landowners, in 1120. Even with some endowments, the community had a struggle to survive and was grateful when, in 1154, they were granted land by Alicia de Romille, Cecilia's daughter, in a more sheltered valley site, down by the River Wharfe, a narrow cleft in the bedrock through which the River Wharfe runs, not far from the notorious Strid. The old tale that Alicia gave the land in memory of her son, William, who is said to have died when jumping the Strid with his greyhound, is belied by the fact that William was a witness to the priory's charter, but his early death in 1164 might well have been, as described in the legend and in Wordsworth's poem 'The Force of Prayer', by drowning in the Strid, the two events, the founding of the Priory and the death of the young lord, becoming inextricably linked in folk memory over many generations.

The picturesque beauty of the priory site was undoubtedly a matter of supreme indifference to the canons, whose objective of spiritual enrichment and religious discipline no doubt came a close second to the realities of physical and economic survival. Fortunately they had generous benefactors, particularly in Alicia de Romille, who gave rights of hunting and access across her lands, whilst a fair at Embsay granted by King Henry II was another source of income. But most important of all was the granting of land, a kind of spiritual insurance policy, by rich nobles, no doubt partly to atone for the hardships imposed on the Anglo-Saxon communities but perhaps too as a safety valve against insurgency. Bolton Priory soon acquired gifts of land at Marton, Storiths, Kildwick and Cononley, as well as churches and livings at Skipton and Long Preston, and later at Harewood.

Such estates, scattered over a wide area, require management, and a system of outlying farms (granges), managed by lay brothers and tenants, was developed, all bringing in income to the parent priory, enabling the business of the priory to continue and indeed be expanded. 'Business' is perhaps the key word, because by the thirteenth century a business it was indeed, with a large number of people involved, both at the parent priory and at outlying granges that in turn administered outlying farms. New building was required, to provide accommodation and facilities, to build the splendid priory church that through happy chance of history still survives as the village of Bolton Abbey's parish church.

We are fortunate in the chance survival of a set of official accounts (Comptus) belonging to Bolton Priory from the period 1286 to 1325 which gives a detailed, and occasionally vivid insight into the life of the priory during this period.

The number of canons, for the size of the house, was surprisingly small, there being only between twelve and nineteen who lived and worked under the rule of a prior. In addition there was a great number of lay brothers, living out and sharing the work of the priory, as well as corrodians, who were wealthy people or those who for a variety of reasons were paid for by the wealth of others, allowed to live at the priory in return for payment of gifts of money or property.

The records suggest that some of the men who became canons were, as evidenced by surnames, local men; others came from a wide catchment area extending over the whole of Yorkshire and including the Midlands and South. For many youths and young men, particularly those of good birth, the monastic life offered a degree of financial and personal security in a difficult and dangerous world, and a career structure of sorts which, if not quite the modern equivalent of the Civil Service, offered the dignity of office. There is also evidence to suggest that rules and vows could be interpreted with differing degrees of severity. At one period in the thirteenth century, for example, the canons were accused of serious laxness, holding a good deal of private property rather than goods in common, spending a good deal of time away from the priory – for example, in hunting the local red deer, and introducing strangers into the cloisters, for what purposes we are not told. Consumption of food, according to the records, could often be quite prodigious and included an allowance of a gallon of ale a day for each canon – thought that was not an excessive amount by common medieval practice.

Even in its lax periods, the priory was a tightly organized community, with both canons and lay brothers undertaking

A view of Raydale, Yorkshire Dales National Park

In the Howardian Hills

Beningborough Hall, near York – *c*.1715. West front

Farming in the Dales – Round-up at Ribblehead. Ingleborough is in the background

Kirkgate and St Mary's
Church, Tadcaster

The Devil's Arrows,
Boroughbridge

Knaresborough –
from
John of Gaunt's
Castle

Castle Howard – Sir John Vanbrugh's masterpiece

Nunnington Hall, a blend of architectural styles and periods make this one of the most fascinating of the National Trust's Yorkshire properties

Rievaulx Abbey

The River Derwent at Kirkham Abbey, Howardian Hills

Helmsley – pattern of pantiles

Helmsley – Market Square with Feversham Memorial

specialized tasks, the lay brothers in particular managing the estates. Crops of wheat, oats, barley, rye and beans were harvested, enough to keep the communities, which included various servants and paupers, well fed with meat and bread and supplied with plenty of ale, and to earn surpluses from their harvests to purchase other requirements from local tradespeople. But most important of all was the management of livestock. Bolton Priory owned three thousand sheep, producing a major cash-crop – wool, which was sold to wealthy Italian merchant princes and taken by packhorse train to be exported through such ports as York. In a good year the priory could earn from its wool in excess of £100, a veritable fortune in the currency of the time. There was also over four hundred head of cattle for beef and dairy produce, the latter dealt with by the priory's own 'vaccaries' (dairies). Crops had to be harvested, transported and stored across the estates.

It was a very considerable business, requiring specialist skills – in agriculture, finance, commerce. It has been estimated that in the fourteenth century more than two hundred people were employed or in some way survived directly because of the economic activity of Bolton Priory, and the overall effect of the priory through the local economy must have been vast. Yet it should be remembered that Bolton was one of the smaller monastic houses in North Yorkshire.

However, disaster could and did happen with alarming speed. In 1315 and 1316 Yorkshire suffered two disastrously wet and cold summers, years in which the grain crops on the high, thin soils did not ripen enough to produce enough grain for seed, in which sheep died in great numbers through disease – the murrain, and in which there was not enough grain harvested to feed cattle through the winter months. The effect on the community was devastating. Property had to be sold, debts were incurred, help was sought from outside. Because most of its lands were poorer lands in the uplands or high in the Dales, Bolton Priory was never as wealthy as the monasteries with great lowland holdings, and two bad harvests or any such natural disaster left the community bankrupt.

Worse was to come. Hardly had the canons recovered from the dreadful harvests of 1315 and 1316 than the English army was defeated by the Scots at Bannockburn, and for ensuing years life in the North of England became intolerable, as bands of marauding Scots came to rob, burn and pillage. In 1318 they came down the Great North Road as far as Pontefract, before turning westwards from Calderdale to Airedale and up Wharfedale. Forewarned, the monks fled to Lancashire, leaving the raiders to loot and plunder. Even Skipton town, in spite of being protected by its massive castle, was burned.

In 1319 it was to happen again. This time there was resistance, at Myton on Swale where Archbishop Melton hastily gathered an army, including monks and clergymen, to defend their lands. But the Archbishop's inexperienced army was no match for the warlike Scots, who once again turned westwards into Wharfedale, doing considerable damage, destroyed crops, livestock and barns, whilst the terrified canons this time fled to safety inside Skipton Castle's impenetrable walls. Only the direct intervention of the King saved the priory, when he took the prior and canons into his protection for a year and appointed lay 'keepers of the goods of the priory' whilst the canons this time were given temporary accommodation at other monastic houses. It was to be more than a decade before Bolton Priory recovered from these devastating years, and then only partially. But recover it did, and prosperity returned, allowing some extensive rebuilding in the mid and late fourteenth century, including an extended choir in the church, new transepts and some fine new windows.

In the sixteenth century the last prior, Moone, began work on a splendid new tower which was destined never to be completed, since Henry VIII, jealous of their wealth and power was to dissolve the monasteries. Notwithstanding a pension of £10 granted to Thomas Cromwell, Henry's minister, in 1538, Prior Moone was forced to surrender the priory on 29 January 1539 – the prior receiving the not ungenerous pension of £40 per year and his fourteen canons pensions that varied from £4 to £6.13s 4d.

But who were the White Monks? Even as early as the end of the eleventh century, many monks felt deep dissatisfaction at the lax way Benedictines and Augustinians were interpreting the Rule of St Benedict. A new spirit of asceticism was abroad. At Cîteaux, in Burgundy, in 1098, a group of monks determined to form a stricter and more rigorously managed body, and rules were drawn up for a new order who would follow a more strictly controlled way of life, living and working not close to existing communities and consequent distractions of the flesh, as Benedictines had, but in remote, isolated, wilderness environments, close to nature, the elements, so that life could be centred on spiritual salvation and scholarship. Their white habits were to symbolize spiritual purity.

The first Cistercian House in England was built in Waverley, in Surrey, in 1128. Three years later St Bernard sent his secretary, William, direct from Clairvaux to the north of England to establish a monastery by the River Rye, at Rievaulx ('Rye Valley') three miles from Helmsley, on land given to the community by Walter l'Espec, Lord of Helmsley. Walter l'Espec's generosity might have been linked to the fact that in 1125 he had also given land at Kirkham, in the Howardian Hills, for an Augustinian priory, reputedly in memory of his son, also christened Walter, who had been killed in a riding accident.

The new monastery, in what is acknowledged to be one of the most beautiful monastic sites in Europe, soon flourished and grew to majestic proportions, thanks to the energy and enterprise of Abbot William. After a mere eleven years, 140 monks, 240 lay brothers and 260 hired men lived or worked at the new monastery.

Work began on a building first to glorify God, and in so doing to glorify the human spirit. Stone for the building was obtained locally, in the Corallian Limestone at Hollin Wood, and transported to the monastery by a little canal, fed by the River Rye, which can still be seen from Bow Bridge, perhaps the oldest surviving industrial canal in England.

By any standards, Rievaulx is an architectural masterpiece, the austere Norman work of the founding fathers yielding to the grace and lightness of thirteenth-century English Gothic style at its most magnificent, particularly in the splendid presbytery, 145 feet long, with seven bays, finely decorated.

But the architectural inheritance, however glorious, is only part of the story. The Cistercian monks brought brilliant organizational skills to bear to create the wealth which lay behind the remarkable building.

Aelred, a young Anglo-Saxon nobleman from Hexham, Northumberland, and courtier of King David of Scotland, visited

Archbishop Thurston at York and, learning of the work of the Cistercians, came to Rievaulx to see for himself. Entranced, the twenty-four-year-old renounced a brilliant wordly career to enter the order, serving his novitiate at Rievaulx before going to Rome. By this time Rievaulx was a major Cistercian missionary centre, establishing monasteries at Melrose, Warden and Dundeena, and Aelred was sent to Lincolnshire in 1143 to establish a monastery at Revesby. In 1147 he was invited to return to become Abbot of Rievaulx, and he proved a gifted administrator and scholar, for a time head of the Cistercian order in England and a driving force behind the expansion of the order.

As at Bolton, the monks soon acquired gifts of land – in Ryedale itself, in the Vale of Mowbray, in the Vale of Pickering, in Bilsdale, as far away as Calderdale. Clever management of these estates and the development of specialized cash-crop farming – at one time Rievaulx owned fourteen thousand sheep – were to open the way to the change from subsistence farming, where peasant farmers barely scratched a living from thin soils, to a modern agricultural economy.

But their innovations did not end there. The Cistercian philosophy of self-reliance brought involvement in many areas – their own fishery, for example, was established at Teesmouth, and they opened iron-mines at Bilsdale and near Wakefield, developing techniques which were to lead directly to the Industrial Revolution. Certainly the Cleveland iron-industry can be traced back to the monastic smithies – from the forge at Laskill in Bilsdale to that at the abbey itself which was situated just to the south of Walk Mill.

Even though the fortunes of the abbey fluctuated over the centuries, owing to the Scottish raids, bad harvests and the Black Death, this pioneering industrial technology continued. In 1540, after the Dissolution, it was no doubt former monastic workmen who improved the dam at Rievaulx to drive a trip-hammer in the forge, which produced around forty-five tons of iron ore a year, using local coppiced woodlands to supply the charcoal required for the furnace. In 1576, at the abbey site, the ironworks were renewed again with the building of the first blast furnace in Yorkshire, capable of producing a hundred tons of pig iron a year.

The impact of Fountains Abbey on modern Yorkshire was every bit as profound as that of Rievaulx.

In 1132 a group of twelve Benedictine monks from St Mary's Abbey, York, gave up their attempt to bring reform and a stricter discipline into their parent abbey and sought the support of the excellent Archbishop Thurston of York. But their own abbot, Geoffrey, refused to discuss the matter with the Archbishop's supporters and followers at a hearing arranged to discuss the grievances, and a crisis of authority developed. The Archbishop saw it as a direct challenge to his authority, and the rebels were therefore given permission to leave St Mary's. They enjoyed accommodation with the Archbishop for three months, after which time, soon after Christmas 1132, they were presented with land belonging to the Archbishop in a narrow wooded gorge of the River Skell. Because of the many springs, some of them mineral springs which flow out of the valley sides, the new abbey, though dedicated to Our Lady, was also known as St Mary of the Springs, Sanctus Maria de Fontibus, soon anglicized to Fountains. Prior Richard, their leader, was elected abbot, and they sought permission from Bernard of Clairvaux to join the Cistercian Order and took the white habit.

For a time it seemed likely that the community would not survive in this bleak and lonely environment by the River Skell. But things changed when Hugh, the urbane and wealthy Dean of York, resigned his post to join the little band, bringing with him his excellent library, brilliant organizational powers and a good deal of wealth. Hugh's immediate influence was to attract other benefactors, and soon the monks were able to start building that glorious structure that rivals Rievaulx in Gothic splendour, the magnificent four-storey tower giving height to the whole architectural group. But the most impressive feature of all at Fountains is perhaps the unique *cellarium,* the storage cellar, whose slender, perfectly proportioned columns give an effect of grace and elegance that make it difficult to realize that the area was used merely for storage of woolsacks.

Dr Arthur Raistrick, the great Dales scholar, has written eloquently of the profound influence the monks of Fountains Abbey had in the development of the Yorkshire wool industry. With extensive holdings of land in Nidderdale, Upper Wharfedale, Malhamdale and Ribblesdale, and even as far away as Borrowdale in the Lake District, it was the monastic farmers who developed the sheepwalks which are still such a dominant feature of the Pennine landscape.

In the Malham area in particular Dr Raistrick indicates the many farms which were managed from the granges at Malham and at Kilnsey, their produce, particularly of wool, finding its way by track and path, notably along the celebrated Mastiles lane from Malhamdale to Wharfedale, to Grassington, Pateley Bridge and Fountains, continuing to York, a source of that great medieval trading city's wealth, as the Yorkshire wool continued its journey to the city states of Florence and Venice, thus establishing a cultural and economic link between the merchant princes of the Italian Renaissance and the Gothic architects and masons of Fountains Abbey. As skilled sheepfarmers and merchants, their initial vows of poverty and simplicity which had tempted Prior Richard and his brothers to the Skell was replaced by commercial acumen. And a very successful enterprise it became too. In one year Florentine merchants bought 27,664 pounds of pure wool from the Cistercians at Fountains alone, their money required to finance the ambitious building programme in the thirteenth and fourteenth centuries.

Such skills were to survive the monastery itself. After the Dissolution, wool production was to remain the staple industry of the Dales, leading directly to the development of the West Riding wool industry as first water-power and later steam-power in the valleys, served by the canal and later still rail transport, brought cheap supplies of coal to drive the millwheels. Modern industrial Yorkshire is a direct result of techniques and processes initiated by the disciples of Aelred of Rievaulx and Hugh of Fountains.

With such splendours as Bolton, Whitby, Selby, Rievaulx and Fountains to enjoy, it is easy to neglect or disregard the many monasteries of North Yorkshire which in less richly endowed counties would be major focal points.

Byland Abbey, for example, has an intriguing history. It was formed by a group of monks from Furness Abbey, in Cumbria, of the Order of Savigny, originating from Normandy and like the Cistercians, seeking an austere alternative to the Benedictines, also with white habits and soon to join the Cistercians in 1147.

These monks had set out to establish an abbey at Calder, in Cumbria, but inevitably were forced to flee south away from the Scots and equally inevitably made for York to seek the help of the good Archbishop Thurston. At Thirsk their plight was brought to the attention of Lady Gundreda, mother of Roger de Mowbray. She persuaded her uncle Robert d'Alney, a former Whitby monk, to share his home with the monks at Hood Grange, near Sutton Bank, from where their abbot obtained release from Furness Abbey. Their numbers having increased, they were given land at Old Byland. Proximity to Rievaulx was a problem for them, so they moved again, this time to Stocking, now Oldstead, where they remained for thirty years before moving once again, in 1177, to the present site of Byland Abbey.

Though the abbey is more of a ruin than either Fountains or Ricvaulx, much remains which is impressive, including part of what had been a magnificent twenty-six-foot rose window and some impressive floorings, of yellow and green tiles set in complex geometric patterns.

Their history, too, was not without incident. In 1322 Edward II's army, harassed by Robert the Bruce, fled south, spending the night at Blackhow Moor above Byland, the King himself staying in the abbey. Next day his forces were routed and the hapless Edward fled to York, leaving the North of England to the pitiless Scots. Amazingly, the abbey survived. Like their Rievaulx brethren, the Byland monks were early industrialists, working the iron ores of Rosedale from the thirteenth to the sixteenth century. They also had extensive property in Upper Nidderdale.

Jervaulx Abbey was another community of the Order of Savigny, originally given land at Fors by Fitzbardolf, Lord of Ravensworth, which is generally assumed to be near Aysgarth, Wensleydale, but which may well be further west in Fossdale, near Hawes, if the evidence of a grave believed to be that of a monk, dug up last century, its occupant clutching a cross, is to be credited. What is certain is that the abbey moved to its present site near Middleham in 1156, to land on a fertile shelf above the River Ure given by Conan, son of Alan, Earl of Richmond. As with Rievaulx, the name Jervaulx is a Norman-French form – this time of Yoredale.

It is reputed that the monks' skill in making cheese with sheep's milk led to the development of the world-famous Wensleydale cheese in the valley, and they also worked coal – and iron-mines and bred horses, a skill which remains in the Middleham area, though race-horses rather than domestic beasts are the focus of attention.

Though the ruins of Jervaulx, dating from the late twelfth century, are not very extensive, they are particularly lovely in spring, covered with masses of purple aubretia that make a vivid contrast with the dark grey sandstones. Jervaulx has a small, and tragic, place in English history for its abbot, Adam Sedbergh, was implicated in the rebellion against the authority of King Henry VIII known as the Pilgrimage of Grace. On the evidence of an informer, a former monk, Ninian Staveley, Sedbergh was arrested and tried for treason. He was imprisoned in the Tower of London where an inscription carved in one of the rooms – 'Adam Sedbar Abbas Jarvall 1537' – recalls his melancholy fate. Abbot Sedbergh died at Tyburn, and the King's soldiers sought a bitter retribution from the abbey itself by expelling the monks, plundering its treasures and blowing it up with gunpowder.

Less than a mile from Richmond, easily reached by level footpath, is Easby Abbey, founded in 1151 from an Order of White Canons, Premonstratensians, an order modelled on the Cistercians but following the Augustinian Rule. Though on a smaller scale than some of the greater Yorkshire abbeys, Easby is a particularly picturesque ruin, and it includes an impressive gatehouse, built in 1300 and virtually intact, with a particularly interesting range of buildings, making excellent use of available land.

Easby's footnote in history came in October in 1346 when the English army, advancing northwards to face King David II at Neville's Cross in County Durham, was billeted in the abbey and inflicted severe damage in so doing, no doubt leaving the abbot to reflect that, with friendly forces such as these, enemies would not be needed. Fortunately the army, led by Henry de Percy and Ralph de Neville, was able to inflict a crushing victory on the Scots, so for most people living in the troubled North of England damage to Easby was more than amply compensated.

For collectors of unusual monastic orders, Malton Priory, a Gilbertine priory, part of which survives at St Mary's Church in Old Malton, is not one to be missed. Gilbertines were the only monastic order to be founded entirely in England, by St Gilbert, a Lincolnshire parish priest, in 1131. He built a small convent next to his church for seven clearly very determined local women. Unable to combine his new community with the Cistercians, Gilbert drew up his own code which offered an intriguing blend of other orders – the nuns followed Benedictine regulations, the canons Augustinian rule, and lay brothers and sisters that of the Cistercians. Many of the Gilbertine monasteries were double, for monks and nuns, the church carefully partitioned to allow nuns to hear Mass without seeing the monks, to avoid any worldly thoughts. Being neither black nor white monks, they adopted a piebald habit – the men with black habits and white cloaks, the nuns with black cloaks and tunics with a white cowl.

At Malton, all that remains of the large priory church is the west part of the nave and two-thirds of the façade, though foundations of other monastic buildings lie under later developments in the town; nevertheless, some impressive late Norman work remains as a relic of this monastic order, native grown and based on gentle English compromise, which could boast only twenty-four houses.

This score is, nevertheless, somewhat better than the Carthusians', as they had only nine houses in Britain. To learn something of their strictly ascetic order is quickly to understand why.

The Carthusians, founded by St Bruno in 1084, originally came to England in the twelfth century but only really flourished in the fourteenth and fifteenth centuries, and Mount Grace, founded by Thomas Holland, Duke of Surrey, who was later beheaded for joining in the rebellion against Henry IV, was built in 1398, the last of their houses to be built.

The Carthusians took a strict vow of silence and seclusion which led to a total separation of one monk from another, a totally ascetic life which takes to an extreme avoidance of human contact. At Mount Grace each monk occupied a separate cell, complete with sleeping-quarters and a little garden, where he could at least see a square of sky before returning to study and contemplation. The cells were built around a central cloister, and carefully constructed hatches allowed food to be passed into each without even the hand being seen. A garderobe (toilet) was attached to each garden. The monks came together only for High Mass, for Vespers and at midnight for Night Office, and they ate together in the small refectory only on Sundays and certain holy days. The rest of the time was to be spent in silent meditation or in manual labour. They were not allowed to speak to each other except during a few minutes each Sunday and were allowed outside the confines of the monastery wall only once a week.

Mount Grace, their ruined priory just off the A19 near Osmotherly, is an intriguing, oddly moving place. Its ruins have nothing of the splendour and grandeur of Fountains, Whitby or Rievaulx but are quite unique in their impact on the visitor who has time to absorb its extraordinary atmosphere. One of the cells there has been restored to give visitors an impression of what life was like. The church was a simple, austere building without any ornamentation and with minimal creature comforts. There was no infirmary, for monks who were sick would be tended in their own cell.

It is impossible not to be impressed by the stoicism and strength of purpose of the monks of Mount Grace. The little group of buildings is situated at the very bottom of the steep, wooded escarpment that forms the western bluff of the Cleveland Hills. Close by traffic on the A19 roars between the A1 and the busy towns of what is now County Cleveland. At Mount Grace, you can simply hear the silence.

# 5

# Pleasure Grounds and Palaces

Four and a half centuries after the Dissolution, controversy must still rage as to the justice, or otherwise of Henry VIII and his ministers, in effectively destroying a major part of the social and economic fabric of Tudor life. In the North, which remained relatively underdeveloped, the political implications of Dissolution were to continue right through the sixteenth century, with disastrous consequences during the abortive Rising of the North in 1569.

Over the centuries the passionate zeal of the founding fathers of monasticism had softened to become a cosy bureaucracy. It wasn't a simple process. In both spiritual and secular terms the able leadership of gifted men often renewed the vision and brought power and influence to cope with the successive periods of tribulation – the Scots' invasions, bad harvest, reckless financial management, which included the sale of produce in advance to powerful merchants, subsequently living beyond their income and falling into the hands of the money-lenders. At Fountains, for example, Abbot Peter Alying in 1276 actually pledged the abbey itself as security to a Florentine company of merchants, and it took the intervention of the King to save the community from total ruin. On the other hand, under the direction of Abbot Marmaduke Huby, in the early sixteenth century, the number of monks at Fountains more than doubled, and the estates were managed with remarkable efficiency and foresight, making it the wealthiest Cistercian house in the land, an obvious target for a monarch looking for a quick financial return. Fountains Abbey's income at the Dissolution was more than £1,000 per annum, a huge sum in the currency values of the time.

Perhaps one has to take the report of Layton, one of the King's inspectors, just a little sceptically, because clearly it was very much to Henry's advantage to discover corruption and waste at the abbey. As Layton was to write to Thomas Cromwell: 'Please your worship to understand that the Abbot of Fountains hath so greatly delapidated his house, wasted ye woods, notoriously keeping six whores and six days before our coming he committed theft and sacrilege, confessing the same; for at midnight he caused his chapleyn to stele the keys of the secton and took out a jewel, a cross with gold stones ... ' In the circumstances Abbot Bradley was fortunate indeed to receive in 1540 a handsome pension of £100 per year, but his monks received only a single payment of between £5 and £8.

The abbey lay empty for some months whilst the Church authorities debated if it should become the cathedral of a vast new bishopric covering parts of Richmondshire and Lancashire. In the event, it was decided to use the Benedictine abbey at Chester for this purpose, and in 1540 glass and lead were being stripped from the abbey for use at Ripon and York. In October 1540 the abbey and part of the estate, and 'the Scite of Swyne Abbey and the Monastry of Nunkeeling, with their church and bells', were sold by the King for £1,163 to Sir Richard Gresham, a London merchant. The abbey seems to have drifted into gentle decay until 1597, when it was bought by Stephen Proctor, son of an early ironmaster. He began work in 1610 on Fountains Hall, using stone from the lay brothers' infirmary.

Fountains Hall is a remarkable and unusual building, unusual in its height, its five storeys necessitated by the steepness of the land immediately behind the site of the house. It is unusual too in that it shows a divergence from the conventions of late Elizabethan and Jacobean architecture (a superb example of which, also built by Proctor, is to be seen at Friar's Head, near Winterburn, Malhamdale), by including a Renaissance classical doorway, balustrade and carefully balanced façade. There is also a magnificent oriel window, with heraldic stained glass, Dutch in origin. Stephen Proctor was later to claim that the Hall had cost

£3,000 to build, notwithstanding the ease of obtaining stone nearby, a prodigious sum in those days and interesting because it represented a quite ostentatious use of wealth at a period when the houses of the landed gentry in the North of England were either simply functional or defensive. Here was new money, from industry, creating not a heavily fortified castle or manor house but an object of beauty, of glory. It was the shape of things to come.

One wonders what Sir Stephen Proctor, as he became, thought of that great, deserted abbey only yards from his fine new house. The whole thing may, indeed, have been little more than a speculative venture because only a few years after the Hall was completed Proctor produced what in effect was an estate agent's description of his house, abbey and estates for what he described as 'this Bargen ... richly woorthe the Price' of £7,000. The description is fascinating and gives insight into the estate as it must have been in the early years of the seventeenth century, each of the granges on the site having fine dwelling houses 'fitt for Farmers of the best sort to dwell in'.

There is also in the Scite of the Abbey many Fishe ponds inclosed in a Wall, and the whole Scite hath been all walled about with a highe Wall of Lyme and hewn stone, and containeth 80 acres. And much of the wall standeth good, the rest is fallen downe, but the stone beinge theire, may be set up with a little Charge, and would be a very pretty Parke, the Ryver runninge in a Valley throughe, from one end to the other, besett with Woods Plaines and Thicketts very Parke like, and most in the Viewe of the House ...

There is Orchards and Walks well furnyshed with deinty Fruits, and the last yere, theire was such abundance of ripe and goodly Grapes hanginge an growinge upon a high Rocke theire, as I thinke the Northe could not have the like.

There is no mention of the actual ruins of the abbey, though a 'goodly Milne' (mill) and 'Garners' (storehouses) 'all of hewn stone' deserve mention to the prospective seventeenth-century purchaser. Nevertheless, the aesthetic attractions of the 'very pretty Parke' had not passed unnoticed. In early seventeenth-century usage, a 'park' was an enclosure, usually for deer, and only gradually began to have the connotation, so clearly indicated here, of a pleasure ground. Gardens were usually small and formal – the 'knot' garden – and enclosed behind high walls, a little bit of peace and order protected against the forces of wilderness and chaos.

From 1627 until 1767 the property was in the hands of the Messenger family before being purchased by one William Aislabie, owner of neighbouring Studley Royal, and incorporated into that estate.

The Aislabies are an interesting family who were to have a profound effect on the landscape of North Yorkshire. They made their fortune through a judicious marriage – George Aislabie, Registrar of the Ecclesiastical Court of York, married Mary, daughter of a wealthy Ripon landowner, Sir John Mallorie. Sir John's son died under age, and Aislabie inherited his father-in-law's fortune. His son, John Aislabie, added fame to that fortune by becoming Mayor of Ripon in 1702 and rising to be Chancellor of the Exchequer of England in 1718, a political career which was to collapse in ruins in 1720 through his involvement with the notorious 'South Sea Bubble', a speculative venture which led to a massive financial scandal and disgrace. Undaunted by the failure of his political ambitions, Aislabie returned to his Yorkshire estate to continue creating a remarkable landscape over the last twenty-two years of his life; the work was continued by his son William, who was finally able to incorporate the abbey itself into the noble scheme. The house they built at Studley Royal was unfortunately destroyed by fire in the 1940s, only the stable block remaining.

What the Aislabies created at Studley Royal and at Fountains was a landscape of European importance, part of a very special English tradition. 'Creating a landscape' may seem a contradiction in terms. Landscape is, after all, the result of the interaction of many forces – geology, climate, vegetation, centuries of human activity, a largely unconscious process. But what eighteenth-century English country gentlemen were putting into practice was very much a conscious process, nature tempered with a good deal of art – art, paradoxically, that seemed so effortless in its effect that it appears no art at all, merely nature herself. Painters were much to blame for the new fashion, creating in the educated mind a sense of an idealized classical landscape, epitomized by the work of the seventeenth-century French painter Claude Lorrain, a landscape carefully proportioned, noble in sentiment, calm in feeling. The contrast in mood came in the brooding rocky gorges and crags of the more romantic Italian master Salvator Rosa – a mysterious, gloomy, threatening kind of landscape.

The horrors of the Civil War behind them, Englishmen of the eighteenth century entered a new 'Augustan' age of peace and prosperity. Apart from occasional trouble from Scots and Jacobites, wars were something that happened overseas. Britain was now a great trading nation, centre of a vast and expanding maritime empire. Fortunes could be made from trade, even from such unsavoury activities as the West Indian slave trade. Fortunes could be made, too, in manufacturing, as first the new turnpike roads and later canals opened up vast new markets. Iron, lead and coal were there to be mined to supply expanding industry.

Profits could be invested in real estate, and land was available for the entrepreneur; alternatively an ancestral estate, hitherto neglected, was there to turn into a vast pleasure garden, a landscape fit for men and women who saw themselves as the modern successors of the sophisticates of Ancient Rome. So armies of workmen were brought in to clear the wilderness and scrub and to plant noble trees, not in the regimented and geometric lines of the gardens of France and Italy but in carefully placed clumps in foreground and background, or fine single specimens. The trees would have a functional purpose too, as a source of shelter and wealth-giving timber, perhaps not for the next generation but for the one after that and subsequent ones to follow – an investment in beauty and in wealth, which above all must please the civilized eye. Becks were to be gouged out, dammed to make lakes, canals or ornamental canals and ponds. Statuary, in the manner of the classical Greeks whom eighteenth-century Englishmen admired, was to be placed on an artificial island, to reflect finely chiselled features in the limpid waters. Little pagan temples were to be erected, whose classical columns would reflect in the waters, or perhaps on a bluff of the hillside, half concealed among trees, just as in a Lorrain painting. Or, in the spirit of Rosa, a grotto or ornamental tunnel might be constructed from rough-hewn stone, something mysterious and romantic, even slightly sinister, a touch of what later became known as 'Gothic'. Splendid, even pompous gateways and lodges would be erected, often carefully placed at the end of a long drive, at exactly the point to enhance a view – as at Studley of Ripon Minster.

You see all this illustrated so perfectly at Studley. The little valley of the Skell where the monks had their fishponds was turned, by the Aislabies, into a kind of living painting – the canal, the Moon Pond, the Half Moon Pond, the lake, all forming the centrepiece around which astonishingly beautiful buildings have been erected. Complex sluices and underground water-channels maintain the mirror-still water-levels, and a rustic cataract, which might almost have come from a stage set, carries the foaming waters of the Half Moon Pond into the canal. You follow paths away from soft green lawns, past the Temple of Piety, climb through a 'Gothic' tunnel to the mock-medieval Octagon Tower, follow the high-level path to the little Temple of Fame, a superb little circular temple, and continue on to Surprise View, a little wooden shelter in the Chinese manner, offering that splendid vista of the abbey itself, with Abbot Huby's great tower reflected in the clear mirror of the canalized stream.

The whole thing is artifice – absurdly so, one might argue, a kind of eighteenth-century Disneyland, but executed with consummate taste and bravado, an echo of classical civilization in cold northern countryside which somehow remains very English in its greenness and its softness.

The abbey itself had now become an object of the picturesque, its function to reflect the more Romantic, Gothic elements in the landscaped gardens, its ruined walls and slender arches echoing the cataract, the tunnel, even the Octagon Tower, its very dilapidation part of its pleasing mystery and melancholia. To illustrate how deep-rooted such a view of the picturesque has become in our consciousness, imagine the outcry if some benevolent millionaire came along with an offer to 'restore' Fountains Abbey to its early sixteenth-century glory, putting back the roof, the windows, the wooden doors. 'Outraged' would be the mildest epithet to describe letters to *The Times* and the *Yorkshire Post*.

Not that William Aislabie suffered any such qualms, proceeding to 'improve' the ruins of the abbey with various bits of neo-Gothic ornamentation subsequently removed by later owners. Thankfully the abbey ruins, though still maintained by the Department of the Environment, and also Studley Royal estate, are now in the care and protection of the National Trust, to be enjoyed by thousands of visitors yet keeping their sense of peace and tranquillity.

Clearly, if you'd got a handy ruin on your estate in the eighteenth-century, preferably a ruined abbey or priory, though a decent castle would do, you had a distinct advantage when it came to creating a landscape to go with it. Bolton Priory, for example, found its way via the Cliffords and the Burlingtons to the Cavendishes, Dukes of Devonshire, who adapted the old monastic gatehouse to a splendid neo-Gothic shooting-lodge whose guests have included prime ministers and royalty – King George V was a frequent guest on what are reputed to be among the finest grouse moors of all England. If Bolton Priory's setting by the Wharfe is superb, the gracious parkland around it is the foil for a jewel that attracted Turner, Girtin, Landseer, Ruskin and others; it was the excellent Reverend William Carr, pioneer of Dales dialect studies and breeder of the Craven heifer, a cow of gargantuan proportions, who laid out the miles of ornamental walks and footpaths which have been enjoyed by generations of visitors.

At Rievaulx it was the money of a London banker and goldsmith, Sir Charles Duncombe, Lord Mayor of London, that acquired the estate and was to lead to another remarkable experiment in the picturesque. Duncombe's great-grandson, Thomas Duncombe III, no doubt inspired by Aislabie's example at Fountains, conceived the idea of creating a great terrace to match an existing one at Duncombe Park, this time with the purpose of opening up a series of remarkable views and vistas of the abbey ruins. At each end of the 'long serpentine walk' which runs along the top of the hillside above the abbey stand two remarkable temples. The first of these, built in 1758, is known as 'the Tuscan Temple' and is a circular structure supported by Doric columns, containing a little summerhouse with a superb painted ceiling – attributed to the Italian Andrea Casali (1700–84). From this architectural masterpiece the visitor enjoys a series of breathtakingly lovely views into Rydedale and across the noble ruins of the abbey – each clearing of the trees offering a self-consciously chosen 'view' to allow the ruins to be seen from a different angle. There can be no finer illustration of the concept of the Picturesque. At the end of the terrace is the elegant 'Ionic Temple', also built in 1758 and probably designed by Sir Thomas Robinson, who helped to complete Castle Howard. This is a little banqueting-house, with glorious frescoes on the ceilings and ceiling coves by Giuseppe Mattia Borgnis (1701–61) and superbly furnished. Like Fountains Abbey and Studley, Rievaulx Terraces are the property of the National Trust and open most days of the year.

A disastrous fire in 1693 destroyed Henderskelf Castle, near Malton, home of Charles Howard, third Earl of Carlisle, only ten years after it had been rebuilt. The Earl decided to replace it with a house worthy of his position as acting Earl Marshal of England – he was cousin to the young Duke of Norfolk who had not yet come of age – and a future First Lord of the Treasury. After quarrelling with his original architect, Talman, he brought to Yorkshire a young soldier-playwright he had met at the fashionable Kit-Kat Club, a man with no previous architectural experience. That Vanbrugh turned out to be an architect of genius was either an accident of fate or a reflection of the perceptiveness of the young Earl. To be fair, too, John Vanbrugh had a collaborator also of astonishing talent – Nicholas Hawksmoor, who doubtless tempered Vanbrugh's flights of fantasy with realism and was to add his own remarkable contribution.

The result of Vanbrugh's and Hawksmoor's work was a magnificent palace without equal in the North of England, and an undoubted masterpiece, perhaps even excelling Vanbrugh's later achievement at Blenheim Palace. It took half a century to complete, from preliminary drawings in 1699 to after the death of Vanbrugh in 1726, Hawksmoor in 1736 and the Earl in 1738, having spent an unbelievable £78,000 on the house – a fortune of many millions at today's prices.

Castle Howard, still the home of the Howard family, is an overwhelming experience, a piece of rhetoric in stone executed in the grandest manner, classical in form, baroque in exuberance, larger than life, the great central dome (destroyed after a fire in 1940 but restored in the 1970s) flanked by massive wings, each vaster than a mansion in its own right. Its sculpture galleries, libraries, tapestries and art treasures provide a feast for the senses that requires several visits to absorb. The great hall is seventy feet high and fifty-two feet square and offers an astonishing sense of space and light.

But Castle Howard is more than a house. It is also set in a richly beautiful landscape which has been created to reflect the majesty and splendour of the overall conception. Great avenues five miles long have been laid out, a huge obelisk at the crossroads. The visitor enters through a massive gateway. There are woods, artificial lakes, a classical bridge which carries nothing more than a cattle-path across the lake, its massive proportions there to add perfection to a view. Statues line terraces, fountains gush splendour, a pyramid caps a hillock. You even find a statue hidden deep in a wood, like something from a Roman legend.

Two of the most remarkable creations are masterpieces of English architecture in their own right, irrespective of their situation in the grounds of Castle Howard. One is Vanbrugh's Temple of the Four Winds, designed and built between 1724 and 1726, a little summerhouse with a dome and four porticos, its interior of richly decorated plasterwork, a building of grace and eloquence and acknowledged to be one of the most beautiful small buildings in England. Just as theatrical, but in a totally different way, is Nicholas Hawksmoor's mausoleum, a circular colonnaded temple of simple but epic grandeur, set on a massive stone podium, dominating the landscape like the temple of the ancient gods. It is the resting-place of the Earls of Carlisle and a building many believe to be Hawksmoor's greatest masterpiece, which, for an architect of his genius, is praise indeed.

What impresses so much about Castle Howard, one of the great showpieces of northern England, is the totality of the house, the gardens, parkland which extends over an area of more than a thousand acres of the Howardian Hills. This is a landscape which epitomizes the eighteenth century at its finest – grand, noble, richly expansive. The very pheasants which leap out of the copses and hedgerows seem to belong to the novels of Henry Fielding; one half expects to meet Parson Adams, tattered Aeschylus under his arm, to come bustling around the corner or to discover Tom Jones and Patridge on the run from some wayside inn.

The nearby village of Whitwell is still very much an estate village. Great country estates and their management are an important aspect of economic life and of society in North

Yorkshire, even though catering for the weekend and summer visitors has now replaced many of the labour-intensive chores that once made up country house life. Visitors are now in the cash crop necessary for a great estate to keep in being; heritage is a business which has to be run professionally and well, and at Castle Howard, with its costume gallery, exhibitions and regular attractions, they do the job particularly well. The glory once the privilege of the few is now shared by many, even though for many people, outside North Yorkshire at last, it has taken a television serial *Brideshead Revisited,* to awaken awareness of what had long been there for the experiencing.

If the glory of Castle Howard is that it reflects the architectural glory of a particular period, many North Yorkshire country houses, like others in Britain, reflect a complex story of additions onto an original medieval or Jacobean house as each generation of a particular family adapted the building to their needs or reflected the fashion of the times, so much so that the house becomes an architectural patchwork quilt requiring an expert eye to decipher particular periods of the fabric. In many respects this can be their greatest charm, a marvellous time-chart whose origins may go back deep into English history.

Such a house is Ripley, near Harrogate, home of the Ingilby family since the mid fourteenth century. Sir Thomas Ingilby, still in his early thirties now continues a line and a tradition which go through the fabric of Yorkshire history like a bright thread. King Edward III, out hunting in the nearby royal forest of Knaresborough in 1355, fell defenceless in front of an injured wild boar but was saved by Thomas de Ingleby, who was duly rewarded by a knighthood, the use of a boar's head as a crest, and such useful privileges as freedom to hunt in the royal forest and a charter to hold an annual market and horsefair in Ripley. A Sir John Ingleby helped to found Mount Grace Priory in 1396, a Sir William Ingleby fought for Henry VII at Flodden Field, and his son in 1558 was appointed Treasurer of the border towns of Berwick-on-Tweed – the town's great treasure-chest is still kept at Ripley Castle. Francis Ingleby was a priest and Catholic martyr who was hanged, drawn and quartered at York, and though the family were ardently Royalists, they had Cromwell himself, no less, staying the night after the Battle of Marston Moor in 1644, sleeping in the library under the watchful eye of

Lady Ingleby, who was armed with two pistols 'in case she missed with the first'.

The house itself dates from the fifteenth century, with a fortified gatehouse which was built in 1415, fortifications being permitted because of the all-too-regular Scottish raids. The old tower was built in 1555 and contains three magnificently panelled rooms; the rest of the house dates from the 1780s, remaining relatively unaltered since that date. Therefore Ripley Castle provides an attractive blend of Tudor and late eighteenth century, making it one of the most interesting and unusual of North Yorkshire country houses.

The extensive parkland and walled gardens were designed by that doyen of English landscape gardeners, Lancelot 'Capability' Brown, in the middle of the eighteenth century, though, curiously, the lakes – formed by damming tiny Thornton Beck – were not dug out until 1844, long after Brown's death. Nevertheless, the parkland has all the hallmarks of its creator – long, romantic views with scattered clumps of trees blending into the Nidderdale landscape and a lake in the foreground that gives an immediate focal point.

Ripley village, a typical estate village, is an even more artificial creation than the parkland itself. In 1827–8 Sir William Amcotts Ingilby had the entire ancient village of Ripley swept away and replaced by a new model village based on one in Alsace-Lorraine, in northern France. Handsome stone houses line a broad cobbled street, and the village hall has the somewhat un-Yorkshire title Hôtel de Ville.

Not far north of Ripley, about four miles north of Ripon, lies Norton Conyers, another North Yorkshire house whose family and fabric date from the remote past. Its initial owners, the Norman family of Conyers, bequeathed the property to the ill-fated Norton family in the 1350s. This powerful and influential Catholic family lost everything in the abortive Rising of the North in 1569, when, through their support of the rebellious Northern Earls against Elizabeth, Richard 'Old' Norton and several of his sons had to flee abroad to escape execution. Others less fortunate were executed. The property was acquired in 1624 by the Graham family, Scottish Borderers turned English courtiers, and they have remained there ever since. The house has its origin in a fortified manor house built in

1490, with extensive alterations including some fine Dutch gables, in the seventeenth century, and further extensions in the 1780s. There is even the bedroom and the actual bed used by the future James II and his wife when as Duke and Duchess of York they stayed in Norton Conyers *en route* to Scotland.

But Norton Conyers' most remarkable association is undoubtedly with Charlotte Brontë and *Jane Eyre*. In 1839, when Charlotte was governess to the 'riotous, perverse' children of the Sidgwick family, she visited the Grahams at Norton Conyers and was deeply impressed by the family's legend of a mad woman: during the previous century the mad woman had been confined to one of the top attics in the house. The story captured Charlotte's imagination and was later to emerge in those frightening episodes in *Jane Eyre*. Similarities exist between Norton Conyers and Thornfield, the house that provides much of the setting of *Jane Eyre*, but it is likely that the fictional house contains elements of several atmospheric houses that Charlotte knew well.

Nunnington Hall, in Ryedale, some 4½ miles south of Helmsley, is another house whose origins as a Norman, or perhaps pre-Norman, manor house go back into early North Yorkshire history, situated as it is on a curve of the River Rye, with obvious defensive purpose. The present house, now owned by the National Trust, dates from Tudor times but with considerable addition and extension in the late seventeenth century. Inside are a splendid panelled hall and staircase, and fine porcelain and tapestries together with period furniture add to Nunnington's dignified charm. The National Trust have used extensive attics to house the outstanding Carlisle collection of miniature house rooms, each decorated with meticulous attention to period detail.

The National Trust's greatest house in North Yorkshire is Beningborough Hall near Newton-on-Ouse, five miles north-west of York, a magnificent Palladian house designed by William Thornton, the York carpenter-architect, for John Bourchier, a descendant of one of the Parliamentarians who put their signature to the death warrant of King Charles I. The Hall was acquired by the Earl and Countess of Chesterfield in 1917, before eventually becoming the property of the National Trust in 1959. Of mellow brick with elegant pilasters and decorated frieze work,

Beningborough reflects the true Augustan spirit, and the splendid decorated woodwork, including a superb oak staircase, makes it a showpiece of eighteenth-century craftsmanship. The great saloon, with its gilded Corinthian pilasters, overlooks 375 acres of parkland leading down to the River Ouse. The National Trust, realizing the potential of the house, have a major interpretative display illustrating the development of the country house in England, while a carefully restored Victorian laundry gives a vivid insight into the hours of effort which went to maintain the pristine dignity of an aristocratic family.

The spirit of the eighteenth century, though on a much more intimate scale, pervades Sutton Park, a Georgian house eight miles north of York, whose elegant, uncluttered proportions enjoy a setting created by the master himself – 'Capability' Brown. The house contains splendid plasterwork by Cortese, furniture by such masters as Chippendale and Sheraton. The gardens are unusually fine.

Pride of place, however, among houses regularly open to visitors in North Yorkshire must go to Newby Hall, just off the Ripon-Boroughbridge road, near the village of Skelton.

If Castle Howard epitomizes the eighteenth-century's Grand Manner, Newby Hall tames eighteenth-century grandeur with that period's sense of style and elegance. Basically an early eighteenth-century house in the manner of Sir Christopher Wren, it was acquired in the mid eighteenth century by William Weddell, an enthusiastic art-collector and aesthete who had no less a figure than the great Robert Adam, between 1765 and 1783, to enlarge the house. (Adam also built the Boroughbridge lodges and stable blocks). Weddell's main concern was to have somewhere to house his magnificent collection of antique Greek and Roman sculpture. Adam accepted the challenge and created a house whose interior and exterior afford an astonishing artistic unity. Whether it was a room in which to display the magnificent Gobelin tapestries or the sumptuously elegant entrance hall or the splendid sculpture gallery, attention to detail in furnishing, plasterwork, proportion and colour was Adam's hallmark. Later additions and extensions, particularly in Victorian times, though they have taken something away from Adam's single-mindedness of purpose, have left most of the glories intact, and fine furniture, some outstandingly fine paintings and ceramics, together with the famous tapestries and statuary, make Newby one of the most important artistic collections in the county. But Newby remains a home, in scale and in conception somewhere to live, as indeed the Compton family, who inherited the estate from the Vyners of Studley, still do.

Beyond the house itself lies what is perhaps the finest garden in Yorkshire. Sweeping down to the River Ure are long herbaceous borders and pathways leading to sunken Italian gardens, pergolas, alpine and rose gardens and an extensive arboretum. To broaden its visitor attractions, a steamboat on the river, a narrow-gauge passenger-carrying steam railway through the gardens, an imaginative children's adventure garden and an interpretative centre, together with the usual cafeteria and restaurant make Newby Hall an enterprise determined to make the most of tourism. It is a heritage conserved by the income tourism brings but in ways that do not detract from the glory of its setting or the integrity of its artistic achievement.

Around the house and gardens extends a great expanse of parkland. A huge equestrian statue of Carrara marble, brought by a member of the Vyner family from Leghorn and supposed to represent the Polish King John Sobiesk; trampling on a Turk, stands outside the main entrance to the house. It was originally placed at the Old Stocks Market in London, on the site of the present Mansion House, but its head reputedly changed to that of Charles II trampling on the vanquished figure of the unfortunate Oliver Cromwell – an interesting re-interpretation of history.

In the park is a church, now Skelton's parish church, dedicated to Christ the Consoler, in High Victorian style, richly decorated in marble. Its history is inexpressibly sad. It was built in 1871–2 by Lady Mary Vyner in memory of her son, Frederick Grantham Vyner, who perished when making a Grand Tour on the Continent in 1870. The young man was captured by brigands and a ransom placed on his head, but before the money could be paid he had already been murdered by his captors. Heart-broken, Lady Mary used the ransom money to build this church in his memory.

'High Victorian' was, until recently, a term of abuse in architecture. Yet for sheer, romantic bravura nothing in North Yorkshire matches Carlton Towers, tucked away in the south of the county just off the A1041 between Selby and Snaith. It was the creation in the 1870s of two remarkable English eccentrics, Henry, ninth Lord Beaumont, and Edward Welby Pugin, son of that famous High Anglican architect of Victorian England A.G. Pugin. Both men died bankrupt in their early forties but only after changing a fairly conventional Jacobean and eighteenth-century house into a riot of mock-medieval, something between the Houses of Parliament and St Pancras railway station, covering the older house with turrets, battlements, gargoyles, curving flight of steps and heraldry. Above the house soars a massive clocktower. Inner rooms are like medieval banqueting-halls, decorated by a gifted church architect, John Francis Bentley, who executed his work with skill, creating gloriously rich decorated ceilings, a minstrels' gallery and a huge Venetian drawing-room.

In some ways Carlton Towers is a gigantic folly. In other ways it is a triumph of Victorian imagination. Just as Vanbrugh at Castle Howard tried to re-create the glories of Rome, so Pugin and Bentley re-created a Victorian version of a medieval or baronial castle, a fantasy mixed with aesthetic and even religious beliefs, a flirtation with medievalism and the Catholic Revival. But at the same time the building of Carlton Towers illustrated the technical brilliance and engineering virtuosity of the Age of Steam, a period when, if you could afford it, architects and engineers could turn your most bizarre flight of fantasy into an extravaganza of iron, marble, tiles, stone and glass. It was the spirit of the Crystal Palace placed in the flat countryside of the Vale of York, and in its way a remarkable piece of architecture. Now the Yorkshire home of the Duke of Norfolk, and welcoming visitors throughout the summer months, Carlton Towers is, in country house terms, something totally different, something to be experienced for its own sake.

But architecture and landscape – rich men's creations – do not end at great park gates. Just as the echoes of the great houses of Yorkshire continued to be heard in the style, and the pretensions, of scores of lesser houses, in town and country, throughout North Yorkshire, even in quite modest dwellings, there can be seen traces of the great landscape gardens and parks in many much smaller gardens and estates. A clump of trees here, a shelter belt there, an avenue of trees leading into a village, by a church, the curve of a stream, the shape of a copse, the richness of a hedgerow, ornamentation on a bridge.

As we shall see in Chapter 9, the kind of farming which produced that kind of landscape – the patchwork-quilt effect of fields and woodlands – has been overtaken by economic and technological change. There is no longer the need for small enclosed fields, perhaps not even for hedgerows and small woodlands – at least not in the narrow cost-accounting system of agricultural economics that seems to determine so much which once required the judgements of good husbandry and management of land for the next generation.

Thankfully North Yorkshire is still a vast, conservative, slow changing region. Maybe innate conservatism is a protection against change, especially if it involves an old-fashioned love and respect for the land and the communities who live in it.

Change and loss there will be, even in North Yorkshire, as elsewhere. But it would be unthinkable to allow the great houses of North Yorkshire – the Castle Howards, Newbys, Beningboroughs, Nunningtons, Carltons and others too numerous to name – to decay into dereliction because of economic and social change. Likewise the countryside that reflected the great house way of life – the parkland, estate land, needs protection as a uniquely English heritage.

However the system is managed, whatever system of grants, concessions or trusts we can devise, whatever benevolent institutions we can support – and the National Trust and the two National Parks are perhaps the supreme examples of institutions able to protect and manage great landscapes – we've got to ensure that enough of North Yorkshire is there for people in the next century to enjoy. And that's as much a matter of economics as of ethics.

# 6

## Water and Wheels

The evolution of transport has left a considerable mark on North Yorkshire. The ways people have devised to get themselves and their goods around has not only produced much to look at and discover, which is interesting in its own right, but shaped, to quite an extraordinary degree, the kind of county which it has become.

Take the coast and the rivers. From the very earliest times it was always a lot easier and cheaper to get your goods around in a boat, whether propelled by sail, muscle or engine. North Yorkshire's two principal ports, Scarborough and Whitby, were from medieval times important not just for importing goods from the Continent and exporting local produce but for transport within the UK by means of coastal shipping, in many cases quicker and less hazardous than travelling overland.

Scarborough, with its great natural harbour, which was improved, after some difficulty, as a result of a 1546 Act, imported timber, hemp and flax from the Baltic, brandy and wines from Portugal, but coastal shipping brought corn, butter, ham, bacon and salt fish. By the eighteenth century the Newcastle coal trade was an extremely important part of Scarborough's commercial activity.

Whitby, of course, was also Yorkshire's great whaling port, reaching its zenith in the later years of the eighteenth century and the early nineteenth when up to twenty whalers would leave port, each with at least twenty-five local men and boys on board, and a whole land-based industry developed to deal with the blubber, whalebone and sealskin as ships returned from voyages to Greenland and the Arctic Circle. Suitable ocean-going boats had to be built, repaired, provisioned, equipped in the local harbour. For the whalemen it was a hazardous, violent life, coping with the hardship of the voyage, totally dependent on a worthwhile catch for survival.

The development of these ports, and such minor ports and fishing villages as Filey, Robin Hood's Bay, Runswick Bay and Sandsend along the North Yorkshire coast, provided an important trade link between Yorkshire and the rest of Britain.

What is less obvious, perhaps, is the degree to which inland waterways – initially rivers and later canals – helped to develop the county. For most of human history roads in North Yorkshire, with rare exceptions, were little more than beaten earth tracks, muddy quagmires in wet weather, and for most of the winter months taking anything by wheeled vehicles any distance was difficult. A cart or haywain might indeed rumble its load between granary and mill, but a journey over any distance was slow and expensive. Much, of course, could be carried purely on the hoof, either as livestock which used the great drove roads such as Hambleton Drove Road across the edge of the North York Moors or those in the Pennines, or on packhorse, trains of a score or more tough 'jagger' ponies carrying packs or panniers across country, using miles of packhorseway and bridlepath that can still be followed, mile after mile along the stone causeways of the North York Moors or the green ways of the Pennine Dales. But as a general principle, if you were a merchant or manufacturer, just as soon as you could get your produce onto a boat and navigable river, so the time and cost of transport declined dramatically.

Yorkshire's great river system, particularly those rivers draining into the Humber, constituted important trade routes from earliest times, and the position of many modern towns is due entirely to their being situated on the highest navigable point of the river or, in some cases, the highest point for the berthing of decent-sized sea-going vessels. It was here that the wharves and warehouses would be built to permit transshipment from wagon to boat. It was here, too, that trade, banking and commerce flourished.

Take the River Ouse. The highest point for commercial navigation to this very day is the city of York, and a reason for York's pre-eminence as a trading centre was because it was, and to a degree still is, an inland port, the Ouse being tidal as far as Naburn. You'll still see lighters and small barges from the city's Lendal Bridge, loaded with cargo.

York shares pre-eminence on the Ouse with another ancient North Yorkshire inland port, Selby. Selby could, of course, take much larger vessels, and it became an important sea-going port without the need for expensive and time-wasting trans-shipment, an important factor in the years leading to the Industrial Revolution as York declined in relative importance as a port. Tadcaster, likewise, was the highest navigable point on the River Wharfe, a fact which had a significance when the superb Magnesian Limestone rock found in the locality was quarried and transported down the Wharfe and up the Ouse to York for use in the city walls and the Minster.

It didn't take a lot for merchants and tradesmen to realize the potential offered by river improvement, broadening and deepening the river bed to take larger craft and, most important, avoiding hazards like rapids, awkward bends or weirs where a local miller had harnessed the water-power (a major hazard) by building a stretch of artificial waterway or cut, to bypass the problem, with locks to maintain the water-level.

By the eighteenth century, when trade was booming and bad roads were a major brake on economic growth, measures were being taken in many parts of the country to create 'navigations' by improving rivers. Companies were formed for the purpose, deriving their income from tolls paid by users. The growing city of Leeds, highest navigable point on the River Aire, received a major boost to its fortunes in 1699 when the Aire and Calder Navigation Act was passed to improve the River Ouse. Further improvements took place in the early years of the eighteenth century, but the entire stretch between Knottingley and Goole was replaced by a fine new canal, surveyed by Rennie and built by a Leeds engineer, George Leather, in the early nineteenth century, of what is now North Yorkshire from Great Heck to Kellingley, close to the present M62. This developed into perhaps the most important commercial waterway in the North of England and still carries substantial commercial traffic between West Yorkshire and the Humber ports.

One of the most interesting canal projects purely in North

Yorkshire was initiated by the Ripon Canal Act which received the royal assent in 1767. The purpose of this Act was to make the River Ure navigable from its junction with the River Swale near Myton on Swale, through Boroughbridge (passing Newby Hall) to Ox Close near the centre of Ripon, from where a 2½-mile entirely new stretch of waterway – a 'canal' – was built to Ripon city. The navigation of the canal took three years to complete, between 1770 and 1773, and about 1¼ miles remain in use, used by Ripon Boat Club, the top sections having been 'cascaded' with the locks removed.

The opening of the original length of the Aire and Calder Navigation left the port of Selby somewhat isolated and badly placed away from the growing traffic between Wakefield and Leeds and the Humber, so in 1775 the canal engineer William Jessop was hired to construct the Selby Canal, a 5½-mile length between Haddersley on the Aire to Selby, and in so doing to make Selby the nearest point for interchange between river or canal barge and sea-going vessel. The canal remains open for pleasure craft though little commercial traffic uses it at the present time, a quiet, meandering route through pleasant, undramatic countryside, and one that deserves to be better known.

The Derwent, Yorkshire's longest river, seventy-five miles from its source to the Ouse, has long been an important river for navigation. In 1701 it was made fully navigable over thirty-eight miles from its confluence with the River Ouse at Drax, from where it forms the present North Yorkshire county boundary to Stamford Bridge, before continuing to Kirkham and Malton, the navigation being extended in 1805 as far as Yedingham, in the Vale of Pickering. Cargo carried on the Derwent during its commercial years included coal, timber, lime and a variety of agricultural produce.

There were even ambitious attempts to improve the River Swale, following a 1761 Act, as far as Marton Bridge, near Northallerton, and plans to improve Bedale Beck to bring barges to Bedale, and even along the little Cod Beck from the Swale to Thirsk.

The most ambitious, and successful waterway venture to run through North Yorkshire was, of course, the Leeds-Liverpool Canal, one of the heroic achievements of the Canal Age as it

follows the natural contours through the Aire Gap, through the
Central Pennines, albeit with some spectacular bits of civil
engineering. Work began on the canal in 1770 but by 1777, after
it had reached Gargrave, money ran out, and it was not
completed until 1816, some forty-six years after the project had
commenced – a delay largely owing to the financial depression
caused by the Napoleonic Wars.

The sections that run through North Yorkshire are particularly fine, winding their way along the southern flank of
Rombalds Moor from Kildwick via Bradley to Skipton, where the
little Springs Branch, going to old limestone quarries behind
Skipton Castle, forms a dramatic feature in its own right, as well
as being the focal point of an attractive canal basin and marina
in the centre of Skipton. The canal then winds its way through
the glacial drumline of the upper Aire valley, passing the
warehouses at Gargrave where the Duke of Devonshire brought
his ingots of lead from the Grassington Moor mines, and Lord
Ribblesdale's calamine (zinc ore) from the Malham mines, the
latter bound for Staffordshire. The canal then ascends through
locks at Bank Newton to an extraordinary serpentine section
where it closely follows the contours before swinging southwards,
past the unusual twin-arch bridge at East Marton and the
summit pond at Greenbers near Burnley in Lancashire. A huge
reservoir stretches from Winterburn to Greenbers through an
extended aqueduct – it is over ten miles long.

It is difficult to exaggerate the importance of canals as a
stimulator of economic growth during the Industrial Revolution,
bringing down the cost of raw materials, enabling new factory
technologies to develop. Of all the towns in North Yorkshire,
nowhere demonstrates the impact of the Canal Age better than
Skipton, with the old warehouses and factories clustered along
the water's edge, where ease of access to supplies of raw material
– coal, cotton, wool – simplified the industrial process. Many of
the factories and warehouses are now empty and facing an
uncertain future, but others have been converted to a boating
centre, a restaurant, an outdoor shop, giving new life to Skipton's
waterfront.

Both river navigation and canals carried a good number of
passengers: a steam-packet boat service ran from York and Selby
to London, and regular passenger services were opened on the

Leeds-Liverpool canal. It was, however, hardly a fast mode of travel, moving at little more than walking pace.

By the mid eighteenth century the chronic state of Britain's roads was forcing even *laissez-faire* governments to do something, and the system of setting up turnpike trusts, in effect consortia of local landowners, businessmen and tradespeople, to raise the capital to rebuild the neglected highways, grudgingly accepted after considerable civic disturbances in the eighteenth century, brought dramatic improvements. The trustees used a system of tolls paid by users – largely on the principle of how much potential damage the wheels of your vehicle would do to the road, to get their capital returned and to raise sufficient money to keep the roads in good repair.

The first turnpikes opened in Yorkshire produced riots by local mobs, angry at the loss of the inalienable right to travel freely. But the need to create a decent system of roads overrode such protests, and the mobs were put down by the local militia. Fine engineers, such as Blind Jack of Knaresborough (blinded by smallpox as a child but capable of feeling his way with a great staff in his hand to survey the route for a new road) and Robert McAdam (whose system of binding small, loose stones with tar produced 'tarmac' – a word which has been absorbed into the language) were available to be hired.

Turnpike roads are so familiar a part of the landscape that we are probably not even aware we've been travelling on them all our lives. Open any 1:50,000 Ordnance Survey map of Yorkshire. Most of the red lines on that map, and the brown ones too, are former turnpike roads, still readily identifiable by the fine old stone or cast-iron milestones which give the name of the road 'Keighley and Kendal', 'Dudley Hill and Killinghall', 'Lancaster and Richmond', and the distance to the next town or towns on each side. You can still find, too, a few surviving examples of tollbooths, usually square, single-storey buildings, perhaps even with a pay window. Because many of them jutted out across the pavement into the roadway, they are early targets of county surveyors' road-widening schemes. A few do survive, such as ones at Settle and at Gargrave on the Keighley-Kendal turnpike, now the A65. Even where the tollbooth has long vanished, the name 'Bar' survives, an intriguing clue to an old tollbooth or turnpike bar. The most famous in North Yorkshire is

Leeming Bar on the Great North Road, but countless other examples exist.

With any large-scale Ordnance Survey Map it is easy to trace those 'main' roads which crisscross the county, the milestones still marked, now generally class A or B roads, which were the old turnpikes. But you can detect an older pattern of narrow lanes and ways, many of which formed the pre-turnpike highways, some of them perhaps still keeping their vehicular rights, but others which are now mere green tracks, between hedgerows or stone walls, sometimes a mere bridleway across fields. Parallel to the B6265 Skipton-Cracoe road (a turnpike which met the Duke of Devonshire's new road from the lead-mines to Gargrave wharves) a green path, now little more than a bridleway, leaves Sandy Beck Bar, where a ruined tollhouse actually has a rear window designed to catch anyone sneaking by on the old road without paying their toll.

The real significance of turnpikes lay in the development of much faster road transport, in particular that brief but glorious era which was to have a lasting impact on many small North Yorkshire towns – the stage-coach era. Like the modern motor-coach, their more democratic successor, stage-coaches carried passengers who paid by the stage, prebooked from innkeepers who worked closely with the coaching companies to service coaches and their occupants with fresh horses and refreshment. So important did coaching become, in a period of about a century from the mid eighteenth century until the 1840s, that a whole new industry and whole new townships developed to cater for this trade. The inns required large stables, kitchens, bedrooms, servants, stable lads, ostlers, and the towns required many associated tradespeople to supply those inns – bakers, brewers, farriers, blacksmiths.

You didn't catch a coach by number but by name. In the 1820s *The Courier,* for example, would leave Town Hall Inn, Richmond, at 5 a.m. every Monday, Wednesday and Friday, calling at the Mason's Arms, Bedale, at 7 a.m. the Black Bull, Ripon, at 9.30 a.m. continuing via Harrogate to reach the Rose and Crown, Leeds, at 2 p.m. *The Diligence* would leave the Swan Inn, Harrogate, every day at 9 a.m. returning from the Golden Lion, Leeds, at 3 p.m. with a fare of 5 shillings 'in', 3 shillings 'out'. The Wensleydale coach, later known as *The Umpire,* left

York every Tuesday, Thursday and Saturday, calling at the Malt Shovel, Boroughbridge, the Black Bull of Ripon, the Lord Nelson at Masham and the Black Swan at Middleham, returning by the same route the following day.

The crack coaches were, of course, the mails, introduced by John Palmer in 1780 to provide a fast, highly efficient service for the post. The mail coaches charged premium fares and, by the standards of the day, were extremely fast, travelling through day and night, the coachman blowing the posthorn to warn tollkeepers of his approach and stable lads to be ready for a rapid change of horses. The Glasgow Mail, for example, followed the Great North Road from London to Catterick, via Barnard Castle and Bowes to Appleby.

By the 1830s mail coaches were averaging 10 m.p.h. or more – an astonishing speed bearing in mind gradients and time required for changing horses. All along the Great North Road, now bypassed by the A1 (M) lie the old coaching towns with their great inns, some of them converted to other uses, some of them prospering in the motor-car era. Boroughbridge is a case in point where the old vast inns seem to echo to the ghostly sounds of posthorns. If the A1 bypass has taken the ghastly nightmare of non-stop traffic away, it has also taken a good deal of Boroughbridge life and purpose away with it, leaving it to drift into a quiet obscurity, its days of greatness behind.

The Great North Road itself, which once had huge droves of cattle travelling along it more than a mile long, encapsulates much of North Yorkshire's and England's history, an ancient Ridgeway through the Vale of York, along the old line of a glacial moraine, developed by the Romans to become a well-drained 'high' way to offer visibility. (Until recent years fragments of the old Roman road could be clearly seen running in fields by the A1; these precious relics have almost entirely vanished under the plough). Many of the older towns, such as Ripon, Tadcaster, Thirsk and Northallerton, lay on branches to and from the Great North Road itself, and they also share something of the faded magic of the coaching era.

Thirsk is a particularly fine example of a North Yorkshire town whose links with coaching are very evident, with coaching inns such as the Fleece, the Crown and the Three Tuns once served by the London-Newcastle, London-Edinburgh coaches, undertakings with such solid names as *The North Briton* and *The Defence*, and *The Northern Highflyer* from Leeds. Modern motor-coaches between the Midlands, South Yorkshire and Tyneside now park on the cobbled square as passengers call in cafés for refreshment, most of them probably totally unware of the fact that they travel along the wheelprints of the old-time stage-coaches.

It is easy to see the coaching era through spectacles coated with sugary sentimentality, the Christmas-card snow-and-Robin scenario. Reality was a little different. Competition between rival operators along profitable routes was cut-throat, horses were beaten and driven to the point of exhaustion, even death – one Ralph Soulsby is reported to have driven three out of his four horses to death on the stage between Great Smeaton and Northallerton, racing a rival coach. Sentimentalists would have found the suffering of animals of the golden years of coaching difficult to forget or forgive: the welts, wounds, sores, suffering.

Nor was life all that easy for passengers. Journeys could last for days, even the best-sprung coaches were nightmarish by modern standards, and unless you were wealthy and fortunate you were exposed to the worst of North Yorkshire weather on the outside of the swaying vehicle. You had to be fairly wealthy to afford to travel at all. For most people coach travel was a luxury comparable to scheduled air travel today. To get around the country, the vast majority of people had no alternative to walking except perhaps the local, unsprung carriers' carts with the bags of flour, hens and pigs.

The coaching era ended in its actual heyday with dramatic and astonishing suddenness – the coming of the railway. The speed and ease of steam-railway travel from the 1830s onwards totally destroyed the crack coaching routes, and within a matter of four or five years coach travel dwindled to providing connecting links to railheads (even with through coach and train tickets in some instances) and on routes where the railway hadn't yet penetrated. But as soon as a branch line opened, the coach route suffered rapid extinction.

It was a sad end to a great industry. One by one the coaches along the Great North Road quickly went out of business. By the early 1840s only the *Wellington* from Newcastle to London struggled against the inevitable tide. Finally the day came when the *Wellington* left Newcastle empty and reached Darlington empty. At Northallerton too, no one got on or off, and it rolled empty into Thirsk. The end had come.

It wasn't only the drivers and innkeepers who suffered but the whole paraphernalia of servants and craftsmen maintaining the coaches, looking after the horse and passengers. Whole communities lost their way of life. Great inns, once packed with action and life, overnight became mausoleums, their rooms eventually rented off as lodgings or flats, their great stable blocks deserted.

So many of our North Yorkshire towns – Northallerton, Thirsk, Richmond, Ripon, Middleham, Malton, Pickering, Helmsley, Settle, Tadcaster, Skipton and Selby – have retained, in the fine old inns, cobbled courtyards and an indefinable atmosphere, a feeling and a flavour of the coaching era. It's an essential part of their character and essence. Long after the last stage-coach rattled its way into a museum, you can sense that presence. A new era of road usage, usurping the railways themselves, hasn't changed this, though the old inns enjoy a new prosperity.

Railway mania afflicted North Yorkshire from the very beginning. As early as 1833 the merchants and men of commerce of Whitby, having seen the little port decline as the great whaling days came to an end and having jealously watched the success of the Stockton and Darlington Railway, extended to Middlesbrough in 1830, scrapped a plan for a canal through Newtondale and hired the great George Stephenson, no less, to build them a railway line to Pickering.

Opened in 1836, the Whitby and Pickering Railway began life as a horse-drawn tramway, a single horse hauling a coach which could hold forty people, supplemented by a second horse at steeper sections of the line. At Beck Hole, however, a 1 in 15 incline to the little town of Goathland required an elaborate system of ropes and water-filled tanks to haul the coach up to the summit, later replaced by a steam-driven winding-engine. Steam locomotives didn't appear on the line until 1847, and after a fatal accident the incline was replaced by a deviation in 1865 to enable steam-locomotive operation on the line throughout.

Though the historic Whitby-Pickering Railway was an early victim, south of Grosmont, of the Beeching Axe in 1965, it was re-opened on 2 February 1969 as the North York Moors Railway, using vintage steam and diesel locomotives between Grosmont and Pickering. At Grosmont you can still see the original tunnel used by horse-drawn carriages, whilst at Beck Hole the incline survives as a footpath, with the original stone sleepers still to be seen in a nearby cottage garden.

The Whitby-Pickering, if one of North Yorkshire's most romantic lines, cutting as it does through the great glacial overflow channel of Newtondale, was not quite the first railway in North Yorkshire. The accolade goes to the Leeds-Selby line opened in 1834 and designed to speed the journey for freight and passengers to Hull, giving the port of Selby an important new lease of life. The problems of embarkation and tides made it inevitable that the line be extended through to Hull, which it did by 1840.

The railway which really sounded the death knell of the stage-coach was the line from York to Darlington, opened in 1841, part of the York and North Midland Railway, and with it the remarkable, charismatic figure of George Hudson.

Part visionary, part entrepreneur, part villain, Hudson emerged with his York and North Midland Railway, devouring other, smaller companies in its path through a process of wheeler-dealing and shady speculation of such rashness that eventually his ruin resulted. But Hudson, almost single-handed, had created the basis of the railway system of North Yorkshire, forged what was soon to become the mighty North Eastern Railway, its main line through the centre of North Yorkshire becoming one of Britain's most important, high-speed railway arteries, the East Coast Main Line.

It was Hudson's vision, more than anything else, that turned Scarborough from being a sleepy little fishing port to that great creation of the Railway Age, the seaside resort. The line between York and Scarborough, with a branch from Malton to link with the old Whitby-Pickering line, was opened in 1845. With typical aplomb, Hudson gave free rides to everyone on the first day of the operation, packing the trains and Scarborough as well, and the success of the line, and of Scarborough itself, was assured from that point on.

Scarborough shows its railway inheritance more clearly than any other town in North Yorkshire, with the notable exception of

York. The line from York curves majestically through the Howardian Hills, cutting along the side of the Derwent, close to Kirkham Priory, to Malton, then across the Vale of Pickering with the Wolds to the right, the Moors to the left. As it swings north to enter Scarborough through a narrow cleft in the hills, you are aware of approaching a railway terminus of some importance. You pass sidings, isolated platforms, the site of Londesborough Road Excursion terminus, long since closed, and finally the old grand station itself. It still impresses, those long, curving platforms designed for huge trains, the high stonework, arches, glass, the paintwork bleached by sun and salt wind. Even the toilets are on a rather grand scale, more like a public hall than a public convenience, massive fittings, polished brass. The great stone clocktower, in baroque style, above the station building, would dignify a smaller town hall. It isn't difficult to imagine the lines of horse-drawn barouches, the charabancs, lined up outside the wide station entrance for excursions to local beauty spots. It isn't quite like that now. The refreshment rooms seem a little apologetic, the information office full of empty spaces. The excursion coaches no longer leave from outside. They've even taken the lines completely up from some of the far platforms, surplus to requirements. The miles of sidings, once needed to house countless excursion trains, have mostly vanished.

They've closed the coastal line to Whitby, too, one of the most beautiful scenic coastal lines in Britain, serving Robin Hood's Bay where until the mid 1960s diesel railcars provided a marvellous service for holidaymakers. To destroy such an enormously valuable tourist asset for such comparative modest savings was an act of bewildering stupidity and shortsightedness. Thankfully, after several closure attempts but effective local opposition, the Hull-Scarborough line, which leaves the main line at Seamer for Filey, Bridlington, Beverley and Hull, continues to flourish, linking Scarborough with Humberside and retaining Filey's precious rail link.

Although the railway once had a near monopoly of travel into Scarborough, which is now shared with bus, coach and above all the private car, it remains important. Just as in the past, when, for thousands of people from West Riding towns in particular, a trip to Scarborough by train was their only way of seeing

Yorkshire's glorious coast and experiencing the sea, the train is still the best way of transporting large numbers of people, quickly, easily and with minimal congestion, part of a national transport network. Many people, for reasons of health, age, income, sex – the majority of women still don't have driving licences – or mere inclination, don't have access to a car, and for long journeys buses are no substitute. Without the railway people won't come, and without the money they bring to hotels, guest-houses, cafés, pubs, shops, Scarborough's income would suffer.

One nice development in recent years has been the re-introduction of steam trains on the York-Scarborough line during the main holiday period – the Scarborough Spa Express, and improved services with more comfortable long-distance locomotive-hauled trains have increased traffic. Whether this more optimistic scenario can be maintained at a time of savage cut-backs in the level of financial support available for the rail network is less certain. Because its traffic is concentrated into the summer months, the Scarborough line is seen as vulnerable should further rail closures to meet Government financial targets be demanded. In such circumstances the tourist industry of North Yorkshire's coast would suffer a serious blow, for continuation of the railway to Scarborough is vital to the town's future.

As indeed it is to Filey, which once had a direct line into its holiday camp further down the coast, and Whitby, which kept its railway by a quirk of a politician's pen, not the busy main line from Leeds and York via Malton and Pickering but the winding, twisting, bending and reversing little branch line from Middlesbrough along the beautiful Esk Valley, serving villages whose tiny stations are as lovely as their names. The Esk Valley branch is really a patchwork of different rural railway lines, most of which are long vanished. The line has survived to take children to school from villages where roads are too steep for buses to run. It is kept alive because of its economic and social value to the local community and to the resort of Whitby itself. Recent attempts to market the line for recreational trips, and to link with the North York Moors Railway at Grosmont, have produced worthwhile increases in traffic which, whilst not exactly guaranteeing a future for the line, offer hope that it might yet survive, as it should, as one of North Yorkshire's major tourist assets.

But the survival of the Esk Valley line has proved the exception rather than the rule in North Yorkshire, as elsewhere in England. At the peak of the Railway Age, say the 1890s, before electric tramways in urban areas and motor-buses in the countryside began to make an impact on traffic, North Yorkshire was a dense network of country railways. There was hardly a village beyond walking distance of a station or out of earshot of the familiar shriek of a steam-locomotive whistle. You could travel by train all the way along the North Yorkshire coast, virtually along the clifftops, from Saltburn to Whitby, Robin Hood's Bay and Scarborough, a route of superb scenic interest which, if it had survived, would have been a great tourist attraction.

There was a meandering line through the Vale of Pickering, with stations in the Forge Valley and at Thornton-le-Dale, meeting the Whitby-Pickering line at Pickering itself and continuing to Kirkby Moorside, Helmsley and Gilling, where it met a line from Malton which carved its way through the Howardian Hills, calling at such stations as Hovingham Spa, Ampleforth and Coxwold. From Malton too a railway wandered through the soft chalk wolds on its way to Driffield through the Burdale tunnel. There were lines from Knaresborough to Boroughbridge, to Catterick and Richmond, to Masham, from Harrogate and Pateley Bridge, between Selby and Cawood, whilst further west the Yorkshire Dales Railway ran from Skipton to Grassington, meeting the Ilkley-Bolton Abbey-Skipton line just west of Embsay. The Wensleydale line left the East Coast Main Line at Northallerton and made its way via Bedale and Leyburn to Redmire, where it survives as a freight branch serving the Preston-under-Scar limestone quarries. Beyond Redmire the tracks are lifted and only a thick strip of shale and scrub marks the line to Aysgarth, Askrigg and Hawes that meets the famous Settle-Carlisle line at Garsdale.

Some of the lines, now vanished, enjoyed a fascinating history. Some even kept their independence well after the nationalization of Britain's railways in 1948. Among these, for example, was the little Easingwold Railway, less than $2\frac{1}{2}$ miles long, between Alne, on the East Coast Main Line and Easingwold village. Opened in

1891, it kept going till 1957 as a freight line, though its passenger service – a single ancient coach behind a little tank engine – gave up the ghost in 1948. The Derwent Valley Light Railway survived right until the 1980s. It ran from York at a little station at Layerthorpe in the east of the city, originally to Cliff Common on the Selby-Market Weighton line. Passenger services ceased in the 1920s, but for another half century or so the railway provided an important service for the community, though gradually being truncated until only $4\frac{1}{2}$ miles of track were left between York and Dunnington.

It is difficult to imagine that the little town of Pateley Bridge in Upper Nidderdale once boasted two distinct railways, the fourteen-mile branch from Harrogate already mentioned and a remarkable little mountain line, the Nidd Valley Light Railway, built for the construction and servicing of Bradford Corporation's great series of reservoirs in Upper Nidderdale at Angram and Scar House. Passenger services began in 1907, with four trains a day hauled by former Metropolitan Railway tank engines originally built for the London Underground but enjoying a somewhat contrasting environment in the Yorkshire Dales. Stations were opened at Wath, Ramsgill and Lofthouse, and the line remained open for passengers until 1929 and for freight until the completion of the Scar House Reservoir in 1936, when the line was closed and the track removed. Much of the trackbed survives as a footpath, and its route can be easily traced by anyone with a large-scale Ordnance Survey Map, with surviving station buildings and old warehouses now private houses or put to other functional use.

One of the most curious lines of all in North Yorkshire was the Sand Hutton Light Railway, built during the 1920s by Sir Robert Walker of Sand Hutton Hall, as an eighteen-inch narrow-gauge line from Warthill on the York-Market Weighton line through his estate to Bossal, a distance of $4\frac{1}{2}$ miles. The line was used mainly to carry agricultural produce but also had a passenger service on Saturdays and on market days. It survived until 1932.

North Yorkshire's most famous railway, shared between three northern counties, is, of course, the Leeds-Settle-Carlisle line which runs directly through the heartlands of the Pennines. Built by the Midland Railway to provide a direct link between the towns and cities of the Midlands, South and West Yorkshire and Scotland, the Settle-Carlisle has been described as 'one of the wonders of the north' and 'the high watermark of Victorian railway engineering' and offers a superb scenic journey through the Yorkshire Dales and the Eden district of Cumbria. Stations on the line which had been closed in 1970 have since 1975 enjoyed a new lease of life, specially re-opened on certain weekends of the year to provide the widely acclaimed *Dales Rail* service. This is perhaps the most successful transport recreational scheme in the United Kingdom, bringing people from Greater Manchester, Lancashire and West Yorkshire into the Yorkshire Dales National Park, but it also takes Dalesfolk out into the cities for shopping and sightseeing. The Settle-Carlisle is also recognized by steam preservationists from throughout the British Isles as the most spectacular line in England for steam-locomotive operation, the notorious 'Long Drag' between Settle Junction in the Ribble Valley and Ais Gill summit in Cumbria being a stern test of men and machine and a glorious opportunity for the railway photographer.

Unhappily, changing economic circumstances and a general decline of rail freight traffic have led British Rail planners to determine that the line is no longer required in the new streamlined British Rail system. Since closure proposals were announced, 23,000 objections have been received and with them unprecedented publicity. The trains which once ran empty are now bursting at the seams, and extra trains have had to be supplied to meet the demand as people of all ages, from all parts of Britain and even from overseas, enjoy the thrill of travelling over this spectacular line. Even though British Rail engineers have pointed out that millions of pounds worth of essential repairs are required on the line, particularly to such great viaducts as Ribblehead, a fact that few experts dispute in principle, it is difficult to imagine any government willing to face the political odium of sanctioning the closure of what must now be Britain's best-loved railway. The Settle-Carlisle railway, as the late Bishop of Wakefield, Eric Treacy, has pointed out, is a part of Yorkshire's heritage, and no bureaucrat is going to get away with destroying that.

For many people, the decline of the railways in North Yorkshire, the closure first of all the branch lines and then even of some of the main lines, such as the direct line from York to

Hull via Market Weighton, and the Harrogate-Northallerton line which served the city of Ripon and provided the most direct line between Leeds and the North East, is a simple matter of economics, for if first of all the motor-bus and then the private car had taken away the traffic, the lines should indeed have closed. But life is rarely as simple as economics. Without their railway, many communities have suffered severely – young people, old people, have moved away, economic growth has been affected, the quality of life has been worsened. It took society a long time to realize such truths, and by this time many railways, and even the bus services which had replaced them, had gone. By the late 1960s and the 1968 Transport Act a slow recognition had emerged that Britain wanted, and needed, a railway network. Many of the surviving lines were saved and, like the Esk Valley line, have continued to serve the communities they were built to serve.

It is still possible to get around a good deal of North Yorkshire by train, and to enjoy fine countryside in so doing, and the electrification of the East Coast Main Line from London to York and Newcastle, which will also serve Thirsk and Northallerton, provides a gleam of hope. Better mainline services demand better branch connections.

Already, one North Yorkshire line which survived by the skin of its teeth in the Beeching era, from Leeds and Harrogate to Knaresborough and York, now enjoys an improved service with the new Class 141 diesel railbus on a much more frequent and regular service through from Leeds. Crossing as it does the great expanse of Marston Moor, where Cromwell inflicted a crushing defeat on Charles I's troops, there is a sudden dramatic view of the Nidd Gorge at Knaresborough, whilst the great viaducts across the Crimple Beck, just south of Harrogate, and across the Wharfe at Arthington on the Harrogate-Leeds section not only are major landmarks but offer the rail traveller some spectacular views.

The York-Malton-Scarborough and Esk Valley lines have already been mentioned as worth travelling along for the trip alone. The Esk Valley (Middlesbrough-Whitby) in particular not only offers glorious scenery, richly wooded in places, with the Esk tumbling in and around the valley floor crossed by railway tracks, but provides excellent access to the North York Moors National Park.

Over in the west, both the Leeds-Settle-Carlisle line, which has a well-timed daily service, with extra trains, including a Sunday service, in summer, and the Leeds-Skipton-Morecambe line offer superb scenic journeys. Pride of place has to go to the Settle-Carlisle, with breathtaking views along the whole of Ribblesdale and on through Dentdale, Garsdale and the Eden Valley, but the Leeds-Morecambe line should not therefore be underrated. Cutting across the undulating countryside between the Yorkshire Dales National Park and the Forest of Bowland, there are some unforgettable views, particularly across to Ingleborough Mountain, which is seen from several angles, and, around Clapham, vistas across to the Bowland Fells. The Leeds-Morecambe line still has its local stations open for a daily service, again providing excellent access to the Yorkshire Dales, particularly from such stations as Gargrave, Hellifields, Giggleswick and Clapham.

There are too, in North Yorkshire, two interesting preserved lines well worth visiting. The North York Moors Railway, between Pickering and Grosmont, already mentioned, marketed as Moors Rail, is a major preservation enterprise and tourist attraction, enjoying widespread public and private support. Trains operate along a full seventeen miles of single track, through the great Newtondale gorge, serving the important tourist centre of Goathland. With good linking bus services between Malton and Pickering (though the closure of the Malton-Pickering section must rank high on the list of railway crimes) and integration with the British Rail services at the Grosmont end, the North York Moors Railway is a full-scale transport service. It is also about experiencing the Moors and the railway, with not only the existing stations but a fine new station in the forest in Newtondale, available to take visitors into the heartland of the Moors, and a visitor centre, interpreting the railway within the landscape, exists at Pickering station. The other preserved railway is on a much smaller scale and cannot match the professionalism or resources available to the Moors Line. This is the Yorkshire Dales Railway at Embsay, where limitless enthusiasm and energy have got a station re-opened, several hundred yards of track re-laid and weekend steam-trains offering nostalgia if not transport. A small museum of railway material and an excellent bookshop are at Embsay station.

For the intrepid public transport user, particularly during the summer months and especially at summer weekends, there are some outstandingly fine bus routes, most notably the Dales Bus and Moors Bus networks through the two National Parks, and suitable bargain tickets offering unlimited travel for a fixed sum are available, such as Explorer Ticket (purely bus) and Dales Wayfarer (bus and rail) in the Yorkshire Dales.

But for most people visiting North Yorkshire the car is the means of getting there and getting around. A car means, after all, going where you want when you want, and given the sheer vastness of the county, with so much to see and do, a car gives the flexibility and the freedom which even the best public transport service cannot match. Surprisingly, for such a gigantic county, North Yorkshire has hardly any motorway, only a few short miles of the M62 which slice across the bottom stem of the county between West Yorkshire and Humberside. On the other hand the Great North Road, the A1, is a motorway in almost everything but name, and this dissects the county, a high-speed route. Other major routes, such as the A64 between Leeds, York and Scarborough, have been improved, with so much widening and a series of major bypasses that its origin as a turnpike road is obliterated; like many such trunk roads, it is fast and convenient if somewhat boring.

Better, then, to get back to the old byways, the network of quieter lanes and minor roads, those which were quiet before the railway came and are quiet now that the railway has retreated. They are all maintained in North Yorkshire to a surprisingly high standard, and parking in most North Yorkshire towns is rarely a problem, even though large, unsightly car-parks often take up too much space in an otherwise compact town centre, and disc schemes, convenient though they are, allow sidestreets to be quickly cluttered. Nevertheless, there are few places in England better than North Yorkshire to enjoy motoring or a motoring holiday, with miles of quiet but scenic roads. Only the popular villages in the two National Parks suffer anything like what would, in other parts of England, be described as traffic congestion, and then only on a very few days of the year – summer Sundays and Bank Holidays. Visitors, however, have to take the lanes as they find them, being prepared to drive carefully and to take their time behind the occasional tractor or even a herd of cows, or, on roads where overtaking is impossible, behind a tourist cruising along at 20 m.p.h. In North Yorkshire you must be prepared to be patient.

How do changing patterns of transport affect people who live and work in Yorkshire?

Car-ownership levels are high. To an extent this reflects better-than-average income levels, but it also disguises the fact that many people, in smaller towns and villages, are reluctant owners of an elderly car, suitably patched and mended by a local garage, that they can't really afford to run but can't afford to be without.

The country bus networks which evolved in the 1930s, following the passage of the Road Traffic Act, 1930, have broadly provided for many essential rural needs – work, school, shopping and leisure trips, the same buses which serve local communities also being available for tourist use during the summer months. Over the years two large companies, National Bus subsidiaries, have emerged from numerous amalgamations and take-overs of smaller companies, the Darlington-based United Automobile Company in the north and east of the county, and West Yorkshire Road Car Company, Harrogate based, in the west, with Ribble Motors penetrating the fringes of the county along the Lancashire and Cumbria border, and one or two independents such as Pennine Motors in Craven and the York Pullman Bus Company in Ryedale keeping certain routes.

As car-ownership levels rose and bus ridership declined, North Yorkshire County Council, as a public transport authority, has taken seriously its duties to maintain an adequate public service, and over the years local authority subsidy, in the form of revenue support, has risen markedly, though it remains only a fraction of the total bill for highway maintenance. However, new Government legislation, aimed at wiping away the big company monopoly on rural bus routes, ending the system of cross-subsidy of unprofitable country routes by profitable runs along the busy main roads and opening up rural services to more competition, will change this. Few experts outside Government circles predict anything but a loss of services as the big companies pull out of loss-making rural routes to protect their profitable inter-urban business, and as small companies struggle to make ends meet in rural areas. Savings to the public purse will be trivial, but loss to rural communities could be high as more people, particularly less affluent families, are forced to leave. North Yorkshire stands to suffer acutely from the loss of the country bus network if plans as they stand at present are carried out – hardship that could prove even worse than that caused by the Beeching closures because, when the railway went, there was, at least in theory, a replacement or alternative bus.

At the end of the day it comes down to what kind of society and what kind of civilization we want to see in a county like North Yorkshire. Quality of civilization can be measured by the quality of compassion shown by members of that society to the less fortunate. Transport, whether you live in a town or a country village, is a vital necessity. A good public transport service, which all people, of all ages, sexes and income, have available to meet their needs is a hallmark of a civilized society. Many parts of Europe – France, Italy, Germany, Austria, Switzerland, Scandinavia – have kept their rural rail network when in Britain it has dwindled. Now country buses are threatened with the axe.

Maybe new solutions are required, such as car-sharing schemes being tried out in Upper Nidderdale and the postbus service in Masham and Rosedale. But these are only partial solutions and if, as many experts predict, current legislation proves a social and commercial failure, new measures will be required to re-create a decent transport network. Long-term predictions of energy and resource crises, whilst they may take decades to fulfil, may well dictate a less profligate use of our limited resources than policies based on high car-ownership and usage, considerations of social justice apart.

Nor is it mere nostalgia to regret the passing of the country railway threading its way through the landscape with minimal intrusion and considerable convenience, or the scarlet bus, its meeting of countryfolk a social occasion lost to the speeding motorist.

At the very least, everyone who loves North Yorkshire's life and landscape is going to have to be vigilant to keep those surviving but important services.

# 7

## Queen of Spas

Some time in the latter part of the sixteenth century, an Elizabethan gentleman, William Slingsby, was walking over the rough common not far from his home in Knaresborough and close to a scatter of cottages known as Haregate and noticed a spring bubbling from a crevice in the rock. Something about its appearance and bitter taste reminded him of waters he had tasted at 'Spaw' in the Belgian Ardennes. He arranged for the little spring to be paved and walled, for it was indeed a chalybeate spring of pure water but rich in iron.

Expert opinion soon confirmed, the medicinal value of the spring, soon to be known as Tewit Well because of the 'tewits' (prewits) often seen and heard nearby. One Dr Timothy Bright, an able physician and rector of Barwick-in-Elmet, near Leeds, was among those who supported Slingsby's view that this well was as good as anything an Englishman could find overseas, and he gave the well the name 'the English Spaw'. Dr Bright not only recommended the waters to others but indicated he would use them himself in the summer season.

By the early seventeenth century the fame of the 'Knaresborough Spaw', as Tewit Well and other springs in the neighbourhood were soon known (Haregate being too insignificant a hamlet to be of any significance) had spread. Two important pieces of propaganda about the remarkable springs were published in 1626 – Michael Stanhope's *Newes out of Yorkshire* which was subtitled 'An account of the true discovery of a soveraigne Minerall, Medicinall Water, in the West Riding of Yorkshire, neere an ancient Towne called Knaresborough, not inferior to the Spa in Germany', and Dr Edmund Deane's important *Spadacrene Anglica.*

Dr Deane's claims for the remarkable powers of the waters of the Tewit Well must have excited an audience still accustomed to the claims of wizardry and witchcraft: 'It dries the too moist brain, and helps rheums, catarrhs, palsies, cramps etc. It's good against inveterate headaches, megrims, vertigo, epilepsy, convulsions, and the like cold and moist diseases of the head. It cheers the spirits, strengthens the stomach, causes a good and quick appetite, and promotes digestion. It's good in the black and yellow jaundice and hippo, as also in cachexy, and beginning dropsy, seeing it opens obstructions and expels redundant seriousities' – plus a dozen or so other serious maladies that the wonder waters could cure. Michael Stanhope gives a list of people who enjoyed remarkable cures because of the drinking water. The Countess of Buckingham, no less, came and had her asthma cured, Lady Hoyh of York was relieved of terrible swellings after the birth of her children, Mrs Sadler enjoyed relief from dreadful headaches.

Now miraculous cures after drinking waters from certain wells were nothing new. There is a long and ancient tradition, extending back into pagan times, of the magic powers of 'halikeld' – holy wells, Christianized in later years with well-dressing ceremonies and continuing even into present times with the custom of tossing a coin into a well or spring 'for good luck'. Deane himself mentions two wells near Knaresborough, St Mungo's Well at Copgrove and St Robert's Well near Knaresborough consisting of ordinary plain water, sought out by the poor and ignorant for miracle cures. Even though, as a reputed man of medicine, Deane saw the mineral content of the waters as the important factor, faith in the healing powers of the newly discovered springs remained an important element in what was to become a new fashion.

As well as Tewit Well, Deane describes three other important mineral springs in use in the 1620s – the sulphur wells in Bilton Park and at Starbeck and a powerful spring 'beyond a place called Hargate Head in a bottom on the right hand of it, as you goe and almost in the side of a little brook' – that most important spring soon to be known as Old Sulphur Well.

Sulphur wells must have been known to local people a long time because of their unmistakable stench: 'They are called by the populace *Stinking* wells because they have a fetid smell, consisting most of sulphur vive ... These are sulphureous fountains, and cast forth a stinking smell afar off, in the winter season and cold weather especially. They are very cold, and have no manifest heat, because their mines and veins of brimstone are not kindled under the earth, being hindered by the mixture of salt therewith. Such as drink the water verily believe there is gunpowder in it, and they vomit it up again. They leave upon grass leaves and sticks in their currents a grey slimy substance, which being on fire has the smell of common sulphur.'

It was these evil-smelling waters which were to provide the basis of a new industry around which one of the North Yorkshire's most famous towns was to grow. An accident of geology, a fracturing of the earth's crust along a north-west south-west line across what is now modern Harrogate, associated faulting and mineralization of the rocks, and lines of vigorous springs, were to create the basis of a whole new way of life.

Michael Stanhope, in another book, *Cures without Care,* published in 1632, was quick to present to an astonished public what could happen if you drank or bathed in the 'fetid' waters. Weakness, palsy, scurvy, tumours, worms, ulcers, all could be banished with frequent immersions or drinking well water: 'One Smith, a shoemaker in York was so over-run with the scurvy, that his life was in danger, medecines being of no service, was prevailed upon to drink the sulphur water at home, in the middle of the winter, which cured him in a month. There is nothing more common than for people to frequent this sulphur well and get cured of their ulcers and sores by washing in it.'

Such was the power of the written word in the seventeenth century that, with the notable exception of the Civil War period, the new wells were soon attracting a large and diverse clientele, who, hearing of the reputation of the 'miraculous' springs, would come to sample the waters, not without mixed impressions. The famous naturalist John Ray noted in his diary, in 1661, a visit to the wells: 'We went to the Spaw at Harrogate, and drunk of the water. It is not unpleasant to the taste, somewhat acid and vitriolock. Then we visited the sulphur well, whose water, though it be pellucid enough, yet stinks noisomely like rotten eggs or sulphur auratum diaphoreticum.' Marmaduke Rawdon, of York, noted a visit to the Old Sulphur Well in 1664: 'Wednesday, July 20th, they went to the Spaw at Knaresborough; there are two wells, which they call the Sulphurous Spaw, of a most unpleasant smell and taste and stinks like the smell of a sinke or rotten eggs, but is very medicinable for many diseases ... '

Another famous visitor to the Wells was that intrepid traveller Celia Fiennes, who recorded details of her experience in her trip to 'Haragate' in 1697 in her famous *Journeys:* 'From thence [Knaresborough] we went to Haragate which is just by the Spaw, two mile further over a Common that belongs to Knaresborough, its all marshy and wet and here in the compass of 2 miles is 4 very different springs of water: there is the Sulpher or Stinking spaw, not improperly termed for the Smell being so very strong and offensive I could not force my horse near the Well ... I dranke a quart in a morning for two days and hold them to be a good sort of Purge if you can hold your breath so as to drink them down.'

The number of visitors and patients seeking the waters in what was still a wild, boggy stretch of common was causing certain problems. There was little protection for invalids in the ice-cold winds and rain prevalent for much of the year, nowhere to change and, above all, no toilet facilities, which could be a major problem given the purgative effects of the sulphur waters in particular. Michael Stanhope pointed out the lack of hygiene when the poor and sick coming to the spa cast off their 'putrid rags', in some cases fouling the water that others would drink.

Knaresborough was too far away to be of any use for immediate shelter. Thus cottages, lodgings and eventually bathing-houses and inns were built close to the spring – what became known as 'Low Harrogate' around the Old Sulphur Well, at the bottom of what is now the Valley Gardens by the Old Pump Room (built over the Old Sulphur Well in 1842), and at 'High Harrogate', close to the Tewit Well and near John's Well, or the Sweet Spa, discovered in 1631 by Michael Stanhope, another salt-free chalybeate well. Many of these houses were originally built as encroachments on the ancient common land, fines for encroachment eventually being regarded as a form of rent as the demand for accommodation and facilities increased. Inns were soon built, the Queen's Head in 1687, the Dragon and the Granby in High Harrogate some time before 1700.

With the cottages in the twin spa villages came a burgeoning industry. Entrepreneurial medical men, such as George Neale of Leeds, were quick to see the opportunities to improve facilities and attract a good clientele. The wells were improved – given decent stone basins to catch the waters, stone shelters above them to protect imbibers from the unpredictable climate. New springs were explored, such as those at Bog Field, rich in sulphur and salts, and the bogs were drained. Neale developed a practice of treatment based on heating the sulphur water for hot baths, followed by sweating in hot blankets, a treatment considered excellent for rheumatism, sciatica and gout. Hogsheads of sulphur water were brought from the wells to be heated in vast cauldrons and kettles for guests. Some visitors would take baths during the day, others would stay overnight, taking the hot bath treatment in the evening and drinking the waters the following day.

By the eighteenth century the annual influx of visitors had grown to such an extent that a whole army of hoteliers and boarding-house keepers, cooks and chambermaids, stable lads and shopkeepers, was required to look after the guests. The celebrated springs were now bringing the rich and famous from throughout the land.

Not that Harrogate was without its rivals, in particular Cheltenham, Buxton, Tunbridge Wells and Bath itself, and even Scarborough on the east coast, but the excellence and variety of Harrogate's wells, its healthy situation and the effectiveness of its advocates kept it in the forefront of medical science and fashionable taste.

There was another element too. The 'season', which began in May, continued through June, increased dramatically in July and August and tailed away in September, was now as much a social as a medical event. Harrogate was a fashionable place to visit. To cater for spiritual as well as physical needs, a Church of England chapel, dedicated to St John, was erected on the common in High Harrogate in 1749. The new turnpike road system, making travel very much quicker and easier by a network of stage-coach routes, reached Harrogate in 1752 with the Leeds-Harrogate-Ripon turnpike, the Wetherby (Great North Road) Skipton turnpike in 1759, and High Harrogate –

Blubberhouses – Skipton Road in 1777. A theatre was opened in High Harrogate in the 1760s and rebuilt in more commodious premises in 1788, offering a wide choice of plays.

One of the most remarkable and forward-looking decisions concerning the future of Harrogate was taken in 1770, when the enclosure of the ancient common lands of the Forest of Knaresborough took place. It was considered essential to preserve the open walks which had an attractive part of the amenity of the spa. Two hundred acres of land were therefore laid out as stinted common pasture to which the public had access, and were to include both Tewit Well and John's Well and to extend as close as possible to the Old Sulphur Well in Low Harrogate Spa. This area, originally rough common and scrub but later carefully managed to become that most important and most precious green open space known as 'the Stray', was therefore deliberately planned to protect and enhance the vicinity of the spas. All mining and quarrying on the Stray, works which might damage the precious mineral springs, were expressly forbidden. So that magnificent area of open space which now forms a crucial part of the attractiveness of Harrogate as a town – and which now is helping to determine its economic future – resulted from an awareness that protection of amenity was vital to the new spa.

Such vision was not always typical of the town's expansion. 'Queen of the Spas' Harrogate might consider itself to be, and many visitors enjoyed its rustic charm, but well into Regency times the welfare of visitors who came to enjoy the waters was considered a matter for private hotel-owners rather than for public enterprise or concern. Roads were not paved, and there were no paved sidewalks or footpaths, resulting in muddy ways in wet weather, clouds of dust in summer. The twin spas of Low and High Harrogate were not even connected by road, and the links were by footpath across field or common, with long queues at the stiles in the busy time of year. Amazing as it now seems, Regency men and women, with all their delicacy of manners, taste and refinement, could tolerate open sewers leading into open becks and streams that stank most foully in hot or dry weather.

Nevertheless, people did come to enjoy not only Harrogate itself but also the many 'curiosities' and attractions around the area. A *Tourist's Companion* to Ripon, Harrogate and Fountains Abbey, published in Ripon in 1818, lists no fewer than nine inns and hotels at High and Low Harrogate – the Granby, Dragon, Queen's Head, Hope Inn and 'a Hotel' at High Harrogate, Crown, White Hart, Crescent and Swan Inns in Low Harrogate, 'all elegantly fitted up' with 'spacious' breakfast – and dining-rooms, to attract a 'great resort of company from all parts of England'. There were numerous lodging-houses besides. The little guidebook lists more than a dozen attractions all within a day's excursion of Harrogate and Ripon: Fountains Abbey (complete with detailed plan), Studley Park, Hackfall, Brimham Crags, Newby Hall, Boroughbridge, Aldborough, Newby Hall, Knaresborough, Plumpton Rocks, Harewood House, Bolton Abbey.

To give an idea of the growth of Harrogate's popularity in Regency times an estimated 1,556 visitors per annum in 1781 had become 2,486 by 1795; this had doubled to 5,858 in 1810. Lord Byron was among the visitors staying at the Crown, and in the early years of Queen Victoria's reign there were estimated to be ten thousand visitors per year – this figure did not, of course, include the many servants of the visitors.

Discovery of new springs, some of them chalybeate, others of saline iron, led to the development of what was originally known as the Cheltenham Saline Spring because of its similarity to Cheltenham water. To provide for visitors to the new springs an elegant salon, known as the Royal Promenade and Cheltenham Pump Room, later the Royal Spa Concert Room, opened in 1835 with a grand firework display and fancy dress ball. John Thackwray, owner of the Crown Hotel, caused a scandal by attempting to tap off the Old Sulphur Well springs to the east of his hotel. After controversy and legal action, matters were rectified. Thackwray built new public baths of tile and marble and installed a small steam-engine to pump water from no fewer than six different springs, including one of a strong, saline iron, known as Kissingen Water. These later became the Montpellier Baths and Gardens.

Both concern felt over the Thackwray affair and a growing contrast between the splendour of the new private establishments and the somewhat wretched public facilities finally led, in 1841, to the setting-up of the Harrogate Improvement

Commissioners, established by Act of Parliament. This was an elected body with powers, albeit limited, to give Harrogate some badly needed new facilities. The first of these was a splendid and stylish new octagonal building designed by Isaac Shutt large enough to hold 150 people erected in 1842 over the Old Sulphur Well, known as the Royal Pump Room. The old building over the wellhead was itself re-erected at Tewit Well, whilst another new building was erected over John Well. The sulphur waters were available to visitors on sale or by subscriptions, but a free supply was available and continues to be available outside the building. The women who had previously officiated at the old wells were allowed to continue at the new Pump Room, and they included the aged and indomitable Betty Lupton, by now in her eighties, and something of a legend.

An entertaining account of a visitor to the wells, just before the opening of the Old Pump Room in 1842, gives a graphic description not only of Old Betty but of the reaction of innocents coming to drink the celebrated waters for the first time:

Most of the visitors are early risers. At seven o'clock, or soon after, they flock down to the Old Sulphur Well, the waters of which are distributed by eight or ten nymphs, whose personal attractions are not calculated to make one insensible to the nauseous flavour of the draught which they bestow. The lady paramount at the fount is an old dame styled 'Old Betty – The Queen of Harrogate' over whose head some eighty summers have passed without diminishing her activity or garrulity. She is a privileged person, and dispenses the waters and quodlibets with equal liberality. It is curious to observe the various effects which these draughts produce upon the countenances of those who partake of them. Disgust is expressed in a thousand ludicrous ways, and those who have accomplished the task may be generally observed consoling themselves with the somewhat uncharitable contemplation of the ludicrous distress of others. The scene is not unfrequently heightened by the very unsophisticated exclamations of some burly novice from the wilds of Yorkshire, or the classic districts of Bolton, Oldham etc ... who imbibes the waters for the first time.

By this period High Harrogate had fifty-one hotels and lodging houses, Low Harrogate seventy-nine and central Harrogate, which was beginning to be developed, twenty-one. The population was increasing, most of them to service the 'harvest that never failed' – the summer visitors.

It has been suggested that by early Victorian times the rich came mainly for social reasons to Harrogate, the poor for medical reasons. A charitable fund was established in the early nineteenth century and, amounting to around £200 per year, was available to give treatment to the poor suffering from skin diseases; this led to the establishment of the Baths Hospital, founded by Lord Harewood in 1826, close to the Bog Field springs. King George IV himself gave 50 guineas to its foundation, with further donations from local worthies. However, the hospital closed between July and September to allow all the Bog's Field water to be used for visitors – as the Hospital Trust could not afford to antagonize their many benefactors from among the Harrogate hotel trade and wealthy visitors. But the Royal Baths Hospital, rebuilt on its present site in 1889, soon acquired the national reputation which it still enjoys for its treatment of rheumatic and muscular complaints, and it still uses local mineral rich muds to treat diseases of the joints.

The Harrogate season, according to one commentator, followed an interesting pattern. In the early part of the summer, in May, June and July, visitors were predominantly the *nouveaux riches* of the nearby manufacturing towns – Halifax and Bradford wool men, Leeds clothiers, ironmasters and cutlers from Sheffield, cotton men and merchants from Manchester. Later in the season came the aristocracy – the baronets, the lords, the MPs and their ladies, the landed gentry to stay at the fashionable hotels. Celebrated visitors to Harrogate included Charles Dickens, Lord Tennyson and Clive of India. The middle classes – shopkeepers, clerks, accountants – were more likely to stay in one of the numerous lodging-houses, themselves homes of shopkeepers, drapers and the like, anxious to take advantage of a short but profitable season.

As in all tourist-related economies, Victorian Harrogate relied heavily on seasonal labour, the winter months being devoted to preparation for the season ahead, together with some subsidiary activity such as bottling water and manufacturing bathing – or liver-salts from the mineral-rich springs. As in modern tourist economies, too, the success of the season was very much dependent on the general economic climate. Booms and slumps in nearby manufacturing centres were reflected in numbers of visitors and in visitor spending. So when the mills of the Blackburn, Halifax and Bradford area were doing well, Harrogate would enjoy a good season. Depression and silent looms meant fewer visitors through the Pump Room doors, in the baths, in the coffee-houses, in the tea-rooms, in the theatre. The state of the economy mattered even more than the weather.

Harrogate entered the Railway Age on 20 July 1848, when a branch of George Hudson's York & North Midland Railway from Church Fenton via Wetherby arrived at the old Brunswick Station on the Stray; the North Eastern Railway, with fast, direct links to Leeds, York and London, opened its Central Station in 1862, the old Brunswick terminus closing soon afterwards and now marked only by a stone on the Stray near Trinity Methodist Church.

The effect on Harrogate was immediate and dramatic. The number of staying visitors tripled to an estimated thirty thousand per annum, many of them now coming from much further afield and brought to Harrogate by 'railway speed'. By reducing the time and cost of travel from anywhere in the United Kingdom and even from overseas, railways made Harrogate an international resort and spa in the way it could not be when travel was limited to the speed of a horse on a turnpike road. It also brought in large numbers of day visitors, increasing trade. But, most significant of all, it led to Harrogate's becoming a place to commute from, especially into the new centres of the West Riding, Leeds in particular. Fast, convenient trains made it possible to enjoy living in a comfortable villa so that one's wife and daughters could enjoy the amenities of Harrogate all the year round, yet one could travel into an office or factory in Leeds or Bradford quickly and easily every day.

A new kind of middle-class resident was now living in Harrogate, enjoying its facilities but also demanding higher standards of service all the year round. No longer was it a question of providing for summer visitors. Shops had a clientele in winter as well as summer. New services were demanded and obtained. Dusty and muddy sidewalks were made into flagged pavements in 1863. Fine new roads through the centre of Harrogate were laid. Smart new shopping parades were built. A public market hall was erected to allow people to shop in comfort. Within thirty years, between the 1860s and 1890, the population and the number of houses in Harrogate trebled. Harrogate boomed. Schools were opened, new churches and chapels endowed. All the many, complex, interrelated factors of a modern urban economy were at work. The people with power, wealth and influence in the town were no longer the hotel-keepers, important though they remained. The new men of property in Harrogate were just that – the builders and developers, the shopkeepers, men awake to the building boom and opportunity for commercial expansion.

But what of the old spa town during this period of innovation and change? A new society had new ideas. Forms of medical treatment were changing. Among the most important of these new ideas were those of Vincent Priessnitz of Grafenberg in Austria (now Jesenick in Czechoslovakia), using techniques which relied on a combination of cold baths, cold compresses, douches and vigorous exercise. Hydropathy as it was known quickly became fashionable, and establishments for the new water cure were established at Malvern and at nearby Ben Rhydding in Wharfedale at Ilkley.

Harrogate was quick to respond to the challenge. The Swan Hotel was purchased by a new body with the grand title of the Harrogate Hydropathic Company. Huge extensions to the hotel in the 1890s provided 75 new bedrooms, a dining-room to seat 250, and a 2,400-square-foot Winter Gardens. The bathing facilities included Turkish and cold baths. Similar establishments followed in the 1890s, including the Cairn Hydro and Harlow Manor Hydro. There was even a fashion for electrotherapy, with Mr W. Hardy's 'Electric Baths' in which patients received a mild electric shock whilst in a bath or strapped to a chair – a somewhat gruesome activity, exploited with terrifying effect in the filmed biography of Agatha Christie, set on location, naturally enough, in Harrogate.

The enormous challenges now facing the growing township made it inevitable that something more elaborate than 'Improvement Commissioners' was required for Harrogate's administration, and it was decided to apply for incorporation as a municipal borough – not without a great deal of argument, however, from those who feared such new status would simply mean a rise in the rates. But in 1884 incorporated it was, and the motto *'Arx Celebris Fontibus'* was chosen – 'A citadel famous for its springs.'

The new council began to look at once to the improvements that could be made to Harrogate's public facilities. Amongst the first measures taken was the acquisition of the land between the Royal Pump Room and the somewhat inelegantly named Bogs Field. New storage reservoirs were made for the waters of no fewer than thirty-six different mineral springs, and the land was laid out as fine new pleasure garden, complete with bandstand and walks, in time for Queen Victoria's Golden Jubilee of 1887, and named Valley Gardens.

Never insular, the guardians of Harrogate decided in the same year to send their Borough Engineer, Mr Harry, with two medical experts, Dr Oliver and Dr Black, on a tour of a number of leading Continental spas, including Aix-les-Bains, Wiesbaden and Baden-Baden, to report on what was needed to bring Harrogate into the front line of European practice. On their return they recommended the rebuilding of the old Victoria Baths to incorporate many improvements. But instead of this, the council determined to build a complete new suite of baths. There followed some years of nervous deliberation, and then, in a way which has become typical of Harrogate over the years, the bold step was taken – the building of the Royal Baths, at a cost of £118,000, a considerable sum for the 1890s. The building included a large suite of baths opening to a central hall where a choice of mineral waters would be offered and a glass-roofed Winter Garden available for exhibitions and events.

Opened in 1897, the Royal Baths were equipped without constraint to expertise. Water was pumped directly there from several different springs. There was even a peat bath, and a brine bath with seawater brought specially from Teesside by rail. Almost forty different kinds of bath were provided, using plain and mineral water, steam, peat, electricity, douches, massages; diseases treated included gout, rheumatism, arthritis, sciatica, lumbago, neurasthenia, skin disease, liver and kidney conditions.

The town had a number of halls and concert rooms and small theatres to provide a wide variety of entertainment. In 1900 the ambitious Grand Opera House was built in Oxford Street, a fine and properly equipped theatre which still serves North Yorkshire as the excellent Harrogate Theatre. But there was still a lack of a large concert hall: the town already had a thriving municipal orchestra but no decent place for them to perform. In 1898 it was proposed that Harrogate, like other European spas, should have a 'kursaal', a concert hall big enough to seat two to three thousand people, together with adjacent newsroom, games room, cloakrooms and facilities. Once again, Harrogate looked to the Continent, and deputations looked at several such 'kursaals' in Europe before deciding to go ahead with a fine rococo hall, the foundation stone being laid in 1902 and the hall opened in 1903. From the beginning, the Kursaal, which changed its name to Royal Hall at the outbreak of the First World War (though the original name can still be seen in the ornamental stonework), became a centre of artistic excellence, with such legendary names as Fritz Kreisler, Busoni, Paderewski, Sarah Bernhardt and Nelly Melba appearing on its bills in the years before 1914.

Edwardian times were perhaps the high-water mark of Harrogate's prosperity as a spa. Over 75,000 visitors a year were estimated to be coming to the town to enjoy its amenities, and in August 1911 no fewer than three eminent dowagers came to enjoy the waters in the Queen of Spas – Britain's Queen Alexandra, her sister the Empress Marie Feodrovna of Russia and Queen Amelie of Portugal.

The traumas of the First World War did not, at first, seem to have long-term effects on Harrogate's fortunes, the spa enjoying something of a boom in the immediate post-war years, with both an older generation retiring to relive an Edwardian youth and the shattered survivors of the war seeking peace, rest and treatment. As late as 1926 fifteen hundred glasses of sulphur water were served from the Old Pump Rooms one morning.

But change was to come. Though Harrogate was used to the effect of periodic slumps, the great international slump of 1929 affected it savagely. Income from both the baths and the wells plummeted overnight. One by one profitable public enterprises sank into deficit and debt. The Victoria Baths had to be closed in 1930. The Pump Room, enjoying record takings in the 1920s, was in the early '30s losing money, and even the Royal Baths suffered a dismal loss of £832 by 1933. The municipal orchestra was disbanded in 1930, never to reform.

Things were looking serious. The council fought back with

improvements to the Valley Gardens, including the erection, in 1933, of the Sun Pavilion and Sun Colonnade along the length of the north side of the gardens. The old Winter Gardens in the Royal Baths were converted into the more modern Lounge Hall and Fountains Court. A research department was set up to produce regular scientific papers proving the excellence and value of the mineral waters.

But the decline of the spa continued. Drinking the waters was no longer fashionable. Medical men, whilst not doubting the efficacy of the cures, could provide them in ways very much cheaper and easier than by a trip to Harrogate. Taking a few iron tablets was, after all, a cheaper way of absorbing the mineral than travelling to Harrogate to swallow gallons of chalybeate water. Ointments and lotions could replicate the effects of the sulphur water. Rest, fresh air and relaxation could be achieved without travelling from home. Many of the highly praised 'scientific' hydropathic cures were questioned by a younger generation of medical men – science, after all, has its fashions like anything else. Whilst water cures of various kinds continued, and still continue, to be extremely popular on the Continent, in Britain they lost favour. In spite of improvements and new facilities at the Royal Baths, including the building of a gymnasium and a deep pool, the number of patients continued to decline. The Spa Rooms were finally demolished in 1939. The Royal Pump Room was disused for years, or simply used for storage, its fine octagonal servery moved to the Royal Baths. The building was used for a time as a municipal restaurant and became a museum in 1953, which it still is, specializing in the story of the spa and in historic costumes – despite the heavy sulphur content of the air which quickly tarnishes any metal, silver in particular.

The final blow to the spa came in 1964, when the Hospital Board, which for a number of years had used the facilities at the Royal Baths for the treatment of rheumatism, gave notice to Harrogate Corporation that it intended to terminate its contract in 1968. The corporation struggled on, trying to run the baths as a treatment centre for private patients for another year, but on 31 March 1969 the Royal Baths closed with the exception of the elegantly decorated Turkish baths, a sauna and the inevitable solarium, which remain open, leaving the splendid entrance hall,

Pump Room and Lounge Hall as a suite of public rooms, thus ending an era for Harrogate which had lasted four hundred years.

It is still possible to taste Harrogate sulphur water at the Royal Pump Room's outside drinking-fountain or better still within the Royal Pump Room Museum, where the attendant will conduct you down the steep and narrow steps to the Old Pump itself and the silent, glass-covered well contained in its crumbling stone walls. Here, in an atmosphere heavy with sulphur, you'll be given a glass of water, clear and pellucid but with a characteristic smell and a strong, salty, tangy taste which is quite unforgettable. You will soon admire the stamina of those who drank two quarts a day!

For many communities, the decline of the spa would have been a tragedy from which they would not have been able to recover, but underneath the elegant exterior, Harrogate has a touch of the same grit in its collective personality that makes up the bedrock from which the springs emerge. As early as the 1930s, seeing what lay ahead, Harrogate has determined to change the bathchair image from which it was beginning to suffer. New light industries were developed, to absorb labour no longer required by the vast hotels and bath-houses. Industrial estates to the south and east side of the town provided room for expansion close to road and rail networks. A major step forward came when ICI decided to establish a large part of its fibres division administrative centre in Hookstone, Harrogate, to be followed by Dunlopillo and the Milk Marketing Board's regional offices. The environmental attractions of Harrogate, for executives and their families, were a bonus which brought industry in.

But Harrogate wasn't content to let its reputation as an inland resort drift away into light industrial development, welcome as the new jobs and economic investments were. An annual spring flower show held in the sheltered Valley Gardens was followed by the establishment of the annual summer Festival of the Arts and Science, an ambitious project making full use of the concert hall and exhibition centre facilities to bring internationally famous artistes to the town for an imaginative programme and art exhibitions. Not only are the obvious venues such as the Royal Hall and the Lounge Hall and Harrogate Theatre used for major events, but the larger hotels have proved particularly excellent for smaller-scale lectures by distinguished scholars and writers,

Thixendale,
in the North
Yorkshire Wolds

Appleton le Moors

A distant view of
York from the
Howardian Hills

Hovingham

Carlton Towers, near Selby

Scarborough: The Spa

Bay Town and the cliffs – Robin Hood's Bay

Whitby, from the
New Bridge

*(Opposite)* Scarth
Nick near
Osmotherley

A rural railway in
action – Battersby
Junction on the Esk
Valley line

Richmond Market Place from the Castle Keep


The Golden Fleece, a famous coaching inn, Thirsk

# 8

## Queen of the Coast

Scarborough's reputation as a seaside watering-place began as Harrogate's had, with a casual discovery on a morning stroll. In 1626 Mrs Tomyzin Farrer, a respectable Scarborough housewife, noticed the russet colour of a stream which trickled from the base of the clay cliffs onto the sandy beach as she walked by. She tasted the water, noticing its acidic flavour. Realizing that this came from no common spring and might perhaps have medicinal properties, she collected some of the water and tested it out on herself and her friends. It did indeed appear to have the ability to help a number of complaints, and its use soon became popular with local townspeople.

The fame of the chalybeate spring soon extended as far as York, persons of quality being prepared to make the journey to the little fishing port to sample the miraculous waters, a process accelerated by publication of a booklet, *Scarborough Spaw*, in 1660 by one Dr Wittie.

The indefatigable Celia Fiennes reached Scarborough in 1697 and noticed how everyone visiting the 'Spaw' would, twice a day, at ebb tide, walk along the sands to the spring – the sea, she suggests, leaving 'a brackish and a saltness' in the spring water which 'makes it purge pretty much'.

In 1698, the year after Celia Fiennes visit, a little 'spaw house' was built round the stone cisterns placed to gather the spring waters, and the whole area was protected from the sea by a staithe of stone and timber, all of which prevented high tides covering the springs. The work was undertaken by a remarkable

129

individual by the name of Richard 'Dicky' Dickinson. Though badly deformed, he had energy, imagination and wit. Dickinson rented the site and carried out improvements to such good effect that he can be rightly regarded as the founding father of Scarborough, one of the world's first seaside resorts. He also built facilities on the site for both gentlemen and ladies and charged visitors the fairly substantial sum of 7s.6d. for the use of facilities for a season, 2s.6d. of which went to impoverished fishermen's widows, of which Scarborough must have had more than its fair share, who looked after the needs of the guests. 'Dicky' was also a shrewd enough entrepreneur to realize the potential of bottling and selling the mineral waters. Bottles retailed for 5 shillings per dozen in local shops but 7s.6d. per dozen in London, and the waters were soon widely advertised.

In 1737 the spa nearly vanished in a catastrophe. A sudden landslip caused almost an acre of land 'with cattle grazing upon it' on the clifftop to collapse about twelve feet, with a corresponding fall of earth pushing out the cliffs and lifting the little spa building some two yards above its former position and twenty yards further forward. Painfully the springs had to be dug out and restored.

Two springs had been identified, flowing only a few feet apart but of a differing mineral composition. The North Well, as it was known, was a chalybeate spring, whilst the South Well, or 'purging water', was rich in magnesian salts. Little wonder it was the custom to take the Scarborough water mixed with wine.

An entertaining record of a visit to the newly flourishing little resort is given in a letter by a gentleman, Edward Withers, to his clergyman brother in 1773. It is clear from his letter, however, that already it was other attractions apart from the spa waters which were bringing quite large numbers of people to Scarborough. He notes how people 'divert themselves' in the Spa House or on the sands whilst drinking the waters, and freely intermingle 'where is no difference or distinction made of Quality; but High and Low equally priveleged, pass & repass, mix and separate, as if it were the Elisian fields'. What really entranced the company, especially the ladies, was a fine new salon, built on a 'high Eminency' at the south part of the town where the 'Quality and gentry of both sexes' would meet every evening, elegantly dressed, for dancing, cards and social intercourse. Withers notes that each evening there would rarely be fewer than a hundred people present, and during his stay such celebrities as the Dukes of Rutland and Argyle, the Marquis of Louden and the Earls of Chesterfield, Marchmont and Hunting-don were to be seen mingling with the assembled guests. He notes, too, large numbers of Scottish aristocracy – a tradition of Scottish visitors to Scarborough continues to the present day.

What was happening, of course, was that the spa waters, as in Harrogate, merely provided an excellent, worthy excuse for the passing of several days in pleasant surroundings and agreeable, fashionable company. Once that company began to include the highest in the land, the royal family, everyone with any social pretensions wanted to be seen there. So when in 1761 no less a personage than Edward Augustus, Duke of York, a younger brother of the King, came to enjoy the Scarborough season, even more nobility followed in his footsteps. In 1762 five duchesses, ten noblemen and a bishop were there for celebrity-spotters to note. Scarborough in the 1760s was an approximate equivalent of Cannes or St Tropez in the 1970s, if you were to substitute peers of the realm for movie stars.

If Harrogate had the advantage over Scarborough purely as a spa, with the range and variety of its mineral springs, Scarborough had a quite different and potentially more exciting attraction – the sea.

Fashion for sea-bathing was, of course, related to the fact that, like spa water, sea water was rich in mineral salts. It was even suggested that half a wine-glass of the stuff each day would cure scurvy, jaundice, and gout. But if actual immersion in mineral springs was considered beneficial, sea-bathing could only have an even better effect. How much you indulged depended on your age and sex. If you were a fit and healthy male, you should have five minutes before breakfast every day. The so-called 'weaker sex', invalids and children should wait till three hours after breakfast for a dip of only two minutes duration three times a week. You were warned not to get too cold before going into the water and to get back to your lodgings as soon as you could for hot soup or mulled wine, a culinary treat almost worth getting wet for.

For the convenience of sea-bathers, the once familiar 'bathing-machines' could be hired at a cost of a shilling per bathe. This was a simple form of horse-drawn box on wheels, in

which you could undress as you were being taken out to a
suitable point in the water for your short dip in the brine. The
earliest record of Scarborough bathing-machines dates from the
1730s, and by 1787 twenty-six were in use on South Bay sands,
forty by the year 1800.

What to wear whilst bathing was a problem. In the more
liberal days of the eighteenth and even well into the nineteenth
century, most men bathed nude, dispensing with bathing-
machine and costume, whilst women had their freedom
encumbered by a voluminous gown of flannel material,
utilitarian rather than fashionable. Flannel, when wet, clings to
the figure, and the phenomenon of young beaux with
opera-glasses eyeing their partners of yesterday evening's dance
as they took to the waters, was something a young female visitor
to Scarborough had to tolerate.

Slightly more practical and, in the event, more modest
costumes, consisting of a tunic with belt and short sleeves, and
long trousers down to the ankle, were devised by the 1850s,
designed with more of an eye to fashion. Made from flannel,
serge, alpaca or twilled cotton, they could be bought for the
style-conscious Miss in a variety of colours, and so dressed,
together with stockings, matching shoes and a cap of linen or
oiled silk, she could at least be an object worthy to be ogled.

It was, however, somewhat difficult to keep men in drawers,
mainly because nude bathing was traditional and it was
considered that any form of costume hindered movement when
swimming, but also because of the nature of the materials
available at the time for costumes which were subject to severe
stretching when wet. This meant nothing would stay on for long
in the water anyhow. All this outraged Victorian sensibilities and
sense of moral rectitude. By-laws were passed to regulate sea
bathing in 1861. In 1866 the *Scarborough Gazette* thundered its
disapproval of nude bathing and indecent exposure on
Scarborough beaches, comparing the town unfavourably with
resorts elsewhere in Britain and particularly on the Continent –
an ironic twist in view of the development of topless and even
nude beaches on the Continent in the 1970s and '80s. Not that
the measures proposed didn't meet with some resistance. The
Reverend Francis Kilbert, presumably a pillar of the Victorian
establishment, complained in his diary in 1847: 'If ladies don't

like to see men naked, why don't they keep away from the sight. To-day I had a pair of drawers given me which I could not keep on. The rough waves stripped them off and tore them down my ankles.' The problem of keeping a costume on no doubt led to the development of the one-piece drawers-and-singlet bathing costume in late Victorian and Edwardian times.

Respectability was to win the day with 1892 bye-laws passed for Scarborough imposing a set of fearful rules which, had they been strictly imposed, would have killed the resort stone dead. Bathers had to be twenty-five yards from a bather of the opposite sex. All bathers, except boys under the age of twelve years, had to cover themselves, the men with drawers, the women with gowns – and sexes had to be strictly segregated to sections of the beach for their use. A bathing inspector sought offenders who could be fined up to 40 shillings for the offence.

A more attractive, and doubtless more accurate, picture of Victorian Scarborough is provided by Walter White, a London journalist whose popular *Month in Yorkshire* was published in 1858:

– here all is life, gaiety, and fashion. Long rows of handsome houses, of clean, light-coloured sandstone, with glittering windows and ornamental balconies, all looking out on the broad, heaving sea. In front, from end to end, stretches a well kept road, where seats, fixed at frequent intervals, afford a pleasurable resting place; and from this a great slope descends to the beach, all embowered with trees and shrubs, through which here and there you get a glimpse of a gravelled path to the domed roof of a summer house. And there, two hundred below, is the Spa – a castellated building protected by the sea-wall, within which a broad road slopes gently to the sands. You see visitors descending through the grove for their morning draught of mineral water, or assisting the effect of a 'constitutional' on the promenade beneath; whilst hundreds beside stroll on the sands, where troops of children under the charge of nursemaids dig holes with little wooden spades. And here on the esplanade elegant pony barouches, driven by natty little postilions, are starting every few minutes from the aristocratic looking hotel to air gay parties of squires and dames round the neighbourhood. And turning again to the beach, there you see rows of bathing machines gay with red and green strips, standing near the opening of the valley, and now and then one starts at a slow pace with bathers to meet the rising tide. And beyond these the piers stretch out, and the harbour is crowded

with masts, and two steamers rock at their moorings, waiting for
'excursionists'; the whole backed by houses of the Old Town rising
picturesquely one above the other, and crowning the castle heights.

What Walter White captures so vividly here is that very
Victorian creation, the seaside resort; the picture is immediately
and easily recognizable. It was where you came with your family
and stayed in hotel or boarding-house for a week or more, and the
focal point was the beach, children enjoying the sand.

A more famous visitor to Scarborough, who was to end her
tragically short life here, on 28 May 1849, having enjoyed one last
ride along the sands and one last sunset from the Castle Cliffs,
was Anne Brontë. In *Agnes Grey* she describes 'a fashionable
watering-place' where her heroine could enjoy the 'deep clear
azure of the sky and ocean, the bright morning sunshine on the
semi-circular barrier of craggy cliffe surmounted by the green
swelling hills and on the smooth, wide sands, and the low rocks
out at sea … ' and above all else 'unspeakable purity and
freshness of the air', a phrase redolent with meaning given the
unspeakable filth and pollution of the smoke-laden air in
Victorian towns. Anne notes, too, the great water-cart lumbering
up the beach collecting sea water for the baths, and the
movement of the bathing-machines into the water.

By early Victorian times, Scarborough was in effect two towns
– the Old Town, the ancient, formerly walled town of steep,
narrow streets, red-pantiled cottages and taverns huddled round
the harbour, under the castle, smelling of fish, and an elegant
new spa town, of fashionable Georgian and Regency houses and
hotels, spreading along the Ramsdale Valley in South Bay, up
onto the South Cliffs, gracious crescents and villas where people
of rank would stay for the season.

Improvement of various kinds had been put in hand. The old
rough cliff paths were laid out with steps and promenades. A
carriage road was engineered (Bland's Cliff) in 1772 by
agreement between Mr John Bland and the town authorities to
provide a direct route from the fashionable areas to the foreshore.
Until 1826, if you wanted to walk from the old town area to the
South Cliffs, you had to cross the stream running down
Ramsdale. A blind man, Billy Donkin, kept a plank for the
purpose of helping visitors across. This somewhat primitive

arrangement was terminated by 1827 by the Cliff Footbridge, a 414-foot-long iron footbridge, looking like a piece of fine early Railway or Canal Age architecture, and still a popular feature of modern Scarborough.

The development of Scarborough was hindered by poor communications. Coastal steamers brought goods and supplies but inland roads were bad. Bigland, writing in 1812, talks of the decline of the old port and the fishery because of poor access. A canal was even proposed to Pickering, but capital was not available. Though the aristocracy arrived by carriage, the journey could take several days from almost anywhere in England outside Yorkshire. And for the less affluent, Scarborough might as well have been in America for all the chance they had of going there.

All was to change in 1846 with the opening of George Hudson's York to Scarborough Railway, bringing visitors to the resort, in the words of one contemporary observer, at a speed 'something like the flight of an arrow'.

The importance of the coming of the railway to Scarborough is difficult to over-emphasize. It brought visitors in huge numbers in 'monstrous trains' to the heart of the town. In particular, it broadened the social class of visitor, allowing clerks, artisans and millworkers to reach the resort for a week's holiday or a day excursion. It transformed the rather genteel watering-place and somewhat isolated fishing-village into a booming Victorian seaside resort.

Leisure is still what Scarborough is all about. It's about escaping from drab, polluted towns, enjoying oneself in a fantasy land of sea, sky, beach, cliff, a clean, fresh, sharp environment. But as the entrepreneurs of Scarborough were quick to realize, sea and beach were not enough. A pleasure land had to be created for both fair weather and fine, to cater for the needs of the vast new market from Britain's industrial towns.

In 1858 Joseph Paxton, of Crystal Palace fame, no less, was hired to put together certain improvements to appeal to the new audience. Paxton restyled the spa buildings to create a mock-Gothic castle, echoing the genuine castle across the bay. Unfortunately it was burned down in the 1870s and replaced by the present French baroque pavilion between 1877 and 1880. Paxton's little Swiss châlet remains, however, immediately across the Cliff Bridge, as do many of his ornamental gardens around the Spa and below the Esplanade, including the famous Italian Gardens. The criss-crossing walkways and little shelters, all with fine sea views, are a typically Victorian piece of landscaping, transforming rough, inhospitable cliffs into a charming place to sit and stroll, a place for city people to escape to.

When Walter White, in 1857, walked along the clifftop from Filey to Scarborough, he met only two other men on the path, most of the thousands of holidaymakers in Scarborough not venturing away from the safety of paved walks. Scarborough's promenades and carefully constructed footways were an extended, seaside version of that very Victorian phenomenon the town park, complete with beaches, shelters, flowerbeds.

In 1865 someone had the bright idea of bridging the Ramsdale Valley by acquiring a disused lattice bridge from the Ouse at York and placing it across the ravine as a useful carriageway, a tollbridge finally replaced in 1928 by the present motor-road bridge.

In the 1870s the South Cliff Tramway was constructed, the first incline tramway to be constructed in England, three hundred feet in length between the Spa and the Esplanade, powered by the weight of sea water, pumped by electricity, filling gravity tanks. The Central Tramway, a similar piece of engineering, followed in 1881. Both continue to function. A more orthodox electric tramway ran along the entire length of the foreshow from the Spa to the Old Harbour; sadly it has long been abandoned for prosaic (if open-topped) motor-buses.

The creation of the Marine Drive, around the castle headland, between 1897 and 1908, did much to open up the fine North Bay, which has remained the quiet side of town. But the laying-out of Peaseholme Park and Alexandra Gardens in Edwardian times increased the appeal of the north, with a fine Japanese Garden in Peaseholme Park and the Floral Hall Theatre in Alexandra Gardens. Later attractions included a zoo, a model railway in Peaseholme Park and an open-air theatre.

The problem of what to do with visitors in wet weather was one which had long exercised Scarborough's imagination, and in 1887 an imaginative underground aquarium, later known by the grandiose title 'The People's Palace and Aquarium,' was opened.

It was situated at the bottom of Valley Road, almost entirely under the roadway. Although it was lavishly decorated in fashionable oriental style, its aquatic collections didn't succeed in drawing sufficient crowds, and later owners put on a variety of sideshows, exhibitions, concerts, a skating rink and even a zoo to pack in the excursionists. Sadly the People's Palace never really took off as a concept and survives only as an underground car-park – a sad fate for a brave idea.

A fascinating insight into Scarborough in its golden years immediately prior to World War I is given in a special excursion programme and guidebook published for a gargantuan works outing planned on Friday 24 July 1914 by Bass, Ratcliff & Gretton, the Burton-on-Trent brewers. The guidebook has recently been republished by the Bass Museum and is an absorbing social document, giving some idea of the scale of movement of people to and from Scarborough by train, the importance of the influx to the local economy and the ability of Scarborough to handle it all. The fact that the excursion took place a few days before the outbreak of that most tragic war gives added piquancy.

No fewer than fourteen trains from Burton were arranged for the exclusive use of the Bass workforce and their families. The first train left at 3.40 a.m. with special corporation trams laid on from outlying districts of Burton to bring people to the station, and thereafter every ten minutes until 6 a.m. the entire trip taking about four hours. The trains returned from 8.30 p.m. onwards, the last departure not getting back until 3.5 a.m. making it a seaside trip requiring quite extraordinary stamina. Assuming each train held about six hundred people, this meant a total of 8,500 people on the trip, a heroic feat of organization to get on each of the numbered trains. Once in Scarborough, each traveller was issued with the guidebook listing what there was to do and see and a quite staggering list of facilities available – including lunch-rooms capable of taking well over a thousand people at time.

You can see the evidence of the Railway Age wherever you turn in Scarborough. Nowhere better epitomizes it than the Grand Hotel on St Nicholas Cliff, overlooking the sea. There are no fewer than thirteen storeys of it from sea-level to attics. Completed in 1867, it's as grandiose a piece of Victoriana as its

name warrants. Cuthbert Broderick was the architect, celebrated as the architect of Leeds Town Hall. It's as confident,
self-assertive, in 'mixed Renaissance' style as any Leeds
engineer or textile man could wish, and the internal decoration,
with a sweeping staircase, is like that of a palace. After some
uncertainty as to its future, it's now been taken over by the
Butlin organization, the grand rooms echoing to the sound of a
new clientele.

The same sense of confident self-assertion you see in many
other clifftop hotels, some of them affecting Regency or even
classical styles but all part of a period of ebullient growth in the
middle and late decades of last century, reflecting the prosperity
that came to Scarborough on iron rails.

And it isn't just in the grander hotels. You see it away from the
sea front, in the smaller hotels, the great terraces of
'boarding-houses', three or four storeys high, many of them
faced in that white lavatory-tile brick so beloved of the
Victorians. With their big bay windows, they convey an air of
no-nonsense solidity, all gas fires and Empire, extending as
they do around the station, beyond the Valley, on South Cliff,
into North Bay. Away from the seafront stretch the lines of more
modest terraces, where the armies of workers – waiters, cooks,
cleaners, drivers – required to service holidaymakers, lived and
lodged.

Even when the railway dwindled in importance as trippers
took to the roads, to coach, car and motorbike, that influence
persisted. Mass tourism, started by the railway, continues. It has
helped to create a new, largely artificial environment which has
created its own momentum. Even those more permanent
trippers, refugees from the conurbations fortunate enough to be
able to buy a semi-detached or holiday bungalow, if not within
sight, at least a short car trip from the sea, are part of the process
which began when, almost a century and a half ago, the trains
first steamed into Scarborough station.

Scarborough, like every good host, has learned to give the
customer what he or she expects and desires and, if at all
possible, a little more besides. It's a question of showmanship, of
entertainment, and the entertainment business, in many
contrasting forms, has long been important to Scarborough. As
the little spa dwindled to a mere memory, townsfolk anxiously

realized that more was required than sea, beach and local walks. Recreation is, after all, a serious business. The sea provided a partial solution. Trips by paddle-steamers to Whitby and Bridlington were a splendid way of seeing the coast, and even in present years it's usually possible to take a motorboat across the bay. Angling trips for amateur fishermen have long been popular, and in the 1930s there was even a fashion and availability of tunny fishing from Scarborough harbour.

By late Victorian times the beach itself, so quiet when Anne Brontë described it, was, in high summer, a mass of surging humanity. Jugglers, acrobats, buskers, minstrel bands, donkey rides, fortune-tellers, quacks, preachers, photographers competing for every square inch. There was even a couple of sand-modellers, one on North Bay sands, the other on the South. One favourite show among visitors was Will Catlin's Pierrots, in traditional white baggy costumes with black pompons, in later years transferred to the Arcadia Theatre, now part of the Futura complex. Objections from local ratepayers and traders led to the curtailment of much of this activity, with such exceptions as the Punch and Judy and the donkey-ride men.

By then the entire Old Town was as important for fun as for fish. There were, of course, the traditional whelk, crab and kipper stalls, but anything else which could grab attention and a few coppers from the passing tripper soon joined them. The first funfair opened its doors in 1903. Penny peepshows began to appear, harmless vulgarity to delight the newly literate. The first traditional seaside rock was being made and sold in Scarborough in 1909, whilst an American importation, candy floss, made its appearance in 1925. The tradition continues in the assortment of amusement arcades, waxworks, bingo tables, cafés, ghost trains and general mayhem, as British as music hall or pantomime, cheap, cheerful, slightly anachronistic, vulgar or populist depending on your point of view. You love it or you hate it, but you can't ignore it. Scarborough's big enough to allow you to escape it.

Entertainment is equally important at the more genteel ends of the town, in the pavilions and lounges of the Spa and in Peaseholme Park. It is a tradition which dates back to the leisured days of the spa itself, the palm court orchestra that played through morning coffee. And it's a tradition which is very much alive in the Spa Orchestra, where, for over a quarter of a century, Max Jaffa, with his light orchestral arrangements, has delighted successive generations of holidaymakers in the Grand Hall and sun lounges.

Scarborough has had a tradition of theatrical entertainment since the eighteenth century. The first theatre in what is now St Thomas Street opened in 1767 and gave programmes which were a mixture of farce and song. In 1794 its musical director was no less a figure than William Shield, one of the few English composers of the period of note, best remembered for his comic operetta *Rosina*. John and Stephen Kemble appeared in Shakespeare, as did Edmund Kean in 1829, and the theatre flourished throughout the Victorian period, particularly under the managership of Samuel Roxby. Continuing as the Theatre Royal, it survived until 1924.

There was also the Prince of Wales Theatre in North Street, and the Londesborough Theatre in Westborough which performed operetta, with such notable figures as Oscar Wilde, Lillie Langtry, Sarah Bernhardt and Mrs Patrick Campbell treading the boards until its conversion to a cinema in 1913. Another theatre to open in St Thomas Street was the Prince of Wales Circus, built originally in 1876–7 as a wooden structure but rebuilt in 1908 in somewhat grander style as the New Hippodrome. This has now become the Royal Opera House, specializing in the kind of seaside variety show, usually with television entertainers, guaranteed to draw large crowds of holidaymakers.

Legitimate theatre continues in Scarborough in the Futurist Theatre on the foreshore and in the Stephen Joseph Theatre in the Round in the Ramsdale Gardens, where Alan Ayckbourn, one of Britain's most successful and internationally known playwrights, is Director of Productions, each year offering to Scarborough the premier of one of his bitterly sharp comedies before it is seen by West End and international audiences.

If Harrogate suffered a major challenge to its existence as mineral waters lost their appeal in the 1930s, Scarborough's crisis came in the 1970s as such Mediterranean resorts as Benidorm and Rimini, now only a cheap charter flight or even overnight coach ride away, began to draw an affluent working-class away from the cold North Sea. Guaranteed hot sunshine and cheap wine offer a heady alternative to candy floss and bracing winds from the little harbour pier.

Scarborough is adapting to the change. Many of the hotels, inevitably, have become apartments and flats, catering for families who cannot afford full board or a holiday abroad. There have been vigorous attempts, too, to market the resort at the quieter times of the year for that growing section of the population, the retired, who don't necessarily want hot sun and cheap wine to make a holiday a success, and for specialist interests. An international folk and dance festival in June, a summer cricket festival (which has continued for more than a century) and a September carnival are part of this process.

There is, too, a growing awareness in Scarborough that the town has a heritage to be proud of, a history going back many centuries which is worth interpretation, and little blue plaques on many a house wall and a heritage trail will increase the casual visitor's understanding. The town's proximity to countryside of national importance, the North York Moors, is also being recognized, as Scarborough sees itself well placed to be a touring base for the region. Whether this will prove enough remains to be seen. As the long-predicted Age of Leisure comes into being, albeit in not quite the way many people foresaw, the town's superb situation, facilities and above all experience in keeping people entertained will prove the telling factors.

When all's said and done, a traditional seaside resort had a lot to offer in terms of sheer fun. Much of the Victorian and Edwardian vitality Scarborough had is by no means lost. Maybe the answer is to make more of it, to improve the quality of the experience. It'll need a little imagination, and a little nerve. It's all a bit of theatre, using as backcloth that great bay, the castle, the old town, the sea. Keep the style, the elegance. Bring back the pierrots, the jugglers, the seafront trams, the paddle-steamers, a new pier. It might just work.

# 9

## A Working Countryside

'Countryside' really is an urban concept, a product of both industrialization and the growth of Romanticism in the late eighteenth and early nineteenth centuries. 'Countryside' is that which is somehow different from the familiar sight of paved streets, brick, concrete and tarmac. We endow 'countryside' with a special kind of spiritual magic, even a moral force. 'Countryside' is somehow good, innocent, pure, compared with the corruption and pollution, physical and moral, of towns and cities – particularly modern cities torn apart by the hideous effects of traffic and the efforts of engineers and planners to keep that traffic moving at whatever the cost in human and visual terms.

People living in the countryside, especially those born into the countryside, don't always quite see it that way. Refugees from the conurbations might value, deeply, the sense of peace and quiet, the sense of space; a youngster born in a Dales or Moors village, however, may see it as a prison, without access to 'life' – 'life' being defined as shops, pubs, cinemas, discos. And for many countrymen, their surroundings, however idyllic they may seem to the thousands of visitors who pour into the villages each summer by car and coach, are merely a backcloth, pleasant enough, perhaps, to the important business of winning a living from what the land is prepared to give.

It isn't just a question of sensitivity. It's a question of perspective. For an urban visitor a quaint old barn, all heavy timbers and white plasterwork, supporting a roof of rich red pantiles, is – in that telling word – picturesque, something to be captured on canvas or film. For a farmer the same building may be a cold, damp depressing hovel, ill-ventilated, a relic of a harsh and grim past, where stock suffer from cold and disease. Far better to replace it with a light, modern structure of concrete and asbestos, a place which is dry, properly ventilated, with more space for the stock to move around, easier to clean, requiring less time and effort to maintain. Such a building, to a farmer, is more beautiful in the sense of reflecting a prosperous, cared-for countryside.

A field of well-tended cows in a lush pasture is, to the true countryman, a finer sight than the most glorious display of wild orchids, field gentians or saxifrage. To a degree, the farmer is absolutely right. That richly beautiful, man-made countryside of North Yorkshire is a working countryside, producing wealth in the form of food and raw materials. Farmers, are, after all, primary producers of wealth, the starting-point of an economic chain through processors and manufacturers to distribution and service industries and all the many related activities – including tourism and writing guidebooks – that can occur only because someone, somewhere, is prepared to get up at dawn to plough a field, mow a meadow, milk a herd, clip a flock.

Agriculture is, and will probably always remain, North Yorkshire's greatest industry, and the one upon which the country's prosperity is based, employing 26,000 people, a figure exceeded only by tourism, but whereas many tourism jobs are seasonal, part-time and relatively poorly paid, a farmer may work in a highly capital-intensive business, enjoying the rewards of substantial investment in materials and machinery.

The simple statistics of agriculture in North Yorkshire are astonishing. 200,000 hectares of land are under cereal production, mainly barley and wheat. 25,000 hectares of land grow potatoes and sugarbeet. There are also significant areas in the east and south of the country growing what used to be termed as 'market gardening produce' – greens, peas, tomatoes, soft fruit and even mushrooms. Another 100,000 acres of land consist of upland and rough grazing, and livestock supported on this and other land comprise $1\frac{1}{2}$ million sheep (thus for every human being in North Yorkshire there are approximately three sheep), half a million beef cows, half a million pigs, a hundred thousand dairy cows and four million poultry.

In agricultural terms there are broadly three kinds of landscape in North Yorkshire: arable land, which includes the Vales of Cleveland and Mowbray to the north, the Vale of York to the great plain round Selby in the south and the Vale of Pickering to the east, and in much of the Wolds; upland pasture, which begins in the Pennine foothills east of Ripon and Harrogate and includes virtually everything westwards, the valleys and higher slopes of the North York Moors and unimproved parts of the Wolds; and moorland, all the Pennine summits and higher gritstone areas and the heather lands of the North York Moors.

Each kind of countryside has a productive role. In the hills and the pasturelands the primary product is grass, but grass which is quickly transformed to meat, milk or wool through grazing animals. On hill farms especially the carrying-capacity of a farm is determined by the availability of good pasture and the additional nutriment which can be stored in the form of hay or silage from those precious bits of good 'bottom land' along the valley floor, where, in the cool, wet summers, grass grows long and lush. The high fellsides, exposed to winds and suffering from low temperatures, are usually common land – that is, land which has remained unenclosed, even though it has an owner and to which various local villagers and farmers enjoy rights held in common, most obviously grazing rights. Most commons in the Pennines have grazing which is 'stinted' – that is, common holders are allowed a given number of 'gaits' or sheep rights on the moor to prevent overgrazing and consequent deterioration of the pasture. Without such controls overgrazing would mean starving animals and serious environmental deterioration of the moor.

Typical fell sheep include the ubiquitous Swaledale of the northern Dales – tough, wiry, its fleece thick and oily, capable of withstanding the most murderous cold and dampness, its equivalent the equally hardy Scottish Blackface of the Moors, and the Dalesbred, similar to the Swaledale but with its distinctive white flashes around its muzzle, most common in the Craven Dales. These are the true sheep of the fells, age-old breeds descended, it is thought, from wild sheep domesticated by the monks. The uplands have a vital function in the overall farming economy of the British Isles, above all as an area for breeding. Once away from the bleakest summits, in the more sheltered valleys, local sheep are crossbred with softer – thicker-fleeced specimens from the lowlands – Mashams, Suffolks, Lonks.

The remotest and wildest landscapes in North Yorkshire thus show an important multi-purpose use of the land. On a typical high fellside there will be sheep grazing, water catchment, shooting and sporting interests, public access and nature conservation away from intensive farming methods. That such diverse uses can and should co-exist is a mark of a responsible and civilized attitude to our wild places, with no single interest – be it recreational, conservationist or agricultural – being allowed to dominate. Whether within or outside a National Park area, this is a desirable ideal and requires maturity of judgement and willingness to compromise from various interest and pressure groups if it is to be sustained.

Further down the valley sides, where, on the lower side of the fell wall, the rough, wiry grasses, rushes, bracken, sedge and heather give way to well-drained, limed pasture, agriculture is the prime land use, and public access is limited to the network of rights of way – footpaths and bridleways – that provide what is perhaps North Yorkshire's greatest single recreational resource. No finer means exist of discovering North Yorkshire's richly beautiful and diverse countryside than the rights of way, but once in enclosed pasture land or meadow, as much as in arable countryside, the rambler must be particularly aware that he is indeed in a countryman's workshop and, through behaviour which is both responsible and considerate, keep to paths and close gates, with dogs under strict control.

It is the upland farms which perhaps most keenly illustrate the farmer's concern for a prosperous countryside. Where upland farms have prospered, in spite of the many fluctuations in the fortunes of farmers over the last few decades, the landscape has that looked-after, cared-for appearance which to the outsider appears merely as 'natural' beauty. Miles of stone walls and hedgerows are maintained, field gates and stiles are in repair, pastures look clean and free of ugly rush and weed.

Once the fortune of the farm changes, perhaps a farming enterprise being sold, broken up, on the death of an old farmer, the young people having moved away, the land incorporated into other farms as rough grazing, the farmhouse sold as a weekend home or 'hobby' farm with a paddock for a couple of ponies, then you begin to see the changes. They are subtle at first, a wall broken here, the gap not repaired, insidious rushes moving in, moorland taking over. Gradually that lovely soft green, that appearance of harmony and prosperity, begins to change. An air of neglect begins to hang round the place. The farmhouse, perhaps empty except at weekends, is no longer the hub of activity. Barns tumble to ruin.

You can see the process happening in many parts of the uplands – in the Moors, in the South Pennines, in the Dales. It happened to a considerable degree where the old Water Board brought huge tracts of land in areas such as Upper Nidderdale, Colsterdale, in the Forest of Bowland, and in effect sought to sterilize land as the tenant farmers left. It has happened throughout the uplands as men and women have given up the struggle against an often hostile environment, for easier jobs in the cities. It has happened because the farming system and all the paraphernalia of Ministry of Agriculture advice and grants are still prejudiced against young family farmers on small hill farms, working so-called uneconomic farming units.

The answers to these problems are still far from clear, but what is certain is that, to keep the upland areas of North Yorkshire beautiful, people must be encouraged to stay in or return to the hills, to keep communities alive, to have enough hands available to keep walls in good fettle, fences tidy, hedges trimmed.

One particularly acute problem is that of barns. The system of scattered barns in which cattle were wintered, kept warm under their own supplies of fodder stored under the rafters, is for many farmers no longer viable. A single, large, modern cow-house, close to the farm with running water and electricity, saves a long, tiring trudge round the fields with primitive equipment. So old barns fall into disuse. Slates begin to tumble off a roof, the winter rains gets in. What had been a fine example of vernacular architecture becomes a gaunt shell.

Farmers can't be expected to maintain old buildings purely for the joy of it, and unless a new use can be found, the traditional Dales barns will assuredly vanish, leaving unsightly piles of rubble. One possible use, now being developed in the Dales through an imaginative Countryside Commission/National Park experiment, is to turn them into 'Bank House Barns,' simple accommodation for walkers. Excellent as this scheme is, with pioneer conversions along the Dales Way at Barden Tower, Hubberholme, at Cam Houses and at Horton-in-Ribblesdale, the myriad health, safety and building regulations make it an expensive solution and one applicable only to barns with good road access and close to the farmhouse. Whether or not the concept of much simpler 'stone tents' or bothies as an alternative to camp sites could be developed in ways that would keep bureaucracy happy remains to be seen, but the twin objective of retaining traditional upland buildings and helping along a farming enterprise with a bit of tourist money is a thoroughly admirable one, and, furthermore, a way of increasing mutual understanding between town and countryside.

One fate for moorland farms when farming no longer pays is forestry. As distinct from small-scale planting of amenity woods for shelter, for conservation or as a pleasant shoot, forestry is a major land-use change and one which does not require planning permission, a fact which many conservation and amenity bodies regret. Successive governments have given generous grants and tax concessions for forestry schemes, either through the Forestry Commission or through various investment companies, skilled at exploiting a loophole in the Capital Transfer Tax laws. Large-scale afforestation has occurred in the North York Moors and to a much lesser extent in the Yorkshire Dales. Although, in recent years, the Forestry Commission, in particular, have worked hard to reduce the impact of drab, single-species conifer plantation, usually sitka spruce or larch, by more amenity woodland planting, including native hardwoods, many people are disturbed at the long-term social and environmental implications of large-scale afforestation on the traditional upland landscape of North Yorkshire, arguing that, without generous tax-payers' subsidies, such a land-use would not be economic in any sense.

Further down the valleys, in the lower Dales and on the edge of the Pennines and Moors, problems differ. Farmers have worked hard and often prospered – whether with mixed sheep and dairy herds or with 'store' or beef cattle for fattening in the lowlands. The system of guaranteed prices under the EEC common

Agricultural Policy has benefited the better-off perhaps proportionally, even though the cutting back of the milk quotas has affected incomes and is causing some problems, especially when farmers struggle with high interest rates on a mortgaged farm or with new machinery.

It is insufficiently recognized how much the coming of rural railways resulted in the specialization of farming, in the case of North Yorkshire with dairy farming especially. In Wensleydale, for example, a daily milk train bound for the London creameries provided a vital hard cash income, allowing the growth of great dairy herds. In later years the Milk Marketing Boards took over from the individual dairy companies, and the familiar blue-and-white tankers replaced milk churns and trains, calling at farms or, in isolated areas, taking milk from special trailers left at farm track ends.

The complex pricing and quota mechanism for dairy produce is another clear example of that interrelationship between town and country. The cost of a pint of milk and the percentage of our taxes through the EEC farm support system determine the development and direction of farming in the North Yorkshire countryside. Should there be a consumer reaction against dairy produce because of alleged links with heart disease, it could have a serious effect on rural economies; this is the kind of unpredictable problem the industry faces.

Arable farming is equally dependent on the EEC quota system. If the uplands and the foothills of Moors and Pennines have been relatively unaffected by changes in the Common Market, the effect on lowland farming has been much more marked, with heavy investment in equipment and fertilizers to increase yields, particularly of cereals, at guaranteed prices.

It is at this stage that our farmers' argument about a prosperous countryside being a beautiful countryside begins to fail. Lowland farmers have been encouraged, by a system of grants and agricultural support, to intensify production to a point where output per acre has reached quite remarkable levels. 'Productivity' and 'efficiency' are key words likely to strike chords of gladness in the bosom of politicians of all persuasions, and it is generally agreed that British farmers, including farmers in North Yorkshire, are among the most efficient in the world. It is not generally realized that output in recent years has risen so dramatically that Britain is now self-sufficient in the production of most foodstuffs and is a net exporter of cereals. It is only where you begin to look at some of the effects this can have on the landscape that you realize that the price paid for this efficiency may be a very high one.

The most obvious change that has occurred in an area like the Vale of York has been the disappearance of the hedgerows, the creation of a flat and featureless landscape where great machinery, highly efficient, can move across this newly created prairie without hindrance. Some people have claimed, with ingenuity, that this is merely recreating the 'open' medieval landscape, before landowners of the eighteenth century carved up the land into countless patchwork-quilt fields. This is a false analogy. The medieval landscape, as far as we can re-create or imagine it from documentary and archaeological evidence, was a landscape on a human scale, with scattered remnants of woodland everywhere, much of it coppiced for useful timber. The open fields were narrow strip fields, like the ancient Pennine lynchets, cropped in rotation. Above all it was a peopled landscape, with countless human beings, peasant farmers, working in grim conditions and for appalling hours, but whatever time of year, people would have been visible in the landscape – ploughing, sowing, reaping. Mills would have been a focal point, watermills in the hills, windmills in the plain, grinding the oats, the corn. The new landscapes of the lowlands are empty, with a single technician, hardly a farmer in any sense, more likely to be dressed in an engineer's overalls, with ear-muffs to protect his hearing, driving a huge, slowly moving machine across the great, open prairie, a machine that ploughs, fertilizes, sows, harvests.

The other change is less visible: the impoverishment of the soils caused by forcing heavy crops, year after year, from a chemically enriched soil until the soil begins to break down and blow in the wind. Dustbowl conditions are now a common feature of lowland England. It's wrong to blame the farmer or the farming community for this situation. Farmers merely respond to market forces, and the present situation of over-production and surpluses is a result of political miscalculation. Agriculture is an industry responding to those political and market forces.

Not that change isn't desirable and inevitable. A fossilized landscape, a kind of living museum, would be a dead place. But somewhere there's a balance to be struck.

In much of North Yorkshire, as we have seen, the concept of management, the parkland principle, still holds good. Much of the loveliest countryside in North Yorkshire lies in areas like the fringes of the Dales and Moors, the Howardian Hills, where an equilibrium has or can be struck between change and conservation, both in specific reference to landscape and in terms of broader, long-term environmental issues. Much has been lost or destroyed, but much has remained, and one of the most encouraging signs of our times is a growing awareness among the farming and landowning community that environmental issues matter. It must always be remembered, however, that it is only in the context of a prosperous and successful farming industry that the great landscapes of the past were created and can be maintained or improved in the present day.

Having said this, it's wrong to imagine that North Yorkshire's magnificent countryside was created purely for agricultural purposes: conservation and amenity have always had and will always have, a major role to play, and, as we shall see, recreation also forms part of that process.

Nor should one assume that North Yorkshire, in either the past or present, is purely an agricultural county. Far from it. Industries of various kinds have played a tremendous part in the county's history and are of considerable significance at the present time, having shaped, and continuing to shape, the landscape.

Important among these enterprises mainly in the hill country of the Dales and Moors were the extractive industries.

Lead-mining and smelting were, for many centuries, major sources of activity and income in the Yorkshire Dales – in Swaledale and parts of Wensleydale, in Upper Wharfedale and in Nidderdale. Whenever you walk on the moors above Swaledale and Arkengarthdale, above Redmire and Preston-under-Scar, above Kettlewell and Grassington, on Greenhow Moor and above Pateley Bridge, you are aware of great scars in the landscape, like huge wounds only slowly healing, scars of spoil where even to this day neither grass nor weed flourishes. You will see the gaunt remains of chimneys, storehouses, even smelting-wheels, crushing-floors, levels or horizontal passageways leading into hillsides, deep and often highly dangerous shafts vanishing underground.

It is intriguing to realize that so many of the most cherished villages of the Yorkshire Dales – Gunnerside, Reeth, Kettlewell, Grassington, Hebden, even Pateley Bridge – are former lead-mining towns, their tiny cottages once housing lead-miners and their families. In Swaledale, in particular, farming and mining went together. Many hillside cottages had smallholdings where miners could have some relief from the foetid air of the mines, and additional income to balance the fluctuating fortunes of lead-mining.

The story of Dales lead-mining has been well documented, its origins in pre-history, the industry almost certainly flourishing in both Roman and monastic times, the long lines of grassy green bellpits or 'dayholes' witness to that early activity. Then came later years of mechanization from the seventeenth century onwards, with great waterwheels driven by moorland becks to provide the essential power, or, as at Cononley, near Skipton in the South Pennines, massive beam engines built to draw out the ores and pump the mines dry.

The industry rose to heights of technical sophistication in the nineteenth century, with, as on Grassington Moor, advanced smelt furnaces and elaborate flue systems to remove the lead from the mill fumes. But in the 1880s lead-mining suffered its sudden and dramatic collapse, within a decade, as cheap, mainly Spanish imports destroyed the entire market. Whole communities in the Dales suffered dramatic decline at this time, with immigration to Teesside and Tyneside, to the Lancashire cotton towns and above all to the United States as the only means of survival, leaving shattered remnants of communities which made only a gradual recovery as the railways began to bring the first tourists and, in the case of Grassington, communities from Bradford into the Upper Dale.

Another form of mining, in Wensleydale in particular, helped to relieve the depression caused by the collapse of lead-mining, and that was stone-mining. Yoredale sandstones, in large quantities, were mined from levels in Buttersett, near Hawes, and above Sedbusk at the other side of the valley. Quarrying in the Dales had always been important as a source of building-stone, and literally scores of small quarries once existed, now forgotten and grassed over, where stone was cut for building miles of stone walls, the barns, the farms, cottages and even entire villages. However, the developments in the late nineteenth century were on a much larger scale, exporting stone from the Dales to build the boom towns of Lancashire, transporting the material by train from Hawes station via Garsdale and the Settle-Carlisle line.

Large-scale limestone quarrying is a relatively recent phenomenon. Originally lime, like walling stone, was cut from relatively small, local quarries and burned in the many small, scattered lime-kilns for use on the land, sweetening the pasture. Only when the railways were built in the major dales did large-scale extraction begin, using the cheapness of rail transport to take out vast quantities from new sidings. The original small, local companies were soon taken over by much larger concerns, some of them part of the multi-national corporations, and quarries in the Dales have now grown to gargantuan size, with huge, sophisticated extraction and processing machinery. Ironically relatively little now goes out by train, some on the remnants of the Yorkshire Dales Railway from Swinden to Skipton and on to the Wensleydale-Redmire line for use in the steel industry, and from Ribblehead on the Settle-Carlisle as rail ballast. Otherwise everything else goes by road, with ever larger waggons causing increasing nuisance to local residents and other road-users on narrow Dales roads. Most is used in the construction industry, as a cheap but tough form of hardcore, almost all of this being limestone except some very fine, tough Silurian slates from the Helwith Bridge and Ingleton areas which are used for roadstone. The scale of operation in Ribblesdale and Wharfedale is such that it now poses a major threat to the environment of the National Park, and increasing concern is being expressed by conservationists as to the long-term effects of what evolved from a traditional, small-scale, labour-intensive Dales industry. It has to be conceded, however, that quarrying is a major source of employment in the Dales, both for those directly involved in the actual quarrying and for those in road haulage, both for the companies and for those with their own businesses, often just a couple of waggons, on contract. Again, a balance needs to be struck between economic need and conservation of a superb environment.

Across the Vale of York, in the North York Moors, iron rather than lead was the major source of wealth, a fact which was to result in the growth of industrial Teesside, and of the town of Middlesbrough in particular.

Iron had been worked in the Cleveland Hills since monastic times, with the monks of Byland and Rievaulx working in Rosedale and elsewhere, but major discoveries in the nineteenth century led to a tremendous expansion of the industry. Ironstone is found in Jurassic rocks, in the Middle Lias, and in 1836 rich iron deposits were recognized in an outcrop at Grosmont. Before long ore was being carried in huge quantities via the Whitby-Pickering railway to the port at Whitby, and from there by coastal shipping to Tyneside to furnaces at Birtley and Lemmington. Up to 100,000 tons of ore per year were being produced, and a blast furnace was built at Grosmont itself. Soon ore from the same rich seam was being worked elsewhere in the Cleveland Hills and taken to new furnaces in Middlesbrough, the start of the great iron industry of Cleveland.

In 1850 new and immensely rich ironstone deposits were discovered in Rosedale. A high-level railway was constructed across the summit of the Moors. From Battersby junction on the Eskdale line waggons were hauled up a steep incline before following a level route up to the mines in Rosedale and Farndale. The Rosedale Railway continued in use until the 1920s, notorious for its vulnerability to snowstorms at such an altitude. It now enjoys a new fame as part of Lyke Wake Walk, giving walkers who cross in daylight superb views into Rosedale and Farndale. Doubtless it is far better known to generations of Lyke Wake Walkers than it was to the general public in its heyday as a mineral line. The celebrated Rosedale Chimney, situated on the west side of the dale, has recently collapsed, a loss of a famous Moors landmark, but several iron-smelting remains can be traced. The village of Rosedale Abbey itself, gloriously situated in one of the finest settings of the Moors, retains a hint of its industrial past, its cottages built out of bluish ironstone brick.

Nearer the coast, particularly above Sandsend and Lythe, and around Kettleness and Saltwick Nab, alum-making has made a major impact on the landscape. Alum, a double sulphate of potash and alumina, was of great importance in both tanning and dyeing. During the Middle Ages the manufacture of alum was long a closely guarded secret of the Turks and Arabs and in due course became a papal monopoly when alum rock was found near

Rome. Alum shales were found and recognized near Guisborough in 1595. According to tradition, Sir Thomas Challoner smuggled a workman from the papal ironworks in Italy in a cask to Yorkshire to reveal the secrets of iron-making. The Pope thereupon excommunicated Sir Thomas for his breach of papal power. The subsequent royal monopoly ended with the execution of Charles I, and over the next two centuries huge quantities of alum were mined and processed in Cleveland, skilled Continental workers being brought over to develop the industry. In some cases the workings actually altered the coastal landscape as whole sections of cliffside were excavated. The discovery in the late nineteenth century that coal shales also contained vast quantities of similar material led to the abandonment of the Yorkshire alum works for this cheaper substitute, but in its heyday, around 1805, no less than six thousand tons of alum per year were being produced by the Yorkshire works, requiring twenty thousand tons of coal for its manufacture – all brought by coastal shipping. The wharf and seafront at Sandsend were used for the bringing of the coal and the exporting of the finished alum and must have been the scene of extraordinary activity.

One of North Yorkshire's most curious industries, an industry whose fortune fluctuated spectacularly with fashion, was that of jet.

Jet is a form of fossil wood (the fossilized remains of the monkey-puzzle tree), differing in structure from coal, and is found in its finest form in the Upper Lias strata of Jurassic rock. It was discovered on the foreshore of the cliff and worked into ornaments from Bronze Age times and was particularly popular as jewellery and in medieval times for religious ornaments such as crucifixes. It fell out of use in the sixteenth century but enjoyed a revival largely due to the energy and enthusiasm of two local Whitby men, John Carter and Robert Jefferson, who in 1800 started carving the rock and selling it to the tourists who by that time were beginning to come to Whitby. With the coming of the railway in 1836 and an increase in visitors, the fashion for black ornaments and jewellery made from this stone was growing. By 1850 there were over fifty workshops in and around Whitby, and mines were opened and being worked from Sandsend to Runswick Bay, and from as far away as Roseberry Topping. By the 1870s at the height of the trade, more than two hundred little workshops were supplying the nation, employing more than fifteen hundred men, with a further two hundred men seeking jet in more than twenty separate little mines. Queen Victoria's widowhood no doubt played no small part in the growth of the fashion, but by the 1890s fashion had changed and the increasing difficulty of finding good supplies of the rock, together with the influx of cheap supplies from the ironstone mines at Bilbao, Spain, ended the industry. Traces of the old jet workings, usually little more than shallow, grassy pits in the hillsides, can still be seen in northern and western dales, and it is still possible to find, in Whitby shops, what is claimed, at least, to be 'genuine Whitby jet'.

One tends not to associate North Yorkshire, of all counties, with coal-mining, though small outcrops of coal, in the Yoredale Series, have been worked in the higher Dales for generations. But the southern tip of the county penetrates right down into the South Yorkshire coalfield, and such a massive and typical West Yorkshire mine as Kellingley is in fact just within North Yorkshire, across the Aire-Calder Navigation from industrial Knottingley.

The image of a purely rural county is modified to no small extent by the immense coal-fired power stations, feeding into the Central Electricity Generating Board's National Grid, at Eggborough and at Drax, which, with a productive capacity of 41,000 megawatts, is the largest coal-fired power station in Europe. Served by slow-moving 'merry-go-round' freight trains direct from the nearby coalfields to the power stations, these giant producers of power symbolize the industrial heartbeat of England. The great cooling-towers dominate the landscape, giving the flatlands majesty and significance. It is impossible not to be impressed by them, objects of gaunt beauty.

Agriculture and industry combine in novel ways at Drax, with waste heat from the power station used to heat a twenty-acre glasshouse for tomatoes, and young eels are grown in specially heated ponds for the export market.

North Yorkshire also has one of Europe's greatest coalfields at Selby, a source of energy that will extend into the next century, worked by modern mining techniques that will make minimal impact on the landscape. One seam – the Barnsley Seam – is estimated to contain around 600 million tonnes of fine-quality coal, with an expected output from the coalfield as a whole of 10 million tonnes a year well into the twenty-first century. It has been one of the great achievements of North Yorkshire County Council and Selby District Council and their planners that the opening-up of the great Selby coalfield has been done in ways that make minimum visual impact on a predominantly rural landscape. New mine buildings, as at Wistow Mine and at Riccall, are squat and unassuming in the landscape, looking more like architects' offices than the old image of spoil heap and pitwheels. New roads, new rail links, have avoided major environmental disruption. At Gascoigne Wood near Selby huge new rail sidings and automated loading-bays transfer coal to railway hoppers with automated ease. Whatever the trials and tribulations in the mining industry in the recent past, Selby evokes a new era, a great industry being developed to harmonize not conflict with the environment and the local community. Most people travelling through the area will hardly be aware that they pass one of Britain's newest and greatest coal-mining areas, a new source of wealth and power, existing close to the quiet villages and open fields.

So important and vital has been the opening-up of the new reserves of coal that the East Coast Main Line railway, one of Britain's strategic rail arteries, has been diverted, at the expense of the Coal Board, along a new route between York and Doncaster, giving a fast new main line free of subsidence, albeit at the price of isolating the town of Selby from the direct line to London.

Textile manufacture was long a staple industry in North Yorkshire, particularly of the Pennine areas. In the eighteenth century handloom weaving and knitting were of particular importance. In the northern Dales in particular, in Wensleydale and Swaledale, everyone knitted during every spare minute of the day – making gloves, caps, stockings by the thousand. Mechanization in the late eighteenth and early nineteenth centuries destroyed the market for hand-knitted goods, though the custom of making ornamental knitting-sheaths, in which needles were held, continued right through the century, almost a Yorkshire equivalent of the Welsh lovespoon a young man would carve for his girl; each Dale would have its own distinctive style and pattern.

Both cotton and wool were spun and woven in the new mills of the Dales, at first driven by water-power, later by steam-engine.

There was a great cottonmill at Aysgarth, which reputedly made shirts for Garibaldi's army, whilst at Linton, near Grassington, the mill on an ancient site produced woollens, cotton and even man-made fibres before closing in the 1950s, remaining derelict before being demolished by a property speculator in the 1980s; but once it was a major employer.

Ribblesdale had a number of mills, driven by water-power, providing work for communities at Settle and Langcliffe. They survive relatively unchanged, giving remarkable insight into the industrial development of a valley; only one is still a manufacture, the papermill at Langcliffe.

By the early nineteenth century the larger mills lower in the valleys close to canals and railways were able to grow and expand whilst higher Dales struggled to survive. But the growth of Skipton as a manufacturing centre after the Leeds-Liverpool canal reached the town can still be seen in the great canalside mills and warehouses that survive, some of them gaunt ruins. The last direct link with the textile trade, English Sewing Cotton's mill, closed in 1984.

Many villages in the Pennines especially show their origins as textile communities, in some cases their mills surviving, as in Lothersdale where the great mill waterwheel supplied the power, and at Ickornshaw Cononley, Cowling and Cross Hills. Over in the west, at Bentham, on the edge of the Forest of Bowling, silk was until recently spun and woven.

Further east, in Nidderdale, and in Knaresborough in particular, flax-spinning and the linen trade were of considerable importance, with both around Pateley Bridge and Knaresborough having a number of mills. Knaresborough was developed to be a major focal point of linen manufacture, but failure to invest, lack of access to a railway line until relatively late in the century, and Irish competition combined to result in the industry's gradual decline and eventual disappearance, the once powerful Knaresborough overshadowed by its prosperous rival Harrogate.

Reference has already been made to the great era of whaling at Whitby, and the tremendous flourishing of industry around the old port during the years of activity, whilst Selby, because of its excellent rail and water communication developed as a centre for flour-milling and animal feedstuff manufacture, whilst shipbuilding continues to prosper. All larger North Yorkshire market towns have an associated agricultural service and supply sectors where, livestock-feed, seed, fertilizer, tractor servicing and equipment hire can be found.

But the really encouraging aspect of North Yorkshire's industry is that there is growth and development, encouraged by a combination of available land, excellent communication and a superb environment, and indeed by local authorities taking a positive attitude to industrial development on the right sites. At Thirsk, for example, a joint venture by Hambleton District Council and North Yorkshire County Council has resulted in the development of Thirsk Industrial Park – a seventeen-acre site expected soon to support between 350 and 400 jobs close to the A1 and the soon to be electrified East Coast Main Line railway, and within a stone's throw of the Hambleton Hills and the North York Moors National Park. Similar sites are at Pickering, in Rydedale and in Malton. The industries coming to Yorkshire are the new industries likely to offer permanent jobs in the future – precision engineering, electronics, communications. A micro-computer firm prospers in Pateley Bridge.

Yet even this doesn't tell the whole story. The Development Commission and Council for Small Industries in Rural Areas have an imaginative programme of developing small-scale workshop units, often in purpose-built 'Advance Factories' in suitable village locations. Here a variety of incentive schemes encourages the development of small businesses, particularly in manufacturing, firms that may soon take on additional labour.

There is growing evidence, too, that people of talent and skill are prepared, often at some personal financial sacrifice, to quit the comfort and convenience of city life and have a go in the country – whether farming or starting a small service industry or a small manufacturing enterprise. Improved communications not reduced are some of the disadvantages suffered by rural dwellers, though phone bills and petrol bills may well be high. On the other hand, there is the peace and beauty of the countryside (though planning restrictions can often be stiffer than in the towns) and the satisfaction of standing on your own feet and contributing something worthwhile to the community. Already weavers, printers, glassmakers, candlemakers, musical instrument manufacturers, ropemakers and cabinetmakers are joining the more traditional potters and painters in establishing, if not exactly a William Morris handcraft revolution, the basis of a new self-employed small-business economy.

Not all such enterprises will survive. Long North Yorkshire winters which have a habit of extending well into the month of May, can hurt tourist-based activities particularly hard. If the visitors don't come into your workshop or studio, you've got cash-flow problems, and the businesses most likely to survive are perhaps those specialist manufacturers who have found for themselves a niche in the market where they can fill orders for a particular product or service all the year round. Many romantics take a cottage on the coast, or in the Moors or Dales, and assume that an endless queue of visitors will be there to purchase whatever is on offer. This isn't quite the case, as the busy tourist months in many areas are only two, July and August, and in a recession people are extremely careful of what and how they spend.

Tourism has been a major industry in its own right in North Yorkshire from the early days of the coaching inns (a proportion of whose travellers, strange as it may seem, were actually travelling for pleasure) to the package-tour promoters, whose coachloads of visitors from Birmingham, Bermondsey or New York seek the Herriot Country (a term which these days appears to cover just about the whole of North Yorkshire). Evidence is that, as competition between various regions of Britain, and indeed various regions of Europe for the lucrative, but by no means limitless, tourist market begins to intensify, the region which offers best value and highest quality of experience will win the business. Even greater professionalism, expertise and willingness to put the customer first will be needed.

Too often the British have curled their lip towards the tourist, regarding them as a nuisance, crowds, noise, pollution, until the word tourist became a pejorative term. Attitudes are changing, because they have had to change. Britain needs foreign currency, desperately, as its manufacturing base continues to shrink. It is now more readily understood by people in North Yorkshire that tourism benefits the economy as a whole. Each pound spent by a tourist finds its way through many pockets, helping along suppliers and service industries, including small self-employed businesses directly providing a service or making a product to be purchased. It is estimated that tourism has a turnover of no less than £200 million in the North Yorkshire economy.

Tourism can't replace a decent manufacturing base; it's too seasonal and risky for that, and too many of the jobs are seasonal and relatively poorly paid. But it can act as an important regenerator of a local economy and can help create both the resources and the incentive for conservation. As many a small North Yorkshire town Chamber of Trade will tell you, keeping town and local countryside beautiful is essential for the simple reason that it's good for trade. Beauty, in North Yorkshire, means business.

Already the traditional resorts are beginning to show the way – supported by the Yorkshire and Humberside Tourist Board. Scarborough, Whitby, Filey, York and Harrogate are realizing that money spent on facilities means more people in hotels and guest-houses, more cash through shop and garage tills. But other communities and townships, such as Helmsley in the Moors and Grassington in the Dales, are putting on events such as arts festivals or promotions of various kinds to attract a broader spread of visitors. A veritable flood of guidebooks, pamphlets and maps is appearing: District Councils are employing tourist officers, 'history' and 'heritage' are becoming the key words. Gradually the old attitude that tourism is a nuisance is being replaced by a realization that, in a world that no longer owes Yorkshire a living, tourism is economic survival. Even the two National Parks, once fiercely protectionist in their attitudes, now woo visitors with excellent publications, a free or inexpensive newspaper and interpretative services designed to deepen and enrich experience.

A small but significant part of the leisure explosion in recent years has been the growth of Long Distance Footpath Routes in North Yorkshire. Some three decades ago came the Pennine Way, running along the high summits of the western ridges of the Pennines. Then followed the Cleveland Way, which runs from Helmsley to Filey, along the Cleveland Hills, to be followed by the Wolds Way from Filey to North Ferriby on Humberside. Meantime a rash of Recreational Routes, in effect officially recognized long-distance ways without national status, have emerged in North Yorkshire. These have included the Dales Way from Ilkley through the Dales to Windermere, the Ebor Way from Helmsley across the Vale of York to Ilkley, the Yoredale Way from York to Kirby Stephen, the Derwent Way along the River Derwent, and others too numerous to mention.

The walker on a long-distance path is not only in the best position of all to enjoy North Yorkshire's countryside, and its town and villages; he is totally dependent upon the facilities of the area, shops, pubs, inns, farmhouses, guest-houses. Long-distance paths have economic value. Farmers, once hostile to the long-distance footpaths concept, seeing them in terms of potentially more trespass and nuisance, are now beginning to realize that long-distance walkers need food and accommodation or bunkhouse barn conversion, it's a valued source of revenue to help particularly a hillfarming enterprise, a welcome bit of extra income. The staying visitor, increasingly is recognized as the person to be wooed, tempted, persuaded. But however, good the marketing, the product has to be right. In a competitive market-place, standards are having to rise to meet the challenge.

But for North Yorkshire, with a glorious heritage of both natural and man-made beauty, and a history as rich and as complex as anywhere in England, the task need not be too difficult.

# Part II

## *Exploring Some*
## *North Yorkshire Towns*

## Some North Yorkshire Towns

This section of *Portrait of North Yorkshire* is a brief look at a personal choice of North Yorkshire towns.

All the towns I have chosen are inherently interesting, in their growth, development and modern purpose. Many are rich in architectural features, examples of fascinating industrial history or special features. All have something to offer the visitor, and each section of each town selects one or two important features and then suggests a short walk, to take in some of these.

Towns have been chosen to reflect the range and variety of North Yorkshire's town and to offer a reasonable geographic spread. In many cases features of particular towns will cross-refer to earlier chapters of the book.

Inevitably, what is offered in a book of this nature can be no more than the briefest introduction. Towns range in size from the very smallest that can accurately be described as a town (i.e. providing services for surrounding communities), with a population of a few hundred, to the great and famous, with populations of scores of thousands.

In no way can one do anything like justice, particularly to the larger town, in the space available. In no way, furthermore, can one replace or attempt to compete with the many excellent local guides and leaflets which are available from shops and tourist offices in almost every town visited. You will find far more detailed knowledge, by the local expert, usually reflecting a lifetime's knowledge, in such publications, so whilst this section provides a starting point, supplement it with the local guidebook which almost invariably will flesh out the bare bones presented here.

You'll find that almost every one of these towns is easy to reach by public transport. Some still served by North Yorkshire's rail network, others are usually well served by frequent busses from the nearby larger town. Local tourist information centres and bus station enquiry offices will have full timetable information.

A further point. Wherever you go, please respect other people's privacy. There is nothing worse, if you live in a picturesque part of an old North Yorkshire town, than to have visitors, guidebooks in hand, constantly peering over your garden wall or into your dining-room window. Look, observe, but try not to intrude. And particularly, when you visit churches, often requiring tremendous effort of upkeep by small communities, try to ensure a worthwhile contribution in the appropriate box. It's better done this way than through formal entrance charges. Such thoughtfulness will ensure a continued Yorkshire welcome.

# Filey

It lies on the edge of a little wooded ravine above the shores of Filey Bay, one of the most exquisitely beautiful bays of the entire east coast, bounded on one side by Filey Brigg, a promontory of rock stretching out into the sea, on the other by the majestic chalk cliffs of Bempton which extend out to Flamborough Head.

The sea has governed the lives of the local community since the little fishing-village was first settled, probably by Anglian invaders, though the Romans had one of their signal stations on Carr Naze, on the hillside above the Brigg. Legend has it that the Emperor Constantine bathed in a pool by the Brigg.

That later Danish and Viking pirates made their home here is confirmed by the most convincing evidence of all – the traditional small Filey fishing-boat, the 'coble', unique to the Yorkshire coast, which is a direct descendant of the Viking longship. They are still made, small vessels without a keel but with high, deep bows, like the old Viking boats, pointed at both bow and stern, with a large, deep rudder. Their design and making, from larch but with ribs of oak, is by traditional skill and craft rather than from a pattern book, and they are designed to be used and beached in shallow waters, yet are amazingly stable in rough seas. In former times horses were used to launch them off the sands; now the ubiquitous tractor hauls them out to sea.

In the early years of last century it was recorded that between five and six hundred people were living in Filey, almost all of them fishermen and their families, and that regularly the town sent eight 'five-menboats' to the great herring fishery at Yarmouth. By 1897 this had increased to almost four hundred men, employed in fishing, from thirty-four yawls and seventeen large sea-going cobles, as well as sixty-four smaller, inshore cobles. The industry declined steadily during the twentieth

century but in recent years has enjoyed a welcome revival, with
young men going back to the old craft – crabs, lobsters and
salmon being among the most lucrative catches. About fifty men
currently work in the industry in Filey, from about fifteen or
sixteen boats.

Because of the beauty of its situation, Filey soon began to
attract seaside holidaymakers, even by the early years of the
nineteenth century seeking a 'quieter' alternative to sophisticated Scarborough, and so it has remained. Attempts to
develop the village as a spa didn't amount to much, as the waters
of the little chalybeate spring on Carr Naze were too remote to
attract much interest, and Scarborough with its much better
facilities was too close. But the closeness of the village to the
main Hull-Scarborough turnpike road enabled it to get known,
and four inns catered for the coach trade. Fashionable houses
and hotels were developed and, as in Scarborough, building was
given a tremendous boost in 1847 when the railway arrived.
Many Victorian houses and hotels owed their existence to this
success, albeit on a much more modest scale than Scarborough,
and the town remains a resort of considerable period flavour and
charm, with a perfect sandy beach and a superb setting.

*Suggested Walk* (Allow one hour).
As car-parks near the beaches are quickly full in the summer
months, it might be easier to begin from that at the top of
Station Avenue, which also happens to be where the bus station
and, nearby, the railway station are situated, for public
transport users.

Cross Station Avenue, by the little traffic island opposite the
gas showrooms, and continue ahead down Station Road to the
next traffic island. Keep ahead, on the continuation of Station
Road, past the Station Inn.

This leads into the top of Church Street and Queen Street. For
the moment keep in Church Street ahead, passing a row of
attractive cottages; at least one on the left, as a plaque will
reveal, dates from the seventeenth century, having been restored
in 1946.

Church Street descends to a footbridge across the steep
Church Ravine. Until 1974 this was the boundary between the
old East Riding, in which Filey was situated, and the North

Riding and St Oswald's Church, at the end of the footbridge, was therefore in a different county. Someone gravely ill in Filey was referred to with grim humour as 'off't North Riding' where the graveyard was situated.

The church is a massive cruciform building, with a great square central tower. It dates largely from the Early English period and was founded by the Augustinian canons of Bridlington Priory. Additions, included the battlemented parapets, were made in the fifteenth century; an interesting feature is that the chancel is lower than the nave. The building was restored in the 1880s.

Return over the footbridge, up Church Street and back to Queen Street. Turn left into Queen Street. Almost immediately on the right is a white building with small windows. This is the Filey Museum, situated in what were formerly two old cottages, one of them dating from 1696. The museum belongs to Filey Local History Society and contains a mass of material relating to Filey's fishing and farming industries as well as many items and photographs of domestic interest.

The old street is particularly interesting, and though some new building has taken place, the character is retained – once the hub of the fishing community. Foord's Hotel survives from the eighteenth century with its Doric columns, whilst near the bottom of the street a house with a panel depicting a ship above the door was once T'Awd Ship Inn, reputedly a meeting-place for local smugglers.

Note the tall streetlamp at the end of Queen Street with its two bulbs and red panel to guide benighted boats across the bay. Benches at the end of Queen Street overlook the sea and are a favourite place for older inhabitants to sit, enjoy the view and reminisce. Follow the footpath from the end of Queen Street downhill, leaving left on the path down steps, to emerge on the foreshore, below Church Ravine. On your left is the lifeboat station, a constant reminder of the long and often tragic struggle between fishing communities and the sea.

Further left the promenade ends in a scatter of cafés and a curving incline covered with cobles – not the stony kind but the brightly painted fishing-boats. This is Coble Landing and the focal point of the Filey fishing industry.

If you've time and energy (allow a further hour), you can follow either the beach, if the tide is out, or the clifftop path to the Brigg, which is reached up steps to the right of Church Ravine, over Carr Naze. This is a thrilling walk, but care needs to be taken, particularly with incoming tides and heavy seas.

The name 'Brigg' is probably derived from Old Norse *'brygga'* meaning 'landing place'. Geologically it's interesting, a strip of hard, calcareous gritstone emerging from under the softer clays to produce hard, sea-worn crags and steps, a place to scramble around. It has also helped to lose many lives, as ships have foundered on its reef. In wilder and more lawless days it was not unknown for the inhabitants of Filey to profit from such wrecks. When in 1344 a London-bound ship came to grief, Filey men went on board to relieve it of its cargo – led by the local gentry. Similar incidents were recorded in the seventeenth century; in common with most east-coast fishing ports, Filey was a fairly rough and lawless place, isolated from the rest of the country by poor roads.

Unless you are going to the Brigg, follow the promenade, past handsome Victorian and Edwardian hotels and guest-houses. After half a mile or so look for a passageway, right, leading to steps, between the South Downs Hotel and the Downcliffe. These steps climb up to the Crescent, an expanse of gardens, lawns and flowers, with a glorious view of the bay, and a line of solid Georgian hotels. Unless you wish to explore all the gardens, bear right, back towards the older part of the town, past the Sun Lounge, soon coming to Belle Vue Road. A short way along this busy street of shops and cafés is Cliff House, now the Brontë Café where Charlotte Brontë stayed at various times between 1849 and 1852.

Return to the park and follow the path around the large house on your left, a former convent, now council offices and the tourist information centre. This emerges on Cargate Hill, with its extra-ordinary raised pavements. Turn left into Murray Street, another typical busy shopping street but with the pleasant war memorial gardens, and a small aviary, on the right. Keep ahead into Station Avenue for bus station, railway station and car-park.

## Grassington

Some people might dispute Grassington's claim to be a town rather than a large village. But if you take the essential difference between a town and a village as being the provision of services for other villages in the vicinity, Grassington emerges as the most important town in Upper Wharfedale, centre not only of its immediate cluster of villages which share, or shared, the same ancient parish church, namely Linton, Threshfield, Hebden and Conistone, but of an area which extends from Bolton Abbey to Buckden.

Improved communications have, paradoxically, removed the need for its ancient market and fair which were granted by charter to the lord of the manor, Robert de Plumpton, in 1282. The last vestiges of the old 'fair' or 'feast' held early in October vanished in the 1970s when travelling showmen no longer brought the vestiges of their street fair to Grassington Square.

The origins of the town are very much older than that. Extensive hut circles and outlines of little enclosures on limestone pastures above the town, and in nearby woodland, indicate extensive Iron Age and Romano-British settlement. The Anglian invaders were no doubt attracted by the south-facing terraces above the River Wharfe, the sweet limestone soils for pasture and for growing cereals in open-terraced fields.

From earliest times, the rich veins of lead ore to be found on the Moor above the village also attracted interest. Miners from Cornwall and Derbyshire were brought to the area to work the ores from the seventeenth century onwards, applying skilled techniques to extract the ores, to crush, wash and smelt the lead. In a very real sense the village developed into a small lead-mining town, former gardens of crofts being developed into the very Grassington phenomenon of a 'fold' where cottages were squeezed together on every available inch of land to provide accommodation for miners and their families. All around the cobbled Market Square and off the Main Street are these compact 'folds'. Dark, unpleasant and insanitary they must have been. Until well into last century Grassington's only source of water supply was the tiny beck which now flows underground through the square and which the picturesque old pump was erected to draw.

Far from being the idyllic place it now seems. Grassington must have had the appearance of a frontier town – tough, harsh, even rather violent. Recent research into the local school records shows the frequent absenteeism through illness and even death caused by poverty and poor conditions.

Efforts were made to improve the lot of the mining community – the building of chapels to improve morality, a Mechanics' Institute to increase literacy and knowledge, a well-organized general store for material goods. Ironically the closure of the lead-mines in the 1880s led to severe hardship and poverty, with many families forced to leave to find work, the population dropping by two-thirds. And it led, too, to the virtual fossilization of many of the older buildings so that when the Yorkshire Dales Railway arrived in 1902 the cottages were already picturesque. The development of Grassington as a tourist centre because of its glorious countryside and magnificent walks helped to complete the transformation. A century after the closure of the mines, Grassington welcomes visitors at a large National Park car-park and information centre within short walking distance of the Market Square.

*Suggested Walk* (Allow thirty minutes).
Start from the Market Square. On the right-hand side as you look up the square, with its attractive cobbles and trees, most of the cottages, cafés and houses you see are seventeenth or eighteenth century in origin. Note Pletts Fold on the right, a courtyard now containing cottages and flats. The blacksmith's shop is a functioning small craft enterprise.

Grassington House Hotel, on the right, is a beautifully proportioned eighteenth-century merchant's house, built by a Mr Brown in 1755 and for a time owned by the Alcocks of Skipton, supporters of the Grassington-Pateley Bridge turnpike road.

Next to Grassington House is the Upper Wharfedale Museum, occupying what originally were two lead-miners' cottages of the mid seventeenth century. This entirely voluntary museum, started by local people to preserve and understand the past, has many items of local interest, including two pikes used by Wharfedale men at the Battle of Flodden Field, relics of local lead-mining. Farming and cottage life. The museum is open weekend afternoons, daily from April until October and on Tuesday evenings all the year round.

Pass the end of Gills Fold. The tall eighteenth century block on the left, now occupied by a dress shop and a television shop, once was known as 'The Liverpool Warehouse' and was opened by William Cockshott, manager of the textile mill at Linton Falls, to provide his own workers and local lead-miners with a decent, well-stocked general store. From the 1920s to the 1970s it was a café.

Keep right up Garrs Lane, past more cottages and the Black Horse (a former coaching inn) to the little Congregational chapel, built in 1812 in austere, simple style, its cast-iron columns supporting a little balcony reminiscent of a lead-mine; miners were no doubt the builders. Visitors are always welcome, and a contribution to upkeep or purchase of a postcard is equally welcome.

Opposite the little chapel is a cottage entitled Theatre Cottage which once formed part of a barn where Tom Airey's players performed in the village – his actors including the great Edmund Keen and Harriet Mellon.

Keep left into an unmetalled track, Water Lane, which soon reaches a magnificent eighteenth-century barn, one of the finest in Wharfedale, Pletts Barn. This has now been carefully restored and converted into an attractive outdoor centre and photographic exhibition area. Continue to the top of Water Lane to emerge at the town hall and Devonshire Institute. This was originally the Mechanics' Institute, established in 1855 to provide adult education in the village. It has been extended over the years to provide a valued complex of meeting-rooms and village hall, including a stage for plays and concerts. Its attractions during the summer months include a music festival and an art exhibition.

Return left down the top end of Main Street, again noting the number of cottages that began their lives as miners' homes and have been transformed for holiday or retirement purposes. A particularly interesting fold, Chamber End Fold, with a row of unspoiled cottages, is passed on the right.

Descend Main Street past the Foresters and the Devonshire (Grassington once had five public houses!). Between the gentlemen's outfitters and the stationer's is an opening on the right. Go through here; it leads to an ivy-clad passageway, behind the backs of gardens, and in particular the Old Hall, Grassington's original manor house, home of the de Plumptons and dating from the fourteenth century, though now, of course, much altered. This footway is still known as 'jakey', a name denoting its purpose for the disposal of night soil.

This emerges at Wood Lane. Turn left back towards the square, noting the old National School on the right, dating from 1845 but replaced by a modern building on Hebden Road. Back in the square, look at the old cottage-style building on the left, with a date stone of 1694 and the initials SAP. These stand for Stephen and Ann Peart, who built the house as a family home. For many years it was a Temperance Hotel, and Chapman's mail coach left by the time of the clock over the door. Known as Church House, it provides valuable rooms for a number of parish and local meeting purposes and is the most popular place in Grassington for coffee mornings for numerous worthy local causes.

If you've another forty minutes to spare, do not miss the opportunity to walk down to Grassington's ancient parish church, which is actually situated in the next parish, Linton, but serves this and other communities. It is best reached by walking from the National Park car-park in Hebden Road to the kissing-gate in the far corner, down the enclosed path ('Snake Walk') to the metal footbridge ('Tin Bridge') across Linton Falls to the site of Linton Mill. Turn left where the path meets the road for a five-minute walk (car-parking nearby) to reach this little Norman church, 'the Cathedral of the Dales', a particularly lovely building and focal point of centuries of worship and activity for upper Dales communities for over eight hundred years.

## Helmsley

Whichever way you reach Helmsley, it's a delight. From the south or west you cross the rolling Hambleton Hills and are suddenly made aware of the town's beautiful position on the River Rye, the orange-scarlet pantiles and warm cream limestone of the town making a perfect contrast to the rich greens of the surrounding countryside. From the north or east it's the castle's ruined towers that first catch the eye, like something from a romantic tale. You sense, in the spacious Market Square, surrounded by shops, cafés and inns, centuries of peace and prosperity enjoyed within the rich North Yorkshire countryside. In the centre of that square, close to the ancient market cross, stands an elaborate, Gothic monument, erected in 1867 in memory of the second Lord Faversham, of the Duncombe family, later Earls of Faversham, which first came to Helmsley in 1689 when Sir Charles Duncombe, a wealthy London banker, made Lord Mayor of London in 1708, purchased the Helmsley estate for the sum of £90,000 from the heirs of the late Duke of Buckingham.

The Duke, Charles Villiers, (1628–87), a favourite of Charles II, dissipated his fortune and ended his days in Helmsley Castle in comparative poverty. He was immortalized by Dryden in his satire *Absalom and Achitophel,* one of the most wickedly brilliant lampoons in the English language:

Was everything by starts and nothing long;
But in the course of one revolving moon
Was chemist, fiddler, statesman, and buffoon

– an attack which was itself payment for the Duke's having ridiculed Dryden himself in his play *The Rehearsal* in 1671. Villiers died in some squalor after a hunting accident in an inn in Kirkby Moorside in 1687. You can see the Tudor hall where he spent his last days in Helmsley Castle, with oak panelling and a frieze containing the arms of the Duke of Rutland, who owned the castle between 1563 and 1587.

The castle, founded by Walter l'Espec in the twelfth century, is directly behind the town it spawned. It has a thirteenth-century barbican and a tall, fourteenth-century keep, all on huge, elevated earthworks and contained within deep, double-defensive ditches. Despite its size, the castle enjoyed a remarkably uneventful history. Its only action was its last – Sir Jordan Crosland held it against the Parliamentary forces led by that remarkable general Sir Thomas Fairfax. After its surrender in 1644, its defences were destroyed and left in ruins, the Tudor domestic buildings also being abandoned in the early eighteenth century when the Duncombe family built their new house and laid out grand new parkland in Duncombe Park.

Duncombe Park, immediately behind Helmsley, is a private school and not open to the public, but to enter the magnificent landscaped grounds for a small fee permits can be obtained from the Estate Office, situated in Buckingham Square, in the lower part of the town, close to the entrance to the estate. The splendid eighteenth-century house has been attributed to Sir John Vanbrugh, architect of Castle Howard, with additions by the Victorian architect Sir Charles Barry, though much of the house was rebuilt, to original designs, after a disastrous fire in 1879.

*Suggested Walk* (Allow thirty minutes, plus time to see castle and church).

Begin at the old market cross, looking across at the soaring Faversham monument that links town and estate so closely. On the right is the town hall, built in 1901 in approximately Jacobean style. The market-place, surrounded by comfortable old inns, shops and cafés, is one of the loveliest in North Yorkshire.

Turn northwards, crossing to the Black Swan Hotel, a fine Georgian inn. To its immediate left is a rare example in North Yorkshire of half-timbering, in a house of Tudor origin.

Go through the gate into the churchyard, left, and along a flagged path behind the church, under mature oaks. The somewhat restored half-timbered house is Canons' Garth, reputedly haunted. Return to the path which leads left around the church to the church entrance. Though this is a High Victorian church, built in the 1860s, much material from the earlier church has been incorporated in the later building, including the Norman doorway and chancel arch.

Leave the church through the main entrance, turning right into Church Street, a pleasant, broad street of mainly Georgian houses and cottages, the later Faversham Arms on the corner. In the centre of the green appears Etton Gill Beck, which forms the stream through Helmsley.

Return down Church Street, but this time keep ahead into Castlegate, the pleasant back street behind the market-place, with the beck now on the left, the backs of houses, gardens and outbuildings running down to the water, all red pantiles and cream stone and flash of colour from gardens. The entrance into the castle is on the right.

Now under the care of English Heritage, the castle is open daily, and an added advantage of a visit is the view back across the town and over into the surrounding countryside.

Return to Castlegate, turning right past more cottages and another restored half-timbered house. This leads to Buckingham

A view of Wensleydale

Limestone landscape – Cray Gill, north of Buckden, Wharfedale

'City of Wells' leaves Horton-in-Ribblesdale Station on the Settle-Carlisle line with a steam special bound for Carlisle

On the Leeds-
Liverpool Canal,
Springs Branch,
opened in the 1770s
to serve a local
quarry. Skipton
Parish Church is in
the background

The Gatehouse,
Skipton Castle

Industry in the Yorkshire Dales: Grassington Moor Smelt Mill and Chimney

The old Market Cross and stocks, Ripley – a village modelled in the style of Northern France

The Sun Pavilion
and Colonnade in
Harrogate's Valley
Gardens

Where it all began:
Tewit Well, High
Harrogate

Fountains Abbey
from the River Skell

The Marmion
Tower, West
Tanfield, near
Ripon – remains of a
fifteenth-century
gatehouse with fine
oriel window

Grief made
manifest – the
Church of Christ
the Consoler,
Newby Hall

The eighteenth-
century Town Hall,
Ripon

Industry in North Yorkshire — futuristic mine buildings at Riccall, on the Selby Coalfield, one of the biggest in Europe

Eggborough Power Station near the M62

Square, the estate cottage and grounds entrance. Keep left into Bridge Street, noting a fine Georgian house opposite, next to what appears to be a tall coach-house.

Go right towards the bridge over the River Rye, a lovely old structure with pointed arches, though difficult to see from the road – a footpath on the far side gives opportunity to see a little more.

Cross into Ryegate, noting the farm, Bridge Farm, coming into the town centre. Ryegate and Pottergate form a quiet backwater of the town, with mainly nineteenth-century cottages.

But return up Bridge Street, crossing opposite the post office into Borogate, a central old street now enjoying all the benefits of being conserved and revived for tourism as shops and small businesses await the visitor. Ahead the market-place.

## Ingleton

'Beauty spot of the North' proclaims the sign along the main A65 which goes close by the town. Rather improbable hyperbole it might seem, amid the straggle of ribbon development along the main road.

But then Ingleton isn't quite what it might seem at first sight. In fact it's a bit of a contradiction, with remains of industry cheek by jowl with an interesting old township, and with incomparably lovely countryside all around, a kind of topographical Beauty and the Beast, but, as any Ingletonian will tell you (and the signboard defiantly asserts), Beauty wins every time.

Ingleton wasn't a town to earn even a footnote in Dales history until comparatively recent times, though there were a couple of abbots of nearby Sawley, now in Lancashire, who had 'de Ingleton' after their Christian names; the town's name, with connotations of fire ('ingle'), has links with Ingleborough Beacon and doubtless a Celtic past.

The town we know emerged as communications improved, as a staging-post on the important Leeds-Kendal packhorseway, then on the busy Keighley-Kendal turnpike. By the late eighteenth century its annual fair was noted for leather and oatmeal. Industry came too – textiles in the form of a huge woollen-mill, burned down twice, a leather tannery in the Bottoms by the railway viaduct, whose stench could have hardly improved local amenity, and quarries, one of which, Meal Bank threatened the famous Glens, and is only slowly healing back into the landscape. But above all there was coal-mining.

Coal was worked from local, exposed seams for many years. In 1913 an old colliery was modernized, and an entire new 'model village' to the east of the old township was built to house the miners, a crescent of identical homes in best 1920s style, more fitting to Wigan or Barnsley than rural Yorkshire. The seams ran out and the mines closed in 1937 creating hardship, depression and eyesores which have only recently vanished.

Yet Ingleton has survived, and it has even flourished as a tourist centre. It did so because of its location, virtually on the slopes of Ingleborough Mountain, 2,373 feet high and for decades considered the highest mountain in England, a peak which people have climbed ever since the fashion for climbing mountains began.

When you came to Ingleton by stage-coach in the last decades of the eighteenth century, you hired a guide from the village to take you to the terrifying height of the summit or to several of the 'awesome' caves in the vicinity, the other major tourist attraction. By the Railway Age the track up Ingleborough was beaten well enough not to require a guide, but guides awaited you at the entrance to several of the major caves.

These things are all very well but require some stamina and even nerve to sample. In 1885 a group of local enthusiasts and entrepreneurs had the brilliant idea of opening up a continuous footpath through the gloriously beautiful but then hopelessly inaccessible narrow gills through which the two rivers which flow through Ingleton, the Doe and the Twiss, descend before meeting below the town to form the River Greta. The group formed themselves into the Ingleton Improvement Company, raised share capital and employed local men to dig out and construct the paths through the narrow gorges. Within a month, by Easter 1885, the work was done, the Company charging 3d for a walk through each gill.

The waterfalls were a phenomenal success. By Whit Monday crowds were pouring into Ingleton on the regular trains and on excursion trains, and a modest fortune was being earned at the new turnstile. Over the next few weeks success built upon success. For a total of 3d the visitor could see both series of falls, and the Improvement Company had made so much money that they gave £100 for a clock in Ingleton church tower. But before long there were legal wrangles about access to the falls, and litigation, eventually leading to the establishment of a new company for part of the walks. Trains were met at the station by rival companies touting for custom with handbills. Matters were eventually resolved but not without a degree of ill-feeling. Ownership of the walks fell to the descendants of Samuel Worthington, landlord of the Wheatsheaf Hotel and one of the Company founders, and it remains in the hands of the charmingly named 'Ingleton Scenery Company'.

The waterfalls brought prosperity to Ingleton, and that prosperity was linked to the railway. On a fine Bank Holiday up to six thousand people would arrive at Ingleton station by train, from Leeds, Bradford, Lancaster and Nelson, heading for the falls, buying postcards and tea, on busy days 'eating the town out' so that supplies had to be rushed in from surrounding villages.

The waterfalls are still there, as glorious as ever. Sadly the railway closed even before Beeching. Had it been on the direct Midland Railway line to Lancaster, it would have survived and doubtless remained busy and profitable, but it lay on a branch to Tebay. For many years the London and North Western Railway were responsible for running trains from Thornton station, immediately across the great eleven-arch viaduct across the town. Lack of co-operation and rivalry between the two companies at Ingleton led directly to the building of the Settle-Carlisle line in the 1870s, in effect making the Tebay link merely a local branch. By the 1950s services were withdrawn and, though excursion trains used the old station right until the 1960s, the lines were lifted and the station was demolished. Notwithstanding the large sign on the A65 attracting coach and car alike, Ingleton will never see such days again.

*Suggested Walk* (Allow thirty minutes).
Begin at the large car-park at the old station site, signed 'tourist information'. The Ingleborough community centre, focal point of community activity and local culture, has replaced the old

platforms, and car-parking areas lie where the tracks ran. Walk towards the viaduct, a sad failure of imagination here – wired off with warning notices instead of being used as a superb walkway and viewpoint. It still has to be maintained at public expense (this being a far cheaper alternative than demolition) but because no one will accept liability for public safety (the A65 is a far more dangerous place), such a glorious public asset wastes away.

There are steps just to the right leading to the road below. Cross, taking the gap and steps nearly opposite into the Bottoms, under the arches. Keep right by cottages, then left of the cottage ahead by old buildings site of part of the old tannery and cottages by the bridge to find steps onto the road above. Turn left in the road – known as Bell Horse Gate, a link with packhorse days, the 'bell horse' being the first pack pony in the line.

The road leads over the two rivers to the entrance of the falls. Note the fine eighteenth-century cottage on the left, Broadwood Cottage.

This is the entrance to the waterfalls, the full walk requiring at least two hours and an experience not to be missed; care is required in certain places, which can be slippery and dangerous. The Black and White Café, close to the entrance turnstile, has been a popular walkers' café for many years.

Return across the bridge, noting the slaty stone on the left, bridge indicating that this is Thornton Bridge in the Wapentake of Staincross.

Between the two rivers, on the left, is the shell of the mill, now a garage and workshop. Cross the bridge over the Doe, immediately to the far side going onto a footpath by the river, below gardens. Follow the river upstream. An aqueduct, in the form of a wooden trough on stone piers, once carried a millrace across here to drive the waterwheel. The path goes through an attractive wooded area to emerge at Ingleton's swimming-pool – an open-air pool created in 1935 using the labour from soon-to-be-closed coal-mines.

Turn sharp right, uphill, towards steps by tall houses. These reach a little court. Bear right into the churchyard and go around the front of the church – an attractive viewpoint looking across the bottoms and the viaduct to the hills beyond.

Ingleton's parish church of St Mary is a pleasant, typically Victorian country church, though with a surviving fifteenth-century tower. What is particularly thrilling is the remarkable twelfth-century font, elaborately carved with scenes of the life of the Virgin Mary – the church's patron saint. It seems it survived the depredations of Cromwell's Puritans by being rolled down the hillside into the River Doe. In later years it was rescued but used in the churchyard as a receptacle to mix mortar and limewash in, the exterior being so thickly encrusted that its true importance was hidden. The great historian Dr Whitaker recognized it for what it was, and it is restored to its old position and function, an object of rich interest and powerful medieval carving.

Leave the churchyard and enter the narrow High Street. There are several shops and cottages full of character. In the little courtyard of shops on the left, Carefree Fashions, on the right-hand-side, was once the Black Bull Inn, built in 1710.

Continue to the little market-place – Friday is market day. Opposite the Halifax Building Society, almost concealed in the tarmac, is the ancient bullring, where the bull was tied before being baited by dogs, last used for this purpose in the eighteenth century. Continue along the High Street past an attractive, probably late seventeenth-century cottage on the left, to Ingleborough House, once the Ingleborough Hotel, now an old people's rest home. This was built by John Kidd, one of the founder members of the Ingleton Improvement Company, and financed from a family fortune reputedly made from printers' ink.

Ahead is the top of the village, past the Wheatsheaf, where Mr Worthington had a dance pavilion to the rear of the pub, looking at Blue Hall, the house to the left on a low eminence, built in 1688.

Cross at the road junction, noting the date stone, 1711, in the little terrace, named Paradise Row, opposite. Downhill now, past pleasant artisans' houses and the Highways Depot. The path, signed to Moor Garth, left, leads to a mansion which, in late Victorian times, boasted a hydropathic establishment – shades of Ingleton Spa. The smooth green hillside, also to the left, covers the remains of mining slag and pit heaps, now carefully re-landscaped and re-seeded, Beauty slowly recovering from the Beast. Further to the south-east is New Village.

You reach the Back Lane entrance to the car-park on the right.

## Knaresborough

One of the most dazzlingly pretty of all North Yorkshire's towns,
Knaresborough seems to blend every ingredient into half a mile
of steep, riverside gorge. There's the river itself, the Nidd, darkly
beautiful, set against a backcloth of rich woods. There's a
half-ruined medieval castle, placed, as if with an eye for the
picturesque, overlooking the gorge, a notable landmark and
viewpoint. There's a huddle of cottages and houses, some of
them pink – and whitewashed, giving an effect of a Cornish
fishing village, crowding between zigzagging lanes and paths up
the steep hillside. And then crossing the ravine is a tall,
castellated railway viaduct.

'One of the most notable railway crimes of England,' growls
Pevsner, pointing out how it dissects the ancient town. He's
right, of course, and yet it gives that famous view of the town a
deeper perspective, adding a sense of scale, screening part of the
town away.

Whatever you feel, it's as much part of Knaresborough as the
castle or church, and it was the railway that turned
Knaresborough into an inland resort, a place to go to for the day
or afternoon, to take a boat out on the river, to wander along the
waterside, through the woods. Little wonder the riverside soon
became packed with cafés, tea-shops and boat-houses, which
still flourish, crowded every fine Sunday afternoon as the crowds
still come from Leeds by train, bus, car or bicycle.

Knaresborough's far older than such frivolity. Its origins go
back well back into Anglo-Saxon times, and it was an important
place, a royal town long before its upstart neighbour Harrogate
had ever been heard of. As a trading and manufacturing centre it
probably reached its zenith in the eighteenth century, but it
declined after the collapse of the linen industry and the growth of
the major textiles centres of the West Riding in the nineteenth
century leaving a small but prosperous country town that
probably earns as much from tourism as from any other activity.

The castle survives as a massive rectangular keep and
scattered ruins, now contained within attractive gardens. It has
played no small part in English history. It was built originally by
Serlo de Burgh in 1130, and Hugh de Morville, one of the knights
who murdered St Thomas à Becket, was for a time Constable of

the castle; after the slaying of Thomas at Canterbury, Morville and his companions sought refuge here. In 1206 King John stayed here to enjoy the hunting in the nearby Forest of Knaresborough. A century later, in 1307, Edward II gave the castle to Piers Gaveston and soon afterwards visited Knaresborough. In 1310 he granted the town its free market charter. Richard II was held prisoner here, soon to be taken to Pontefract, where he was murdered.

In the Civil War Knaresborough supported the Royalist cause, and the Royalist army led by the brilliant Prince Rupert was cut down by Cromwell's Ironsides at nearby Marston Moor in July 1644. Four months later the Parliamentarians turned on Knaresborough Castle and town, and by December they surrendered. Two years later Cromwell ordered the destruction of the castle to ensure no further insurrection.

The little courthouse in the castle grounds has a floor which dates from the fourteenth century – the rest of the building is seventeenth century and was used to deal with offenders against the rigorous Forest Laws. It is now a small museum illustrating aspects of Knaresborough's long history.

*Suggested Walk* (Allow one hour, 1¾ if a visit to St Robert's Cave is included).
Knaresborough has much to offer that can best be experienced on foot.

Begin at the market-place, smaller than in many towns, with a surviving area of cobbles around the market cross. To the north-eastern side of the market-place is the shop, founded by John Beckith in 1720, that claims to be 'Ye Oldest Chymist Shoppe in England'. The town hall, in classical style, was built in 1862.

One of two streets opposite the chemist's shop will soon bring you into the castle grounds – a justly famous viewpoint into Knaresborough's gorge. The surviving portions of the castle, including the king's chamber and the dungeon, are open during the summer months. To the left of the castle as you look towards the river a path descends through Bebra Gardens to the river. (Bebra is Knaresborough's twin town in Germany).

The great railway viaduct ahead, carrying the Harrogate-York line, was built in 1851, replacing an earlier one after the original almost completed, had collapsed into the river on 11 March 1848.

As you reach the lane which runs along the river, known as Waterside, notice the mill, Castle Mill, ahead. This was built in 1791 as a cottonmill but soon became the basis of Knaresborough's linen trade. Linen-making had started as a cottage industry in Nidderdale but in the later eighteenth and early nineteenth centuries became a major factory industry. In 1824 eight hundred flax-dressers and thirteen hundred linen-weavers were employed in the town, and Knaresborough linen was among the most famous in England. Competition, particularly from Northern Ireland, gradually overtook the industry but Castle Mill continued in production until 1972. Examples of Knaresborough linen are kept in the Courthouse Museum.

Now turn left along Waterside, following the river downstream. This eventually emerges at Low Bridge, a handsome eighteenth-century structure. Cross, continuing along Abbey Road. You are soon aware of limestone cliffs on the left. A gateway on the left leads to St Robert's Chapel, or, more accurately, the Chapel of Our Lady of the Crag, carved out of the rock by John the Mason in 1408 under licence from Henry IV. About ten feet deep, inside is a simple altar and piscina for the priest to wash his hands. A carved figure of a knight drawing his sword guards the entrance, said to be of St Robert, Knaresborough's hermit saint.

Immediately above the chapel steps lead to Fort Montague, better known as 'the House in the Rock'. It was created by a local weaver called Hill, supported by financial help from local aristocratic families, as a kind of elaborate folly. One patron, the Duchess of Buccleuch, in whose honour it was named, gave shrubs and plants for the terraced garden. It is open to the public during the summer months.

Connoisseurs of medieval saints and Victorian murder romances should continue along Abbey Road past Abbey House Farm (so named because it stands on the site of and contains masonry from a Trinitarian priory) and the Straw Boater, a public house. Continue ahead until, past gateways, a continuous stone wall is reached on the right. A gap stile in the wall leads to a path into riverside woods, steeply down to a little area of level rock above the river with a coffin shape hewn from the rock, and a cave on the left. This is St Robert's cell.

Robert Flower was born around 1160 in a wealthy family and relinquished the world to become a monk in Northumberland, then at Fountains Abbey, before eventually finishing his days as a hermit, performing suitable miracles and taming wild animals. King John visited the holy man here in 1216, and when he died two years later, healing oil is reputed to have flown out of the grave carved from the rock.

It was in this cave that the notorious murderer Eugene Aram placed the body of his wife's suspected lover, Daniel Clark, a tale which captured popular imagination and the pens of Thomas Hood and Bulwer-Lytton among others. Aram's body was displayed on the town gibbet originally in a field near the Mother Shipton Inn. Part of the gibbet is now in a wall on Waterside, close to the railway viaduct.

Return to Low Bridge. Cross the bridge and enter the Long Walk immediately to the left of the seventeenth century Mother Shipton Inn. This woodland walk, open from April until November, is through private land, and a small toll is payable at the entrance. Having enjoyed delightful woodland and a riverside view across to the old town, you soon reach the Dropping Well, a spring so rich in lime that objects placed in it, from gloves to top hats and teddy bears, are soon covered, 'petrified', with a coating of creamy limestone deposit, to the delight of tourists. Further along the river is Mother Shipton's Cave. Mother Shipton was a local prophetess, reputedly born in 1488 and able to prophesy most things, usually in doggerel rhyme, including the end of the world. Most of the prophecies are Victorian forgeries.

The Long Walk emerges on the main road into Knaresborough at High Bridge – formerly the medieval bridge into the town but much enlarged. At the far end of the bridge is Queen Victoria's Jubilee fountain from which spa waters, from Bilton, once flowed.

Turn right into Waterside, back past the riverside cafés, soon reaching the Old Manor House on the right. Just before this point, a cobbled lane, Water Bag Bank, rises up left. Go left at the top to reach the parish church of St John, a building which dates largely from the thirteenth, fourteenth and fifteenth centuries, though heavily restored. Here are some interesting tombs, particularly of the Slingsby family; William Slingsby who discovered Harrogate's first spring, Tewit Well, is buried here.

Go sharp right outside the church into Church Lane; the second gate on the right leads into the grounds of Knaresborough House, built in 1768 and now belonging to the district council. Continue through the grounds into the High Street, which also has a number of fine eighteenth-century townhouses and shops, clear evidence of Knaresborough's most prosperous years. Keep right in the High Street until you reach the opening into the market-place.

## Malton

Medieval politics and intrigue have left, at Malton, a divided township. The original town Old Malton, grew up on a bend of the River Derwent, along the Pickering road, where the church of the Gilbertine priory still stands. New Malton, a busy market town, strategically placed on a river crossing close to the Wolds and the Howardian Hills, is more than a mile away to the south-west.

Around 1138 Eustace St John, favourite of the late Henry I and Lord of Malton, supported Henry's daughter in her claim to the throne of England against her cousin Stephen. He joined forces with her ally King David I of Scotland, who, seeing this as an opportunity to annexe Northumberland to Scotland, placed a strong garrison in Malton Castle. The elderly Archbishop Thurston of York, outraged at what he saw as a betrayal of his country, collected an army led by local monks and churchmen who stormed the castle, burning the village to the ground in the process and forcing Eustace and his Scottish allies to flee over the Border, to be defeated by Thurston's forces at the Battle of the Standard. Eustace was subsequently, if a little surprisingly, pardoned and reconciled to King Stephen and returned to Malton to reclaim his lands and rebuild the town – this time on the site of New Malton. Old Malton did recover to a degree, but as little more than a village around the priory.

Now spared the thundering traffic of the A64 York-Scarborough road, Malton is a market town of considerable character, with a large, irregularly shaped market-place with church and town hall in the centre from which interesting old streets and courtways open out. It has a popular Saturday market.

A visit to the Gilbertine priory (see Chapter 5) should not be omitted. Though only about two-thirds of the façade belongs to the original priory church built around 1200, the western wall contains great columns and arches filled in during later periods. The doorway is particularly richly decorated. But the entire buildings has an air of being detached from something larger. Fragments of columns survive, going nowhere.

*Suggested Walk* (Allow fifty minutes).

Start at the little eighteenth-century town hall. This now contains the Malton Museum whose collections include many relics of the Roman fortress of Derventio, an important staging-post on the military road network close to the military camp at Cawthorne and the many coastal forts and signal stations. Note the plaque to Edmund Burke, one of England's greatest Parliamentarians and orators, who was MP for Malton in 1780–94.

From the town hall continue along the market-place to St Michael's, a handsome church, mainly Norman but with a fourteenth-century Perpendicular tower, though it has suffered heavy nineteenth-century restoration.

Continue down Market Street, which has a fine early nineteenth-century inn, the King's Head, and some attractive eighteenth – and nineteenth-century shops. At the bottom of the street, across the main road, Yorkersgate, is a massive early eighteenth-century gabled house, York House. Turn left in Yorkersgate. The bingo hall on the left was formerly the Corn Exchange, built in 1845, later the Palace Cinema.

Go right into Railway Street, towards the bus and railway station. On the left is one of many fine examples in Malton of a warehouse, probably a grain store, a reminder of the importance of the town as a transshipment point for both the Derwent Navigation and the North Eastern Railway. Note the elevator serving the many floors, still in position.

Cross the River Derwent. Evidence of old commercial moorings is hard to find, but pleasure craft will undoubtedly be there, and there's a fine view of this once busy waterway and the back of the town.

Just before you reach the bus station, there is a path up river, again giving interesting views of commercial Malton and the river. This emerges in the road close to where Castlegate, the Scarborough road, crosses the level crossing and enters the village of Norton, a large and quite developed suburb of Malton on the River Derwent and, until 1974, in the East Riding.

Turn left back towards the town centre, but where Castlegate swings left, going up to the traffic lights bear sharp right, heading for the road in front of the fire station, a cul-de-sac. Just to the right of the fire station a gateway leads into a field where large metal footpath sign indicates a junction of paths. Take the path to the left, leading straight ahead by a fine avenue of sycamore.

To your right across Orchard Field, marked by little more than a faint mound in the meadowland, is the site of the Roman fort of Derventio. This fort, of which little trace remains, once covered eight acres, though the excavated site produced important finds, many of which are in Malton Museum. Nothing remains of the Norman fort destroyed by Thurston on the same site.

At the main road turn left along Old Maltongate. (If you wish to walk to the Gilbertine priory either turn right here or follow the footpath which forks right from near the fire station across Derventio and the line of old Malton-Market Weighton Railway to the road. Allow fifteen minutes' walk in each direction).

You immediately pass a row of attractive old houses with high step gables and then a massive, extremely weathered wall and huge and gateway. Behind is Malton Lodge, a grand Jacobean house, in early classical style, built from a mellow stone. This is reputedly only the lodge of a massive Jacobean mansion, built alongside Malton Castle but demolished in 1674. Its demolition is said to be owing to two heiresses who could not agree ownership of the house. They took the matter before a judge who, in manner befitting King Solomon, ordered the demolition of the house and the equal dividing up of the stones, some of which are reputedly used in this lodge.

Continue to the traffic lights. Turn right into Wheelgate, another street of attractive eighteenth- and nineteenth-century shops and inns, some of them painted in pastel stucco.

The Cross Keys Inn, on the left, is unusual for having been built on a medieval undercroft. This is a surviving part of one of three hostels founded in the late twelfth century by Eustace St John and maintained by the canons of Malton Priory for the

benefit of benighted travellers, the sick and the poor.
Turn left into Finkle Street for the market-place.

## Masham

The huge market square that dominates Masham seems almost
too large for the little town that contains it, a sense of space,
punctuated only by the ancient market cross, that dwarfs the
inns, shops and solid townhouses around it.

The sheer size of the square reflects a former commercial
importance which began in 1393 when Stephen le Scrope, Lord of
Mashamshire, was granted a weekly market and a twice yearly
sheep and cattle fair in Masham town. Partly because Masham
was superbly situated on a convenient crossing-point of
moorland tracks and packhorse ways from the higher Dales
leading into Yoredale, and perhaps even more because the fair
was free of tolls, it grew in importance to a point when it was
estimated forty thousand sheep were sold at a single day of the
fair, in later years held in September. A square large enough to
contain such a seething mass of humanity, their beasts and their
stalls was needed. A Wednesday market survives, though now a
much more local affair and hardly sufficient to make the worthy
burghers of nearby Richmond now complain about the unfair
competition from Masham's 'free' market.

If the zenith of Masham's commercial activity lies in the past,
its superb situation in the lovely countryside, much of it
woodland and parkland, that forms the undulating eastern fringe
of the Yorkshire Dales, gives it an assured future as a small tourist
centre. The town lies on a terrace above the River Ure, close to
where little-known Colsterdale and the little River Burn, which
comes from the old Leeds Corporation reservoirs of Roundhill
and Leighton, join forces to meet the River Ure.

Little over a mile from Masham lies Swinton Park, seat of the
remarkable Danby family, of Cavalier sympathy in the Civil
War, great landowners of the eighteenth and early nineteenth
centuries. They were in turn succeeded by the Cunliffe-Lister
family; Samuel Cunliffe-Lister, the Bradford inventor, wool
merchant and industrialist, founded the family fortune to
become the first Lord Masham. Swinton Park remains the home

of his descendant, Lord Swinton, as well as being the Conservative Party College.

The little town enjoys a certain fame as the home of Theakston's brewery. Thomas and Robert Theakston began brewing ale from the Black Bull Yard just over 150 years ago, and until very recently the brewery remained as a family concern, renowned for its excellent traditional ale, until becoming subject to somewhat tempestuous take-over battles from larger rivals. One of its most famous strong, dark ales is known as 'Old Peculier'.

This is, in fact, the name of Masham's ancient ecclesiastical court, which was established after Roger de Mowbray, in the twelfth century, granted the lucrative prebendary living of Masham to York Minster. The Archbishop of York subsequently freed Masham from 'all the customs and claims of his archdeacon and officials', so to deal with any important ecclesiastical or related legal matters a special court was established ('peculier' meaning particular rather than odd) with powers to judge offences of a religious nature, such as non-attendance at church, as well to grant licences to teach and to marry, and probate for wills. The court had real powers to punish offenders, even excommunication for anyone not supporting the Reformed Church.

After the Dissolution of the Monasteries, Henry VIII gave the powers of the ancient court to the Master and Fellows of Trinity College, Cambridge, and College Lane in Masham links the North Yorkshire town with the far-off university. The court's official seal remains the property of the 'Four and Twenty Trustees of the Ancient Parish of Masham' with its depiction of what must surely be a penitent offender, in medieval smock and cap, on his knees in prayer, no doubt awaiting the court's solemn verdict.

*Suggested Walk* (Allow forty minutes plus time to see the church).
From the market cross note the King's Head Inn, on the right as you look towards the church – a fine coaching inn and post-house. Until 1850 it was also the local excise office where certain taxes were collected and licences issued, and the word 'Excise' can still be deciphered over a doorway.

At the side of the King's Head an alleyway leads past stables where, at Uredale Glass in one of the old stable blocks, glass is manufactured and blown. Visitors are welcome to see the process in operation, with craftsmen creating elegant wares from molten glass. A showroom and coffee-shop also welcome visitors.

Return to the square and cross to the church, its elegant spire a notable landmark. It dates from the eleventh century, though the original work is confined to sections of walls and a doorway. The tower dates from around 1140, but the octagonal lantern and soaring spire were added in the fifteenth century. The nave was enlarged in the fourteenth century and the clerestory added in the fifteenth, with the south porch built on in 1520: a mixture of styles perhaps, but a most pleasing mixture, though inevitably Victorian restoration removed some fine original windows.

There are several memorials of local interests, particularly to the Danby family. Especially fine is the life-size effigy of Sir Marmaduke Wyvill and his wife, placed there in 1609 on the occasion of the lady's death. For this reason Sir Marmaduke's eyes are still open, making it an especially moving memorial of the living for the dead. Sir Marmaduke did not join his wife in the vault until 1617.

One of the most remarkable early Christian relics at Masham is the massive, carved stone pillar outside the church door. This is the shaft of an Anglo-Saxon preaching cross that pre-dates the church, elaborately carved. The figures in the upper panels represent the twelve apostles, one of them holding a musical instrument, probably an Anglian harp. Lower panels contain intricate Anglo-Saxon animal scroll motifs. Unfortunately the pillar is much weathered.

Return to the square and cross to the little free school and grammar school, which still serves as the village primary school, founded by William Danby in 1760 and rebuilt by his second wife, Mrs Danby Vernon Harcourt, in 1834.

Visible across the fields a short way along Millgate on the right is Mill House, remnants of the old watermill by the Ure and birthplace in 1815 of William Jackson the celebrated organist and composer.

Return along Millgate, bearing right into the little marketplace where on the left is the handsome town hall, built in 1913 from a bequest by Samuel Cunliffe-Lister, first Lord Masham.

Continue past the Bay Horse Inn, turning right again into Silver Street, past shops worth browsing in. The post office occupies an ornate little building on the left along the street, more like a village institute than a shop.

Keep ahead along Silver Street. On the right is the Holme, a pleasant park and extensive recreation area, reaching as far as the riverside. The land was given by the second Lord Masham as a tribute and most fitting memorial to the young men of Masham who perished in the Great War.

Bear right to the crossroads, and the attractive well-head fountain built to commemorate the Golden Jubilee of Queen Victoria in 1887. Opposite, a little way back from the main road, is the White Bear, one of the few country inns in North Yorkshire destroyed in the Blitz of World War II, when in 1941 a German bomber returning from a raid on industrial Teesside looked down to see a tell-tale light and offloaded two parachute bombs, completely destroying the White Bear Inn, at that time situated on the main road, and killing six people – a fate no less tragic for being unlikely.

Return on the top road to the village, but now turn sharp right before the baker's shop into College Court, going left into College Lane. The building on the right is College House, the former meeting-place of the Peculier Court; a surviving arched window hints at the building's antiquity.

Turn right outside College Lane, going past the Midland Bank, site of the old Mechanics' Institute. The fine house in the long garden to the right, Par House, was probably built on the site of the ancient manor house built by Sir John de Wauton, lord of the manor of Masham in the thirteenth century. The house overlooks Theakston's brewery.

Continue along Park Street, past attractive cottages, turning left into Chapman Lane, the name denoting the travelling pedlars arriving by this route into Masham Market from the moorland tracks and packhorseways. At the corner are almshouses endowed by Mrs Danby Vernon Harcourt in 1853. In a house directly opposite the almshouses Julius Caesar Ibbetson, a landscape painter and recorder of the contemporary scene, of some distinction, once lodged with a Mrs Powell. Ibbetson enjoyed the patronage of William Danby, a great aesthete and patron of the arts, and many of his finest paintings are at Swinton Park. Others are scattered in galleries throughout the region, including Leeds Art Gallery. Ibbetson had a particularly strong feeling for rural life, including rural poverty which he knew at first hand, and his paintings provide a fascinating insight into life in North Yorkshire at the turn of the nineteenth century. It is recalled that he had the habit of putting his latest painting into the cottage window to hear the comments of local children – his most honest critics. He is buried in Masham churchyard. Chapman Lane leads back into the market square.

## Middleham

Middleham's close connection with King Richard III gave this little Wensleydale township a brief period of glory.

The great castle, guarding the pass through Coverdale in Wharfedale and Skipton, was, in the middle years of the fifteenth century, home to one of England's most powerful barons, Richard Neville, Earl of Warwick, the 'Kingmaker'. In 1462 an eleven-year-old boy, son of the Duke of York, came to Middleham under Warwick's guardianship to be trained in the arts of Knighthood.

Less than four years later the boy's brother, King Edward IV, was held prisoner at Middleham by Warwick. After many difficult years, Warwick was finally defeated at the Battle of Barnet in 1471 by Edward, who rewarded his young brother (now Duke of Gloucester) for his skill and valour by giving him substantial lands in Richmondshire, including Warwick's old baronial castle at Middleham.

During the next few years, Richard of Gloucester developed Middleham as his power base, and his son Edward was born here in 1473. Richard had a reputation as a powerful leader, a skilful, if ruthless, politician but a man with a generosity of spirit which is still not forgotten. In 1483 he became King of England, but his success was short-lived. His son, now Prince of Wales, died at Middleham in 1484, his Queen, Anne Neville, shortly afterwards, and Richard himself perished in 1485 at the Battle of Bosworth at the hands of Henry Tudor, his reputation eventually to be vilified by that most brilliant of Tudor propagandists, William Shakespeare.

Though little remains to remind the modern visitor that Middleham was once a royal town, the massive castle notwithstanding, many fine Georgian houses and two market-places indicate that it was once of far greater importance, with stage-coach services and many inns. Its relative decline (or to be more accurate its inability to grow) is in part due to the growth of Leyburn, its neighbour at the far side of the River Ure. Two factors weighed in Leyburn's favour – its weekly market and its railway station, enough to allow Middleham to keep its eighteenth-century charm, whilst Leyburn became the commercial focal point of lower Wensleydale. But in terms of history and architecture Leyburn, pleasant country town though it might be, cannot compare.

Middleham's great eighteenth-century industry, which created the wealth for many of the fine houses in the town, continues to flourish to the present day – racehorses. No fewer than five major stables, home of many a Grand National and Derby winner, flourish in Middleham itself, and the soft turf of Low Moor and High Moor above the town provide perfect conditions for the training of horses. More than four hundred horses are exercised daily in this area, and the industry provides more than 150 jobs in and around the town, making it easily the main source of employment.

The bridge across the River Ure which separates the townships of Middleham and Leyburn was built in 1829 to replace a small ferry, as an elegant little suspension bridge, part of which survives. It was taken over by the county council and replaced by a more utilitarian structure.

Middleham's predominantly fourteenth-century church has associations with a local saint, whose life is curiously intertwined with ancient mythology. She was Alkelda, an Anglo-Saxon noblewoman, apparently strangled by two pagan Danish women near an ancient, pre-Christian holy well (which still survives two hundred yards west of the church). The Viking name for a well is, of course, 'keld', so it is a possibility that the story has become inextricably linked with some folk memory of ancient human sacrifice by a pagan holy well. A plaque on a pillar in the nave indicates where the bones of St Alkelda are reputed to have been buried.

Richard of Gloucester obtained a remarkable endowment for the church to become a college, with a dean and six canons. The college was never built, but the powers to create canons remained in being, forgotten until 1839 when Dean Wood appointed six canons, the last of whom, in 1845, was Charles Kingsley, social reformer and author, now most commonly remembered for *The Water Babies*. Kingsley was a frequent visitor to the area.

*Suggested Walk* (Allow fifty minutes, plus time to see castle and church).

Begin from the weathered old market cross in the market-place. Middleham once enjoyed a wide reputation for its sheep and cattle fair, taking place on 5, 6 and 7 November (the 5th being St Alkelda's Day) and on 30 March each year.

Middleham's importance as a commercial and trading centre can be deduced from the number of inns in the square – the Black Swan, with its impressive sign, the almost equally impressive White Swan, the Black Bull and the Commercial Hotel. Regular stage-coach services ran from here to York, Richmond and Leeds, whilst an important route from Yorkshire to Scotland crossed Park Rash Pass from Kettlewell through Coverdale, still the most direct way into Craven.

Follow the sign to the parish church along Kirkgate. Note the former Wesleyan chapel, dated 1836, the handsome Warwick House on the right, and opposite a curious cottage in late eighteenth-century Gothic style, with a cruciform panel above the door and narrow, almost moorish windows. Kingsley House is the former eighteenth-century rectory.

Turn left following the church sign into Church Street to the church with its lych-gate. As you go into the church porch, look up to see a fourteenth-century carving of the crucifixion. Inside the church there are many features of interest. The font, plain and simple, is of the fourteenth century. To its right is the carved tombstone of Robert Thornton, Abbot of Jervaulx, who died in 1510. The elaborate sculpture is a rebus or pictorial word-play of a bishop's thorn crozier penetrating a tun or barrel. In the western window of the northern nave the stained-glass window contains fragments of fourteenth-century glass, depicting the strangling of the unfortunate St Alkelda by grim-faced Danes. On the other side of the nave, in the west of the south aisle, is a modern window which include portraits of Richard III, his queen and his young son, Edward placed there by the Richard III Society.

Leave the church by the footpath to the right, across the churchyard to the crossroads of paths, taking the left path. This emerges at the west end of town, almost opposite an incredibly worn piece of sculpture on a pedestal above steps. This is Swine Cross, reputed to be Richard III's white boar emblem, worn smooth by five centuries of Dales weather. To the left is the old school, with a tower, now a shop and arts centre.

Stroll along this upper market-place, noting the variety of mainly Georgian houses, some of them distinctly unconventional in shape, suggesting local craftsmen imitating the 'polite' styles of fashionable places such as York and Richmond but not always getting it quite right. But this is the very source of Middleham's charm. Note a very tiny cottage, Birch Cottage, on the extreme right. Return along the top walkway, above gardens, by cottage doors. Go right at the castle, to the castle entrance.

Middleham Castle's most notable feature, like Richmond's, is a massive keep, but it is in a much poorer state of repair. It is a typical Norman structure, tremendous in the width of its walls – ten to twelve feet thick, about the size of an average twentieth-century living-room. There is a chapel and huge curtain walls dominated by great corner towers. The round tower at the south-west, known as Prince's Tower, is reputedly where the tragically short-lived Prince Edward was born.

From the castle turn right into the little track, walking past the castle and new bungalows until you reach the stile in the wall. Cross, walking towards the grassy mounds ahead, through the gate left. It's a steep climb, so take care.

This is William's Mount, probably the site of the first castle built here in the 1070s by Alan the Red, builder of Richmond Castle and first Lord of Middleham – though Alan gave Middleham to his brother Ribald, who may have been the builder. Outlines of the moat survive, and the hillock makes a splendid viewpoint, back across Middleham and its castle, across Wensleydale, with Leyburn directly ahead and, to the south, Coverdale, which winds down from the Pennine summits.

Return the way you have come – this is a public right of way – back to the castle, but this time turn right along a narrow lane, Back Street, which soon becomes cobbled. This goes along the 'backs' of Middleham where attractive alleyways cut through from the market-place. You may be able to detect where masonry from the castle has been used to build some of the cottages and outbuildings. This emerges at the market-place. Turn left to pass the Black Bull and a fine Georgian house. To the left is the market cross.


## Pickering

This compact little town is in the centre of a long line of red-pantiled and soft cream limestone villages which lie like beads on the long string of the A170 Scarborough-Helmsley road, at the very point where the Tabular Hills descend to meet the green and fertile Vale of Pickering. You can quickly appreciate its strategic importance, on the main moorland road from Whitby and the coast to Malton and York, the inevitable Norman castle positioned to keep an eye on both the crossroads and any seaward movement.

Pickering is one of the comfortable, mellow little country towns that you can pass all too quickly through on the main road, not realizing how much it has to offer.

It's been a market town for centuries (Monday is market day) and in the past earned an excellent living through the quality of its bacon and salted pork, much of which found its way to Whitby for mariners, and in the breeding of horses, particularly cab and coach horses, mostly Cleveland Bays, which found their way as far as London when, in the days of horse-drawn trams and buses, a Pickering Cleveland Bay might well have hauled you along the Strand.

In a county rich in castles, Pickering's holds its own, situated above but slightly away from the town, so that Pickering isn't a castle town in the way that Richmond, Skipton and even Scarborough are. The ruins are extensive, with a circular thirteenth-century keep on an elevated motte, and a series of powerful towers including the intriguingly, and romantically, named Rosamond's Tower. Henry III gave the castle and lordship of Pickering to his younger son, Edmund, who, in due course, obtained the market and fair charter from Edward I. But Edmund's son Thomas, Earl of Lancaster, was eventually beheaded for treason.

The glory of Pickering's parish church of St Peter and St Paul isn't so much the architecture – fascinating as this is, revealing every period from the twelfth to the nineteenth century – but a series of astonishing wall paintings executed around 1450 and amongst the finest of their kind in England. They had been lost but preserved under whitewash for many generations before being accidentally discovered and mysteriously lost again in 1851, rediscovered in 1880; though inevitably heavily restored, they still represent an astonishing piece of late medieval art. The frescoes recall the lives of several saints, including St George putting paid to the dragon, St Edmund being pierced with arrows, St Thomas of Canterbury being murdered by his knight, and Christ entering Hades, which is symbolized by a lurid dragon.

If that were not temptation enough to visit Pickering, the town is the terminus of the North York Moors Railway, with a station rich in interest, whilst Beck Isle Museum is a regional museum of some importance.

*Suggested Walk* (Allow thirty minutes, plus time to see church, castle and Beck Isle Museum).
Start at the little Ropery car-park, just by the traffic lights. It's difficult to imagine this was where, until comparatively recently, the railway ran to Malton. Attractively designed loos, walkways and supermarket prove how well modern development can blend in with an old town, providing a green beckside area.

Walk forward to the market-place, turning right at the Midland Bank. This is a broad street of pleasant shops, pubs, banks and offices. Cross to the broad, raised pavement on the left, heading for the church ahead, past the bottom of Bargate and evocatively named Willowgate to enter the churchyard through the little gateway ahead.

Pickering church is situated on a low eminence, the churchyard closely boxed in by houses and cottages to give an unusual, enclosed feeling. The castellated walls around the churchyard date from the fifteenth century. With Norman, Transitional and Decorated work, it is a handsome if not spectacular building, and its most interesting monuments include effigies of Sir David Roecliffe and his lady of the fifteenth century, and a plaque to Robert King and his son whose claim to fame was that they helped to found and plan the city of Washington in the USA. The magnificent frescoes in the nave offer a richness and wealth of detail requiring time to study.

Leaving the church, go directly ahead on the path which leads down steps into Birdgate, continuation of the market-place. A wallside plaque on the Black Swan Hotel in Birdgate informs you that on 20 May 1836 a crowd of seven thousand people was here to witness the opening of the Whitby-Pickering Railway and watch no fewer than three hundred dignitaries make their way to the inn for what must surely have been quite a repast.

Return along Birdgate into the market-place, but opposite Taylor's fish shop cross right into Bargate, a street of pleasant Victorian houses and shops. This continues as Castlegate, which has a number of traditional cottages and an unspoiled village shop. Note the great stone mounting-block on the left outside the Quaker meeting-house, doubtless to enable Friends to mount before a long journey on horseback to outlying villages.

Castlegate broadens to a green. As it swings left by the castle walls, the footpath on the right leads to the entrance, itself a fine viewpoint back towards the town and over the surrounding countryside. About half a mile left, a green mound indicates the site of a former castle, no doubt the original castle said to have been built by the Conqueror himself, perhaps on the site of an earlier defensive fortification.

Take time to see the castle, now under the care of English Heritage and open daily.

On leaving the castle, bear right down the steps, keeping ahead on the signposted path opposite the vine-covered pottery which soon leads into a narrowing into a footpath. There are views across the North York Moors Railway from here, carriages and equipment, assorted warehouses. The path emerges close to the station where, during the summer months, you are quite likely to see a steam locomotive or vintage diesel waiting to depart in front of crowded carriages.

Although Pickering station dates from North Eastern Railway rather the Whitby-Pickering days, it has much of intrinsic interest to the devotees of railwayana, but there is also a well-supplied information centre and an exhibition interpreting not only the railway line but the landscape, well worth seeing even if you do not intend to catch a train.

From the station return to the traffic lights, but this time turn right into Bridge Street, crossing the lovely part-medieval, part-eighteenth-century bridge over Pickering Beck, best viewed from the little grassy area on the right.

Further right, in a fine late Georgian house, is the Beck Isle Museum. It was here that William Marshall (1748–1818), pioneer agricultural improver and educationalist, opened the first agricultural college, and the house has now been converted to a particularly interesting Museum of Rural Life, dealing with many aspects of farming and domestic life in the area.

You now enter Potter Hill, another broad street rising on a low hill, with pleasant greens and trees. There are a number of eighteenth – and nineteenth-century houses here, the town's Roman Catholic church and a Methodist chapel. An interesting Regency house on the right has tall, neo-Gothic windows.

Return to the bottom of Potter Hall, noting two tall warehouses at the end, one with a date stone 1861, guarding a slipway into the beck – a watering-place for cattle on market and fair days. The name 'Potter' means gypsies or tinkers, and no doubt the area was at one time used by travelling people.

An opening, right, at the bottom of Potter Hill leads behind the Old Granary (an early warehouse now converted to a restaurant) to the main road and traffic lights.


## Richmond

Approach Richmond, if you possibly can, along the Hudswell road or the high road from Leyburn that goes by Catterick Camp, the roads meeting before they swing down to John Carr's fine eighteenth-century bridge over the River Swale. As you come round the corner, there it is, in profile, stretched before you – Richmond. The rock, the castle with its mighty keep, the river, the town.

J.M.W. Turner captured and dramatized this very same view with a famous watercolour that transformed Richmond into a mythological Roman or Italian town bathed in rich, golden light. Reality gives Richmond sober Yorkshire greys and greens – grey of crags and castle walls, rooftops, green of the richly wooded valley of the Swale, peat brown of the surging river. But no less satisfying for all that.

This most beautiful of northern towns richly repays exploration and repeated visit. Every corner and turning offers contrast and contradiction. Narrow cobbled alleyways and steep streets – here known as wynds – suddenly open out to romantic, aery, riverside walks and a market square. The finest and perhaps only completely authentic eighteenth-century theatre in England stands opposite an elegant Franciscan church tower. The church in the market square isn't a church. The railway station, protected by a preservation order, doesn't have any trains.

The town was and, due to the proximity of Catterick Camp, still is a garrison town. Alan the Red, a relative of the Duke of Brittany and one of William the Conqueror's cohorts, received Richmondshire no doubt as a reward for services rendered, and proceeded, in 1071, to build the mighty castle on a rocky promontory above the surging Swale. It was further strengthened and enlarged in 1146 by Earl Conan, making the great keep one of the tallest Norman keeps in England.

The purpose of this mighty fortress was surely more than defensive. Richmond, standing at the mouth of a fairly unimportant side valley, was never strategically situated guarding a pass or major route – for example the Great North Road several miles away. But only three miles north of Richmond lies the small and now insignificant village of Gilling West, the wapentake (regional capital) in Anglian times. The great keep of Richmond – the Norman-French derivation of its name is self-evident – was a symbol of authority and power over a subservient people, and the area was dominated by allegiance to France for many years.

The castle, because it never had any strategic importance, was never captured or held under siege, but three kings, two of Scotland and one of England were held prisoner here. William the Lion of Scotland was held until a ransom of £100,000 – a mighty fortune in the currency of the time – was paid, whilst King David II was transported here after his defeat at the Battle of Neville's Cross in 1346. The English monarch was the ill-fated Charles I who was here in 1646 as a prisoner on his way to Holmby House and ultimate execution in London.

There's no finer view of the old town which grew up to service the great castle and its inhabitants than from the summit of the great keep, reached through a steep ascent up narrow staircases, past well-preserved floors. There it is, stretched out before you, the rows of uneven roofs, chimneypots, towers, even the straggle of somewhat drab modern housing which, if much of it lacks imagination, helps to bring Richmond back into the real, workaday world. There's nothing twee about Richmond but all around that glorious countryside, Swaledale, arguably the loveliest of all the Yorkshire Dales, extending westwards, the green foothills rolling into the Vale of Mowbray.

Almost as fine is the view down the great crag into the River Swale from the great grassy terrace that now forms the central courtyard of the castle, seen through the ruined walls and fragments of towers.

Now in the care of English Heritage, Richmond Castle is open daily.

Soldiers are still very much in evidence in Richmond, albeit somewhat friendlier forces from the nearby Catterick garrison, and as you drive about nearby moorland roads you are quite likely to suddenly find yourself staring down the gun turret of a tank as its swings around the corner or to see red flags warning you of artillery ranges. In Trinity Church, in the market-place, where once the curfew bell tolled to keep townfolk off the streets, there is now a fascinating museum telling the history of one of the great British regiments closely associated with Richmond – the Green Howards. The museum was opened in 1973 by King Olav of Norway, Colonel in Chief of the regiment, and it contains many moving relics of campaigns both distinguished and tragic.

Richmond's parish church, St Mary's, is situated outside the ancient city walls (which have now all but vanished) where there was more room to build. It dates back to the twelfth century, with a fifteenth-century tower, though it was heavily restored in the nineteenth century. Perhaps its most interesting features are the choir stalls with their elaborately carved misericords which originally came from nearby Easby Abbey after the Dissolution. A favourite one for visitors depicts a pig playing bagpipes whilst other pigs dance to the strains. A somewhat darker reminder of what life was like in medieval and Tudor times comes from an unmarked stone in the churchyard known as 'the Plague Stone', reputedly indicating the unmarked graves of many of the hundreds of townsfolk who perished between 1597 and 1599 in the terrible plague which afflicted the town. More than a thousand people are known to have died.

The Georgian Theatre Royal, situated in a somewhat ordinary little building which looks more like a warehouse (as indeed it was for many years), was built in 1788 to hold four hundred spectators by the actor/manager/impresario Samuel Butler who had a group of travelling players spending their time between several small theatres in the North. In those days it cost the princely sum of a shilling for a seat in the gallery, 2 shillings in the pit and 3 shillings for the boxes, though if a celebrity was appearing, such as the great Edmund Kean, who began his career in Butler's company and returned to Richmond as a national star in 1819, the stalls were 3 shillings, boxes four.

In 1848 the theatre closed down and was converted to a combination of wine vaults, a corn chandler's store and a furniture store. Thankfully, such alterations as did occur were minimal, and when, in 1960, the true significance of the theatre was realized, a trust was established for its restoration, which was achieved within two years. The original staircases, boxes, galleries, pit and ticket office survive and are still in use, and though (thankfully) only 237 people are now seated in the tiny auditorium, the authentic wooden seats soon make all but the most stoic realize how much tougher eighteenth-century audiences must have been. What is lost in lack of comfort, however, is made up for by a wonderfully intimate atmosphere, ideal for giving the real flavour of Sheridan or Goldsmith.

A small theatrical museum has been created and among its exhibits is a complete collection of painted scenery dating from 1836, reputedly the oldest surviving stage set in the United Kingdom.

*Suggested Walk* (Allow an hour, plus time to see the castle and museums).

Richmond is the kind of town impossible to do justice to in one visit without cultural indigestion. It is a town to return to, to savour. But this initial route gives something of the flavour; if there's more time available, try the excellent Richmond town trail guide on sale at the tourist office in Greyfriars Gardens.

Begin at the obelisk, erected in 1771 to replace the ancient market cross. Traders came from all over the North of England (witness the Lancaster-Richmond turnpike road being built in the eighteenth century) to the market, which was of regional importance, particularly for wool, corn and Swaledale lead.

'The queerest ecclesiastical building one might imagine' is how architectural historian Nikolaus Pevsner described Holy Trinity Chapel in the market-place. Built in the mid twelfth century, it fell into ruin when the parish church was built; it was rebuilt in 1360 but again was ruined by 1439. It was used as a refuge during the 1597–8 plague and has been used as a warehouse for beer, a school, town hall, prison and assize court, and once it even had a tobacconist's shop placed incongruously between the tower and the nave. It now houses the Green Howards Museum.

Many of the fine buildings around the market-place have been spoiled by humdrum commercial development, at least at ground-floor level, but the King's Head survives as a fine eighteenth-century inn, and the town hall, on the south side of the market-place, dates from 1756. The Bishop Blaize is Richmond's oldest surviving inn.

Leave the market-place by the south-west corner by the Talbot Hotel. Don't descend the steep street ahead but bear left along the cobbled way onto Castle Hill. This soon opens out into a fine broad footpath under the crags and castle walls – with seats to enjoy the view – above the River Swale. Return to the market-place by continuing round into Millgate and keeping straight ahead.

Leave the market-place once again by the Talbot, this time going a little further down New Road but bearing left into the Bar, a narrow way once one of the main roads into Richmond. This actually goes under the Bar itself, a narrow medieval gateway, the only survivor of five which penetrated the medieval defensive wall around the town. Permission to build this wall was granted to the burghers of Richmond in 1315 by King Edward II as a defence against Scottish raids.

Follow the footpath downhill, along Cornforth Hill into Bridge Street towards Richmond Bridge, but turn right into the Green, an area of attractive houses and cottages around a fine village green. Directly ahead of you, looking westwards is a strange, ornamental tower. This is Culloden Tower, built on the base of an ancient pele tower in eighteenth-century neo-Gothic style, highly ornamented, to commemorate the defeat of the Scots and Jacobites in 1746. It is not open to the public.

From the Green turn back to Richmond Bridge, going left up Bargate, a steep ascent up one of Richmond's original medieval streets. At the top the period changes abruptly into the eighteenth century again, in Newbiggin, a fine, broad thoroughfare with elegant, Adamesque townhouses, homes of merchants and local gentry, tree-lined and grand.

Return to the town centre along Finkle Street to the market-place, but almost immediately turn sharp left along Friars Wynd, an alleyway which once provided access to the Franciscan friary outside the old town walls.

Turn right in Victoria Road. On your left is the tall, elegant Greyfriars Tower. Franciscan friars settled in Richmond in 1258, but nothing remains of their church except this beautiful, fifteenth-century tower, now preserved in attractive gardens which also serve as the town's war memorial.

Almost immediately on the right is the Royal Georgian Theatre. Details of theatrical performances and opening times of the museum are available from the box office.

Continue to the crossroads and cross to Ryders Wind. Above and to the left, on Pottergate, is Hill House, once home of Frances l'Anson, celebrated in song as 'The Lass of Richmond Hill'. The song was written by one Leonard McNally, a barrister, who married Frances in 1787, his words being set to music by James Hook and performed in Vauxhall Gardens, London, where the song became an immediate success. The tale has a tragic end as Frances died at the early age of twenty-nine in Dublin.

In Ryders Wynd, on the left, is the Richmondshire Museum, a small but fascinating museum which tells something of the long story of Richmond from 1071, together with local archaeological remains and agricultural and local history items. There is a large-scale model of Richmond railway station, closed in 1970 but preserved for its architectural splendour, and a set of the famous BBC television *Herriot* series shown in the locality. The museum, manned by volunteers, is open afternoons from April until October, and mornings during the peak holiday times.

Turn left into Frenchgate – fine views. Local legend has it that its name derives from a French mason and his workmen who first lived in this street, which now contains some fine eighteenth-century townhouses. Turn right off French Gate into Church Wynd leading to the parish church.

Give yourself time to explore the church and churchyard, perhaps finding the gravestones of two veterans of the Battle of Waterloo, William Watson and Augustus Blytheman, and the memorial to Robert Willance, who survived an amazing leap with his horse across Whitcliffe Scar, near Richmond (still known as Willance's Leap).

Once in Station Road it is worth descending to the station, now a garden centre, and the fine new swimming-bath and leisure complex, with a walkway along the old trackbed, perhaps following the riverside path above the Batts to Millgate and the town centre, or, if time presses, from the parish church, simply turn left along Station Road back into Frenchgate and the market-place.

## Ripon

Approach Ripon from the south or east and, if the sun is right, you see the cathedral, like a great ship of pale stone, floating across the plain.

Wilfrid chose the site, on a little headland above the confluence of the River Ure and the little River Skell, around 673, building a little church to serve a group of monks from Melrose Abbey. Only the Anglo-Saxon crypt survives to the present day, a little dungeon-like structure of simple, austere architecture, now used as the cathedral's treasure house.

The cathedral that rises above it was built between 1154 and 1530 and offers a variety of Gothic styles: the simplicity and noble grandeur of the west front, the Transitional north transepts, Perpendicular work in the nave. A particular glory is the magnificent east window, dating from the thirteenth century, with elaborate tracery, and the richly decorated choir stalls, completed in 1494. The misericords are rich in often humorous medieval carvings – dancing pigs, a fox and goose, Jonah and the whale, an owl, a mermaid. Though one of England's smallest, Ripon is one of the most attractive of cathedrals. Detailed guidebooks are available inside.

Enough of the old town has survived, around the cathedral and the market-place, to retain the feeling and flavour of a compact medieval city, as city indeed it is. Its origins go back to Anglo-Saxon times, when King Alfred, no less, is reputed to have granted the town's first charter, in 886, an occasion which inhabitants of Ripon have been enthusiastic to celebrate on its 1100th anniversary in 1986. But it was as a city under the rule of successive archbishops of York that Ripon flourished, having its fair granted in 1108, as well as markets. The town rapidly expanded as a centre for the handling and manufacture of wool.

The coming of the Industrial Revolution and growth of manufacturing in such towns as Halifax and Bradford led Ripon to diversify as a manufacturing centre, and in later years industries included lace-making, linen-manufacture, potteries, clay pipe-making, spur-making ('Ripon spurs' were extremely famous), coach-building and paint varnish manufacture. Varnish was actually invented and continues to be manufactured in the town.

The Wakeman or Watchman of Ripon was in charge of a team of constables responsible for the safety of the city and its citizens. At 9 p.m. each night the 'setting of the Watch' took place, signalled by the sounding of a horn at each corner of the market cross. From this point on the city was in the hands of the Wakeman, and if any robbery was committed, it was the Wakeman's responsibility to capture the villain and bring him to justice, and also to pay compensation to the victim. For this service, every householder had to pay the princely sum of 2d. a year, for each door into his house, a form of insurance which provided value for money on a quite exceptional scale. The Ripon Hornblower continues the custom which has persisted for more than a thousand years by sounding the horn at each corner of the obelisk which replaced the market cross at 9 p.m. sharp, at which time the curfew bell is still rung, and then he departs to sound it at the mayor's house. Unfortunately the payment of 2d.

will no longer make the mayor – successor to the Wakeman – responsible for any burglaries.

Not surprisingly, the horn is still the city's symbol, and the ancient Charter Horn of 886 still survives, encased in velvet and silver. The city takes its past and great tradition very seriously indeed. There is a magnificent collection of silver, a Towne Booke of 1598 outlining the duties of the Wakeman, a Guild Book and three royal charters.

The Wakeman's House in the market square is a half-timbered building, dating from the fourteenth century, now the town museum and tourist office, where displays and exhibitions interpret the long story of Ripon from prehistoric times to the present day.

The market-place, nearly two acres in extent, is a focal point of the town, crowded on Thursdays, market day. The tall stone obelisk, crowned by a weather vane in the form of the Ripon horn, was erected in 1781 to commemorate the completion of local landowner William Aislabie's sixty years as Member of Parliament.

The elegantly proportioned town hall (its classical colonnade crowned by the city motto 'Except ye the Lord keep ye Cittie ye Wakeman Waketh in vain') was originally built by the architect James Wyatt, as a townhouse for Mrs Elizabeth Allanson of Studley Royal. It was granted to the city in 1897 by the Marquess of Ripon to celebrate his year in office as mayor, the previous year.

*Suggested Walk* (Allow fifty minutes, plus time to see cathedral and museums).
From the obelisk in the market-place, bear left down Kirkgate, a narrow street of attractive period shops. As you pass Duck Hill, right, note the restaurant in what was formerly the town lock-up. A new 'Small Shops' arcade fits in well with the sensitive environment. Continue ahead to the cathedral, giving yourself plenty of time to explore it if you haven't already done so, before bearing right down Bedern Bank. Above the high wall to the left as you descend is Minster House, a Georgian house, residence of the Dean of Ripon. There are fine views of the cathedral from this point.

Keep left for a short way into High St Agnesgate. On the right is a building, now a social club, known as Thorpe Prebend, thought to be one of seven livings created out of the vast Ripon parish; this could be the house of one of the priests fortunate enough to hold the living. Mary Queen of Scots, and King James VI and I are reputed to have stayed there. The present building dates from the seventeenth century.

Continue to the little ruin ahead. This is the remains of the chancel of St Anne's hospital church – medieval almshouses dating from the seventeenth century. The present almshouses are much more recent.

Return along High St Agnesgate, turning left to cross New Bridge on the Boroughbridge road to Bondgate Green, a row of early Industrial Revolution cottages restored in 1981 by the Yorkshire Historic Buildings Preservation Trust. Walk ahead to bear right by the significantly named Navigation Inn along Canal Road. The somewhat derelict yard and buildings on the left are the old Ripon canal basin. You soon reach the disused canal, the walls of the old warehouses crumbling visibly, the end of over two centuries of history and, at present at least, a sadly wasted asset.

Return to New Bridge, but keep left before the bridge by Bondgate Cottages to the footpath by the River Skell. Follow the river upstream, soon emerging on King Street by the little church of St John the Baptist, medieval but heavily restored. Cross King Street to the continuation of the riverside path ahead. You soon pass T. & R. Williamson's varnish and enamel factory, founded in 1775. This was the firm that invented varnish to use on the elegant coachwork made in the town. See the little horn medallion on the riverside wall.

The path ends at the bottom of Low Skellgate, close to the evocatively named Barefoot Street. Turn left up Skellgate, only too aware, as you walk, of the pressures of traffic in Ripon that can be relieved only by a bypass. In this narrow thoroughfare, traffic dominates everything.

You emerge in Westgate, opposite the Wakeman's House, but instead of bearing right into the market-place, turn left into West Gate. This soon opens out to a rather fashionable street, with some lovely late Georgian and early Regency houses on the right. As it crosses the bottom of Blossomgate and becomes Park Street, you reach the spa baths on the left.

Built in 1904 this was a late development of the spa era, originally attempting to emulate Harrogate with a fashionable pump room in elaborate *art nouveau* style, all in red brick and yellow terracotta. It is now the town's swimming-baths and sauna. Immediately beyond the spa baths and the spa gardens is an area of lawns, bowling greens, flowerbeds and elegant bandstand, Ripon's bid to be a resort, and a delightful place to sit or stroll.

Return to Westgate, but this time going up Blossomgate, a street with a lovely name but disappointing appearance, once the centre of Ripon's lace-making industry. Turn right into Trinity Road, past the rather attractive church of Holy Trinity, dating from 1832, continuing into Coltsgate, past the Roman Catholic church in High Victorian style, keeping right to North Street.

North Street swings into the northern part of the town, extending to the now-closed railway, with Victorian housing, some large and imposing, and using the white brick favoured in seaside resorts.

But turn right in North Street to Fishergate, then first left along Allhallowsgate, one of the most interesting of Ripon's old streets, with attractive houses and old cottages in local materials and style. On the left you pass Sharow View, former workhouse and now Social Services Centre, a pleasant Victorian building of pleasing proportion. On the right is an elevated stretch of footpath adding to the rural flavour. Turn left at the bottom of Allhallowsgate into St Marygate.

You soon reach, on the left, Ripon Prison and Police Museum. The building, Ripon's House of Correction, dates from the seventeenth century, with nineteenth century additions. After ceasing life as a prison in 1877, it became Ripon police station until closed in 1956, and part of the cell block has now been opened as a remarkable museum of policing and punishment, run by the Ripon Museum Trust.

Continue along St Marygate. The high wall on the right, with a fine gateway in the centre, is known as 'the Gothic Wall' and was built by Abbot Huby of Fountains Abbey to enclose the little Church of St Mary's, which has long since disappeared.

Continue along Minster Road up to the cathedral. Opposite the cathedral is an area of gardens and a little fountain; behind the wall on the right are a number of interesting buildings linked with the cathedral – the old deanery, with its 'stately' seventeenth-century façade, the little stone courthouse, dating from 1832, and the remarkable sixteenth-century old courthouse built over the remains of the medieval courthouse.

Turn right into Kirkgate back to the market-place.


## Selby

The great abbey church, resplendent in gleaming cream stone, seems too grand for this pleasant, unpretentious country town. As you come along the market-place by rows of ordinary shops, banks and pubs, suddenly you are around the curve in the road and facing that great west front, those richly decorated Norman doors, the soaring towers. As you walk past the southern flank of the building, its sheer cathedral size is quite breathtaking. How it came to be situated on this little island port on the River Ouse has been recorded in other pages (p.62). You'll see Benedict's three swans in an escutcheon high over the north porch.

The fact that all the evidence of tradition is that one of William the Conqueror's sons, later Henry I, was born here (as the Queen accompanied her husband to York, in 1070) may not be unconnected with Selby's evident prosperity. Selby's abbot was one of only two mitred abbots north of Trent – the other being the abbot of St Mary's, York.

The abbey church is rightly described as perhaps the finest complete one in England, in excellent state of preservation despite the effects of the tragic fire of 1905. Much of the best work in the abbey dates from the time of Abbot Hugh, from around 1100 and through the twelfth century. Those massive columns are typically Norman, reminiscent of Durham. One, decorated with a trellis pattern, a direct copy of Durham, is known as Abbot Hugh's pillar. You'll also notice that two of the high arches are grotesquely distorted. This was a result of building the great tower too rapidly on the clay foundations, causing the masonry to tilt. Fortunately the movement stabilized and the work could continue, albeit with some loss of symmetry.

There is also much magnificent thirteenth and fourteenth-century work, nothing finer than the glorious east window, a mass of superb tracery and richly coloured stained glass, about a third of it the original fourteenth-century glass. This is the Jesse window, tracing the Old Testament family of Jacob and culminating in a representation of doom. The fifteenth-century cover of the Norman font was one of the few pieces of medieval woodwork to survive the fire. Of especial interest to American visitors in Selby Abbey Church is a piece of fourteenth-century glass containing the arms of the Washington family, undoubtedly the earliest surviving pictorial representation of the stars-and-stripes motif which was to form the national flag of the United States of America.

Outside the church, nothing else survives of the Benedictine community, nor does Selby have anything of the feeling or flavour of a cathedral or ecclesiastical town. Apart from an area in the immediate vicinity of the abbey itself, you have the feeling of being in a port, close to industry and commerce and movement. Maybe that's what makes Selby interesting, its contradiction. It's a town of some potential, and some small-scale environmental improvement schemes, around the abbey itself, and a new shopping precinct and civic centre are beginning to realize that potential.

*Suggested Walk* (Allow fifty minutes).
From the market-place head for the abbey, but take the pathway to the immediate left of the church entrance into Abbey Place, a small, enclosed green fronted by pleasant if unassuming houses. This green is in fact a cholera burial ground, resting-place of victims of the great cholera epidemic of 1848, doubtless a result of insanitary conditions in the old port.

Bear slightly left at the end of Abbey Place into Church Lane, making for the Crown Hotel ahead. There are several new or restored houses in this vicinity, using traditional styles and sympathetic materials – red pantiles and rustic brick – which blend in with the cream Magnesian Limestone of the abbey.

At the end of Church Lane you are on Church Hill, a shopping parade of some character and interest. Ahead is the River Ouse. Cross to the little green ahead, to the right of a solitary surviving waterfront house. On your right is Selby's famous tollbridge. Until 1970 this was a remarkable antique wooden structure which had carried, for a couple of centuries, all Selby's traffic and the main A63, its ancient machinery swinging to permit the passage of ships on the Ouse. It was replaced by the present drawbridge structure. It is worth walking at least part way across to look along the river and at the active wharves and shipbuilding area.

Return to the riverside with its grass and benches, passing in front of the house by the river to rejoin the road by steps at the far corner. Cross the road. On the right is the huge tower of the Ideal Flour Mills complex, now covering the old quayside area. Follow Water Street at the front of the complex, passing decaying warehouses and mill buildings on the right, until you reach Micklegate, a broad street. To your right is the Ideal Mill entrance on the Quay, but notice the number of old buildings or fragments of old buildings in pale stone, which once formed the quayside and port area.

Before going into Micklegate, walk directly ahead into Millgate, keeping ahead beyond Selby Dam. A drainage stream goes under the road, and New Millgate swings off left along the riverside. Long terraces of cottages give a strong feeling of the old port.

Return to Micklegate, a shopping and car-parking area where development of varying quality has not always blended as well as it might in what must surely have been a handsome thoroughfare. It isn't without some interesting buildings, most notably a splendid *art nouveau* public house, the Griffin, on the left.

Continue into the narrower Finkle Street, one of Selby's principal shopping streets, again with a couple of interesting pubs, one with a name – the Black-a-Moor Head – which is typically eighteenth century. This leads back into the market-place. Note the Londesborough Arms on the left, a fine eighteenth-century coaching-house, with a somewhat dissipated satyr, carved in plaster, complete with a bunch of grapes, gazing from the inn wall. Note too, the coach bell, high up on the wall side, there to ring the departure of mail coaches.

The second leg of the stroll looks at more industrial history. This time bear right, past the huge south front of the abbey, but crossing the road to the right at the junction into Park Street. On the left-hand side is a well-kept town park with a tall, very weathered obelisk, looking like a spire detached from the abbey, surrounded by flowerbeds. It is, in fact, no such thing, but a column which stood in the market-place by Finkle Street, moved here in 1960 and looking very much the worse for wear.

Opposite the park is a row of elegant Regency-style buildings, with the appearance of an old Customs House, but now a Salvation Army hostel.

Keep ahead through the park to rejoin the road at the bus station and tourist office, and past the railway station. This isn't Selby's first station but a later version built after the line was extended to Hull. For Yorkshire's oldest surviving station, indeed one of the oldest in the world, keep ahead to the crossroads, turn right underneath the railway bridge for about fifty yards and, past a house on the right, you reach a large warehouse, owned by Dalgety Spillers. This is the original Selby station, built on the Leeds-Selby line in 1834. Although there is strictly no public access to the premises, if you are fortunate enough to arrive when doors are open, you'll see the tall, cast-iron columns supporting a wooden roof, between which tall-chimneyed locomotives hauled carriages filled with crinolined ladies and stovepipe-hatted gentlemen, before they crossed the road to the staithes that once existed, opposite, to board the steamer bound for the Humber and for Hull.

Return under the railway, noting that rather splendid and probably unique railway signal box high above the centre of the tracks, designed to give a view of river as well as railway and operate the swing bridge.

Continue to the road bridge ahead, turning left back into the town centre, past cottages and shops of somewhat faded elegance, and the Crescent, where a couple of pubs show how that elegance could revive. Park House, now a hairdresser's, also points the way.

The abbey and market-place are ahead.


## Settle

Somehow Settle manages to have the best of everything. It isn't too large; the countryside sweeps in close to its very heart; noble limestone crags and green, steep pastures seem to rise out of the very rooftops. It's all so compact with no suburban sprawl or ribbon development, all on a human scale.

Not that there's anything twee or artificially picturesque about Settle. It's got its share of pleasant, dull modern housing, its industrial area, plenty of concrete and pebbledash around, but it's all somehow in balance, not too much of it, a real working community.

So you can enjoy that glorious little town centre, a kaleidoscope of fine little houses, shops, warehouses, chapels without any sense of the artificial. Of course some buildings have been carefully restored, courtyards cleaned, period details re-created. Somehow there's neither too much bad taste nor too much good taste to spoil it. Settle's a functional place; it's about getting on with living.

Go if you can on the Tuesday market day, when the little market-place around the tall pillar which suffices for a market cross is alive with colour and movement, local people mingling with visitors, as many from Lancashire as Yorkshire (Settle is as close to east Lancashire towns as west Yorkshire), farmers' wives mixing with architects from London and ramblers from Bradford. It is an astonishingly rich treasure house of the interesting and unusual.

Take the curious Shambles, in the market-place. There's a row of shops, themselves built over basement lock-up shops, capped by a row of twin-storey gabled cottages, with a balcony. You only build like that where land is scarce. In hill-farming areas good, fertile 'bottom' land is too precious to waste on trivial things like houses, so you build around every little court and alleyway in a place like Settle. You even let the town scramble its way precariously up the hillside, cutting out steps for cottages, chapels, streets.

So it is in Settle. A glorious jumble of little courts and alleyways around the market-place. Many of the houses have a date stone of the seventeenth or eighteenth century over the doorway, indicating a period of growth and prosperity as trade increased after the Civil War, and especially with the coming of the important Keighley-Kendal turnpike in the late eighteenth century, developing Settle as a coaching town, a market town (Henry III granted the town a market charter in 1249). With the coming of the railway in the 1840s on the 'Little' North Western line south of the town and the opening of the famous

Settle-Carlisle line in 1876, its growth received a further boost.

Someone has suggested that Settle has a French atmosphere, perhaps because of the intimate feel of the shops and cafés around its market-place or the ornate, brown stone town hall (containing the tourist office) of 1832 in a supposedly gabled Elizabethan style, which does have a Gallic feel.

Nothing very Gallic about what undoubtedly is Settle's finest building, 'The Folly', built in 1675 but containing an astonishing mixture of Tudor and Renaissance styles, making it a *tour de force* of architectural fancy.

Almost as striking, in Cheapside, at the side of the town hall, is a magnificent neo-classical warehouse, looking more like the façade of a Georgian mansion than such a functional building. Only the crane, high on the wall side, reveals that the three arches forming doors and windows were once mere loading bays.

Settle was an industrial centre too, and interesting early Industrial-Revolution textile mills along the river between Settle and Langcliffe repay exploration.

Two outstanding men born in Settle made a major contribution to human welfare. The first was George Birkbeck (1776–1841), son of a local banker and merchant, who founded the first Mechanics' Institutes in Glasgow and London, which were to prove such a major influence in the education of working men. Birkbeck College, in London University, is named after him. The second was Edwin Waugh, social reformer and philanthropist (1839–1908), whose greatest achievement was the creation of what is now the National Society for the Prevention of Cruelty to Children.

Whilst in Settle, it's worth wandering along Station Road down to Settle station itself, a well-cared-for Midland station on the Settle-Carlisle line. It might even prove possible to combine a trip on the famous line with a visit to Settle. The view from the 'down' platform across to Settle's twin township of Giggleswick, with the copper-domed chapel of Giggleswick School a prominent landmark and across the meandering valley of the Ribble to the lovely hills of Bowland, will surely make the walk worthwhile.

Find time too to see the outstanding *Museum of North Craven Life* in Chapel Place, just off the town centre. This contains excellent interpretative displays of Settle's history and many interesting exhibits, including prehistoric finds from nearby Victoria Cave.

*Suggested Walk* (Allow thirty-five minutes, plus another twenty minutes to ascend Castlebergh).
From the market post cross to the Naked Man Café – so called because of a little carved figurine set into the wall above a doorway. The man holds a carpenter's plane to preserve decency, and he is framed by a coffin and a chair. Dates 1663, this probably indicates it was a joiner's shop.

To the left of the Naked Man, between it and the chemist's, is an alleyway. Follow it through a typical Settle courtyard, with a shop and cottages. Continue through to Kirkgate. There is, in fact, no church in Kirkgate: Settle's early Victorian parish church is at the other end of town, but this road leads from the market-place to the ancient parish church of Giggleswick, which, before the present parish church was built in 1837, served Settle.

You are now opposite Dugdale's the ironmonger's, and in a court on the left is a cottage with the date stone 1664. This is a handloom weaver's cottage, one of many such in Settle. The house named Spread Eagle on the right was once a public house, whilst Settle's main public hall, the Victoria, lies ahead. At the side of the Spread Eagle a long, narrow alleyway, a 'ginnel', leads underneath railway arches to the top end of town and the parish church.

Return to the market-place, this time crossing to the town hall and going by Lambert's shop and the Georgian warehouse, now a shop, towards the Midland Bank, to the right of which is the Trustee Bank. This is the site of the saddler's shop where Edwin Waugh was born.

Turn left on Castle Street behind the bank, between tall buildings, climbing up the street to take the first turn right. Go along here and look for a doorway immediately past the chapel-like building on the left, arched with stone. Through the gate is a footpath which zigzags steeply uphill. This path leads to the summit of Castlebergh, an immense limestone crag jutting out two hundred feet above the town. It's a steep climb, recommended only for the sound in wind and limb, but it offers a superb view of the little town, stretched out below your feet like a great map, showing each road, alleyway and courtyard. Beyond is a magnificent panorama of hills, the splendid limestone scenery of Upper Ribblesdale, scarred by a major quarry, extending to your right.

Return to the road and continue left. This street is known as the Highway and was probably a rather more important thoroughfare before the present main road, the turnpike, was built in 1773. Look for an old milestone set in the walls on the right, and steps right, leading down by small horse troughs into another yard. This emerges by the Folly.

Cross into Chapel Street, almost directly ahead. Chapel Square, now the road leading into the car-park, was once intended to be Settle's canal basin when ambitious plans were drawn up to build an arm of the Leeds-Liverpool Canal to Settle.

Continue past the outdoor shop and police station (on the left) into Duke Street, its name probably a politened form of Duck Street, a wet and boggy lane before the turnpike road was built. Unless you are going to the station (left and first right), turn right back towards the market-place. Linton Court, opposite the Golden Lion, is another eighteenth-century yard with one of its buildings converted to an attractive exhibition centre, photographic and art gallery. A few yards ahead is the market-place.


## Skipton

You might regard Skipton as the last of the main Airedale towns, its close links with West Yorkshire reinforced by canal, railway and busy trunk road. You might also regard it as one of the last of the Lancashire cotton towns, looking south-west towards Barnoldswick and Earby. You might, too, see it as its roadsign declares it, as 'The Gateway to the Dales'. And you'd be right each time.

That's the particular fascination of Skipton. It always has been a crossroads, where Lancashire meets Yorkshire (say it quietly but there's a hint of Lancashire dialect in local speech), where town meets country. It's still Craven's major market town, the focal point of much Dales life.

Crossroads it was in ancient times, where the prehistoric trackways crossed over from Wharfedale. Significantly enough, its river, the Aire, has played virtually no part in the town's history; if Skiptonians think they have a river, they think of the volatile Eller Beck, prone to flashflood the town centre. But then the Aire was never navigable in this part of the Dale and didn't seem to be important for water power.

Sheep were more in Skipton's line, and the Anglian shepherds who kept a few herds on the nearby sweet pastures and limestone slopes gave the township its name and a tradition which flourishes, as a trip to Skipton auction mart any Monday will testify.

The town became a place of some consequence when Robert Clifford, the first Lord Clifford, acquired extensive estates in Craven, including the Romille lands in 1311, and set about building a massive fortress, making use of a steep natural cliff above Eller Beck. Though Clifford was killed only three years later at Bannockburn, later Cliffords, members of one of the most powerful dynasties in the land, developed this massive castle, built around seven virtually impregnable towers. in Elizabethan times the Cliffords were made earls of Cumberland, the third Earl (1558–1605) being a noble adventurer who distinguished himself against the Spanish Armada and for this reason was a favourite of Queen Elizabeth I. The last of the Cliffords, the indomitable Lady Anne (1590–1675), restored the castle after extensive Civil War damage from Cromwell's forces.

The castle, one of the finest and most complete medieval castles in northern England, is now in an excellent state of preservation, with banqueting-hall, dungeon, towers and the splendid conduit court, complete with ancient yew tree in its centre, and has few equals in England. It is open to the public daily.

The town which grew below the castle walls still focused on the broad High Street, from the old market-place to the castle gates, the venerable parish church, resting-place of several of the Cliffords, to its left, Along the High Street houses and the inns, with their characteristic long gardens or 'backs', still form the main shopping and market area, whilst the backs have been in-filled over the centuries with workshops, courtyards, even long terraces of working-class houses for the workforce of the new mills.

The new mills of the Industrial Revolution came to Skipton in 1773 with the extension of the Leeds-Liverpool Canal from

Keighley and Bingley, and the effect of the canal, perhaps even more than the railway in the 1840s, is evident in the growth of mills, warehouses along the canal embankment, an explosion of growth in the early and mid nineteenth century.

Skipton's growth as an industrial town is nowhere better epitomized than in the story of Dewhurst's mill on Broughton Road. Originally built in 1829 by John Dewhurst as a wool-worsted spinning and weaving shed, it was greatly enlarged and extended over the next fifty years and significantly switched to the manufacture of cotton, specializing in sewing-cotton. In its heyday the firm employed over eight hundred operatives, a substantial proportion of the Skipton labour force. By the 1890s Dewhurst's had combined with fourteen other firms to become English Sewing Cotton Co., nationally known as the manufacturers of 'Sylko' sewing threads. The enterprise developed throughout the new century but, almost inevitably, faced severe contraction in the 1980s, until the decision was taken to concentrate manufacture at plant elsewhere, and the Skipton plant was closed in 1984 with the loss of 140 jobs. A greetings-card manufacture has now taken over part of the mill premises.

Like many North Yorkshire towns, Skipton has managed to diversify to a considerable degree, with new light industries able to take up some of the shortfall of the traditional industries in an estate south of the town, which together with expanding service industries and tourism has kept the town relatively prosperous, its strategic position and attractive setting now making it a popular destination for day visitors.

*Suggested Walk* (Allow forty-five minutes, plus time to see the museum and church).

Begin at the bottom end of the High Street. This was the old market-place area, now a busy traffic island, and named Caroline Square after George IV's popular if ill-treated queen.

Walk up the left of the street, across stone setts, to the left of the free-standing block of shops. This is Sheep Street, the block of shops on the right known as Middle Row. Soon on the right you pass a small stone building up steps – this is the old town hall or tollbooth built on the site of Skipton's original moot hall or courthouse. Underneath were the town prison cells, one of which, at the end of Middle Row, is now a restaurant. Until 1862 the Court of Quarter Sessions was held here. Accounts of 1701 record the purchase of a new iron 'engine' for branding felons on the cheek – astonishing barbarism.

As you pass shops on the left, look for several narrow alleys (ginnels) leading into the 'backs'. One of the ginnels now leads to the town and District's fine new tourist office in a handsome, purpose-built stone and glass pavilion.

The cobbled area in front of the shops as you go up the street forms Skipton's market area, and any day but Sunday in Skipton the setts will be crowded with a variety of stalls – a greengrocer's, clothing, cakes, toys, tools, pottery, plants. The Yorkshire Bank on the left was once the Bay Horse Inn with a bull-baiting ring on the forecourt; then there are the offices of the *Craven Herald,* Skipton and Craven's famous old newspaper, one of the few in the country with the courage of its convictions to carry advertisements on the front page and with a wealth of detailed coverage of local events inside, a fine example of a community newspaper. The imposing statue of Sir Matthew Wilson, Skipton's first MP stands opposite the Victorian library and former Mechanics' Institute (now part of the Craven College), whilst the Black Horse, a fine old rambling inn, claims to be on the site of the royal mews of Richard III when that monarch was Lord of the Honour of Skipton.

Bear left along the Gargrave road, past the pie shop and over the canal bridge, going sharp left down narrow, winding stone steps at the end of the bridge to the towpath. This is the Spring branch of the canal. Turn left again under the road bridge to find yourself on a narrow walkway between canal and stream (Eller Beck) which goes past a pleasantly landscaped area, behind the old Skipton corn mill, now a museum, and the great cliff topped by the castle walls. This is an impressive corner of Skipton, the dizzy height of the castle walls, its narrow windows and even privies giving a vivid impression of impregnability. The canal was built to serve Skipton rock quarry as a branch from the Leeds-Liverpool Canal, the stone lowered by incline railway to fill waiting barges.

This path continues along the towpath, parallel to the Eller Beck and the millrace leading to the old corn mill. Follow it up to where it enters the lane. If you turn right, you soon reach the entrance to Skipton Woods, a delightful area of woods and lakes, open every afternoon from 2 p.m. (thirty minutes walk). Otherwise turn left downhill, past the Corn Mill Museum (open most afternoons) to Chapel Hill, where in 1764 John Wesley preached. His associations with Skipton might have been even closer in 1747 when he sought, without success, to become the master of Skipton's grammar school.

Go left in the main road, back up to the High Street past the Castle Inn, but up steps and through a gateway into Skipton churchyard. The church itself dates largely from the fourteenth century, when its living was owned by the canons of Bolton Priory; it was enlarged in the fifteenth century, damaged and restored in the seventeenth and more generally restored in the nineteenth. It is particularly noteworthy for its fine oak roof and the tombs of the Earls of Cumberland.

From the churchyard, keep left across the churchyard to the entrance to the castle, and the majestic twin towers of the gateway carrying the motto *'Desormais'* – 'Henceforth' – across the entrance. Notices outside confirm opening times.

Cross the road here, taking care with fast-moving traffic. The lovely eighteenth-century house opposite is 'The Bailey', formerly the home of Henry Alcock, one of the early partners of Skipton's Craven Bank (now Barclay's) and now a solicitor's. Continue back down the High Street to the handsome, neo-classical town hall, built in 1862 and elegantly proportioned, its balcony a familiar feature of general elections as results are announced there. As well as being District Council offices and meeting-rooms, including an excellent public hall, the first floor houses the Craven Museum, a major collection of material about the Yorkshire Dales, including any important lead-mining relics. The museum is open daily except for Tuesdays and winter Sundays.

Return to the High Street, again passing market areas and shops. Opposite Barclay's Bank once stood the town pillory and the old market cross, whilst in rooms occupied by Ledgard & Winn's store the great Edmund Kean and Harriet Mellon, later the Duchess of St Albans, began their respective theatrical careers with Tom Airey's barnstorming players. It's worth wandering into Craven Court, an alleyway next to Ledgard & Winn's, which has been cleverly restored and incorporated into the store.

Go down the alleyway known as Providence Place by the Skipton Building Society. This passes the Building Society's new offices. The Skipton and District Permanent Benefits Society began life in 1853 and is now, as the Skipton Building Society, the largest in North Yorkshire with assets exceeding £300 million and over fifty branches. It is a major local employer.

Providence Place leads into Court Lane. Turn right here, into Newmarket, where once an overflow from Skipton's market came, now a busy traffic artery. Cross Newmarket into the little alleyway, the Ginnel, by the newsagent's shop. This leads to the little Quaker meeting-house of 1693, a plain, simple building in a quiet garden. Turn right through a pleasant green area, attractively landscaped through the inspiration and energy of Skipton Civic Trust, to cross the wooden footbridge, built with the help of local secondary school children. Notice the steep terraces of housing above, densely populated, amazingly steep streets built in the mid nineteenth century for Skipton's growing working population. The Ginnel Walk emerges in Devonshire Place, a workshop and garage area.

Cross the main Keighley road ahead, soon bearing left into the Waller Hill bus station, opposite the new Co-operative store. Cross to the car-park, bearing left to the footbridge over the canal. Go sharp left over the bridge onto the canal towpath, this the main Leeds-Liverpool Canal and forming part of what is now a popular marina. Left along the towpath now, but take the next flight of stone steps up to Swadford Street, going right over Belmont Bridge but first left into Coach Street. Note the interesting conversions of canal warehouses on the left to outdoors centres and restaurants.

Go ahead to Canal Bridge, where the Springs Branch comes into the town centre. Don't cross the bridge but bear right by the Royal Shepherd Inn along Canal Street. The third turning right, Hallam's Yard, leads past a long, narrow terraced row, through the backs. At the end there is a little workshop and courtyard. Go through the archway and you are back in Sheep Street. Go right into the old market-place, though you may well want to explore the interesting new development around the tourist office, right.

## Stokesley

As you turn the corner to enter Stokesley's extended High Street, it's like stepping back a couple of centuries, to the time of George III. As long ago as 1812 a traveller was able to contrast the peace and quiet with the clamour of nearby Teesside and declare that Stokesley was 'a place well adapted to retirement'. Things haven't changed much to change that opinion. Stokesley has dignity and grace, so very close both to the escarpments of the Cleveland Hills and to the industrial complexes of Cleveland that you can't imagine it has survived unspoiled, an old market town in the fertile countryside of the Vale of Cleveland.

The long main street broadens to contain the market-place but with several groups of free-standing buildings to break up the symmetry and with the softening effect of village greens at the western end. The shape of the little town may well have been defensive – creating a long, linear stockade into which cattle could be herded at those not infrequent times of Scottish raids.

All along the High Street and around the market-place are tall houses, old inns, shops and banks, all giving a surprising unity to the old town. The Saturday market no longer takes place, having been overtaken by competition from Teesside, but the medieval fair survives in the form of the annual September Stokesley Show, one of the most popular events in the Cleveland calendar; in many respects it fulfils a not dissimilar purpose to the medieval event.

The fourteenth-century church has enjoyed its footnotes in history. In 1405 Archbishop Scrope of York impeached King Henry IV as a murderer and usurper and nailed a proclamation on Stokesley church door urging rebellion. The rebellion failed, and the Archbishop paid with his head, but it provided Shakespeare with the theme of one of his greatest history plays. The church tower was used as an armoury in 1588 when England was threatened by invasion by the Spanish Armada, and in 1643 the rector's father organized resistance to Cromwell's army advancing from Helmsley, resistance which must have proved fairly ineffective for the old man was fortunate enough to escape with a fine.

Between 1771 and 1777 Stokesley church was transformed into what it is now, a Georgian church with square nave.

The old manor house next to the church was possibly once fortified, being referred to as 'Stokesley Castle' in times past, and with the remnants of what may have been a moat between it and the church. The present building, now the library and court house, is mid eighteenth century, with handsome gateposts brought from a demolished house nearby.

*Suggested Walk* (Allow thirty minutes).
Stokesley is well supplied with useful wall plaques to guide the visitor. Begin at the town hall, in the centre of the High Street, built in 1853 to replace the old town tollbooth. There's a particularly fine row of houses and inns to the right as you look eastwards towards the manor house, including the Golden Lion, an impressive old coaching inn, and the bow-windowed Midland Bank.

Walk across to the Shambles, opposite the town hall, now an unromantic if functional toilet block, where the old meat market used to be. An area of cobbles between the town hall and the Shambles is where, the plaque informs you, once stood the market cross, and a pattern of squares in the cobbles indicates where the cross stood. Better to have kept the cross.

Cross the road to the opposite side of the High Street. Barclay's Bank occupies an attractive house (why do banks always manage to claim the best houses, one wonders) once belonging to a Dr Yeoman. Turn left and walk towards West Green ahead, past more pleasant eighteenth – or early nineteenth-century houses, with the occasional court, one aptly named Paradise Place.

A cobbled path across the green leads to the town war memorial and the narrower neck of the High Street at the town's West End. There are more period cottages – note the date stone 1770 in the terrace ahead, and the Spread Eagle Inn.

From the end of the town, return left, but fork into a narrow street, Levenside right which follows the little River Leven around the back of the town. This is a beautiful little area, reminiscent of Holland, all river, green, cottages and trees, crossed by footbridges. At one point parallel rows of almost identical cottages create the effect of a little square. Cross the first footbridge to the far side, past the cottages and old mill; an attractive cottage lies ahead with the date stone 1716 and initials

K. and A. H. Cross the elegant, stone footbridge back into the town, a lovely packhorse-style bridge, unfortunately disfigured by an unsightly iron pipe. This leads along a cobbled alleyway into the market-place.

Continue, this time walking towards the manor house, bearing right along the signposted path towards the church and River Leven, taking time to explore this slightly unusual but attractive church.

Return to the footpath and make for the River Leven, crossing the wooden footbridge to the far side. A wall-side plaque will inform you that the avenue of trees here was planted in 1964–5 to commemorate Miss S. Henty, who was born in Stokesley on 8 February 1817 and became the first white woman to settle permanently in the State of Victoria, Australia, in 1836. It hardly seems possible that a whole new nation could develop in such a short time-span, well after Georgian Stokesley had taken its present form.

Follow the tree-lined riverside walk to the end of East Bridge, turning left past the garage back towards the town, noting as you do the fine panoramas of the Cleveland Hills above and behind the town.

At the junction, it's worth going a short way along Springfield Road, right to where, almost opposite the New Tavern, the town's pinfold survives. This was a small compound used for rounding up stray animals until their owner came to collect them, usually upon payment of a small fine. It is rare to see one so perfectly preserved.

But return to the junction and into the top end of the High Street, here known as College Square, presumably taking its name from the little grammar school, all Gothic mock castellation and pointed windows, founded by John Preston in 1805, the town's first grammar school. It stands in the centre of College Square, in an unusual island of buildings, rooms and offices.

Enjoy more pleasant late Georgian or Regency houses around the square to the right. On the far side of the island group is a particularly handsome Regency house, with balconies, now a solicitor's office.

Cross to the town hall ahead.

**Tadcaster**

Two breweries named Smith dominate Tadcaster. You notice it the very moment you get out of the car or bus, a sweet, not unpleasant smell of hops, most noticeable if the air's still or damp.

John Smith's is the bigger of the two Smiths, the tall, cream stone, iron-ringed chimney and high-gabled brewery roof soaring above the town like a medieval castle, the wrought-iron gates proclaiming the Tadcaster Brewery, newer neon signs proclaiming Magnet Ales.

Samuel Smith's brewery, separated from John Smith by a mere stone's throw across New Street, conceals its activity behind an elegant nineteenth-century façade in the High Street, looking more like a fine old country hotel, Old Brewery. Sam Smith's tall black chimney isn't as high as John Smith's, but it gazes defiantly across at its neighbour.

To a degree, Sam Smith stole a march on the upstart John Smith with his Old Brewery Bitter, a real old ale as the pub window flashers tell you, 'drawn from a wooden cask' and soon attracting followers of the Campaign for Real Ale at a time when John Smith's was dismissed as carbonated fizz for the mass market. Undeterred, John Smith struck back with a version of hand-drawn 'real' ale to bend to consumer demand. However, it is certain that devotees of each particular brew will be difficult to dissuade; no doubt, if you live in Tadcaster, loyalties die hard.

It's the hard water from the Magnesian Limestone springs – that lovely creamy rock again – that have made Tadcaster the home of brewers since monastic times, and the monks, with somewhat gargantuan appetite for good old ale, were no doubt shrewd judges. A third, even larger brewery, Bass Charrington, lies just outside town.

Your view of Tadcaster's contribution to the human condition will perhaps depend on whether you take a Falstaffian or a Calvinistic view of life. No doubt as much human happiness as misery has been caused by Tadcaster's fermented waters, but it seems no coincidence that the Methodist chapel, grim-faced and stern, was opened on the opposite side of the High Street to the two breweries, in 1828. As you walk along Tadcaster's High Street there's opportunity enough to sample, and perhaps even compare, the product of the area, for some fine old inns, such as the Bay Horse, the White Swan and the curiously named Angel and White Horse, the latter with a plaster angel as an inn sign, are there to tempt all but the strong-willed.

The High Street, which continues across to the River Wharfe as Bridge Street, is as pleasant an old coaching-town street as you'll see anywhere in North Yorkshire, with several eighteenth- and nineteenth-century shops, many with bow-fronted windows, of mellow brick and creamy limestone, with solid Welsh slate and red-pantiled roofs. Wharfe Bank Terrace, which stretches along each side of Bridge Street, above the river, is a particularly attractive area of houses, shops and workshops, with a through passage upstream to the church and downstream to a footpath through a long avenue of tall poplars. There's a fine view from this embankment back up to the bridge, an eighteenth-century structure said to have been built from stones in the Norman motte-and-bailey castle near the church or perhaps even from the little Roman garrison, situated here at Calcaria, to guard this important crossing-point on the Roman road to York.

*Suggested Walk* (Allow thirty minutes, plus time to see Ark Museum and church).
From the High Street, turn down Kirkgate, soon reaching the Ark Museum on the left (opening times uncertain at time of writing). This little half-timbered house on a stone base dates from the second part of the fifteenth century and was probably a merchant's house. Two heads carved on the sixteenth-century timber at the front were nicknamed 'Mr and Mrs Noah' – hence the name 'Ark House'.

In the seventeenth century the house was owned by one Robert Morley, Tadcaster's first postmaster, and in due course Morley House, as it was known, became a meeting-room for Dissenters. In later years it was divided into two, one part being a dwelling-house, a butcher's shop, a joiner's shop, finally a dwelling house again. The other part became the Falcon Inn and finally a betting shop. During alterations in the 1960s, the age of the building and its importance were discovered, and it has been carefully restored. It is now owned by John Smith's, who for a number of years have kept a small museum in the building, specializing in the history of brewing, with a fascinating range of beer pumps and brewers' apparatus and a fifteenth-century church piscina, together with photographs and memorabilia of great local interest.

Continue along Kirkgate to the church of St Mary's. This church dates mainly from the Perpendicular period, in the fifteenth century, though with some Norman work. In 1875–8 it was painstakingly taken down, stone by stone, and rebuilt on higher land, to take it away from the floodwaters of the Wharfe. There are some fine stained-glass windows, with fifteenth- and sixteenth-century fragments, and examples from the workshop of William Morris. Externally there are some interesting details including well-weathered gargoyles.

Leave the church and follow the footpath to the riverside, and walk along the path up river. Ahead is the town weir, the Wharfe broad and impressive. It was from local quarries, Jackdaw Quarry and Thieves Quarry, that stone was brought and put on barges for York and the building of the Minster and the medieval walls.

Directly ahead is an imposing railway viaduct.

Amazingly, this fine structure never carried a train. It was built in 1846 by 'Railway King' George Hudson, of York, during the years of the railway mania, its purpose to carry a new direct line from York to Leeds via Tadcaster. The financial crash that came before the line was built left the bridge here, with no railway over it, and Tadcaster remained on a meandering branch line between Church Fenton and Wetherby, which closed in 1965, an early victim of the Beeching axe. Had the line been built, it would have shortened the journey time between Leeds and York and placed Tadcaster firmly on the railway map.

To follow the viaduct walk across the river and follow the sign at the viaduct left to a staircase leading onto the viaduct. In the centre a wooden viewing-platform gives a fine view of the river and the old town. You can return by the opposite side of the bridge, following the path along the far embankment, soon bearing away from the river past a Victorian merchant's house – note the glass and iron lean-to of some period charm – before going past warehouses to rejoin the main road at the far side of Tadcaster Bridge.

## Thirsk

Should you approach Thirsk from the north-west (leaving the A168 Northallerton road to come into the town on the B1448 which suddenly sweeps round the corner to pass below the glorious parish church, and into the town itself, by Thirsk Hall and into Kirkgate, all brick and pantile, mellow, glowing in sunlight), you have a sudden vision of what would have been if there'd been no motor cars and ribbon development and semi-detached suburbia.

Spared much of its thundering heavy traffic when the bypass on the A19 was opened a few years ago, Thirsk really is a town worth exploring. It has the advantage of a fine setting. Just to the east is the uplift of the North York Moors escarpments, the Hambleton Hills, for a rich green backcloth guaranteed to make any red-pantiled roof seem a richer shade of vermilion.

That great market-place, with its polished cobbles, is an immediate reminder of Thirsk's importance as a coaching town, with two old and famous coaching inns, the Three Tuns and the Fleece, a direct link with the stage-coach era.

The town remains an important market centre serving a wide catchment, whilst its racecourse, close to the town centre, holds an important place in the racing calendar. Like Northallerton, Thirsk has kept its railway station on the East Coast Main Line; this is, however, more than a mile from the town centre. Thirsk once had a station on the old Leeds-Thirsk railway which closed, first for passengers and finally for freight, many years ago and is commemorated only by the name Railway Terrace opposite the end of Westgate.

A certain literary vet, writing under the pseudonym 'James Herriot', has given the town new fame. The curious can discover in Kirkgate the actual surgery (not that portrayed on television), where the practice continues to flourish, no doubt with as rich an assortment of characters, both human and non-human, as Mr Herriot has made famous.

Thirsk is really two townships, Old Thirsk, a settlement around an extended village green, to the east of Cod Beck, the little tributary of the River Swale which flows through the town, and New Thirsk, around the market-place and the parish church, where most of the commercial development has taken place, and indeed is still taking place. New light industrial estates between the town and the railway are bringing welcome new jobs and economic growth to the area.

The church is by common consent, the finest parish church in North Yorkshire, a magnificent, largely Perpendicular building, built between 1430 and the beginning of the sixteenth century. Its situation on a raised eminence above willow-lined streams gives it a proper sense of drama for soaring tower, aisles and clerestory, all richly decorated. There are splendid details to enjoy, including fiercesome gargoyles and stone heads on the exterior, interesting stained glass, a seventeenth-century wall painting and a superb ceiling.

*Suggested Walk* (Allow thirty minutes, plus time to see church and museum).

Begin at Thirsk's famous clock in the market-place, erected in 1896 to commemorate the marriage of the Duke of York to Her Serene Highness Princess Mary of Teck.

The market-place has an air of importance, several three – and even four-storey buildings giving a feeling of significance. It's worth following the signposted footpath that runs alongside the Fleece Inn for a few yards just to see the extent of the stables, even where they've been partially demolished for car-parking, emphasizing the activity in stage-coach days.

Leave the market-place along the Northallerton road, Kirkgate. Part of the delight of this road is the different heights of the roofs, giving contrast and interest.

On the right you soon reach the town's little museum and tourist office. Because it is manned by volunteers, opening times are limited: mainly weekend afternoons and during the main holiday period. It contains a good range of local exhibits, including some James Herriot material (and why not?) and well-researched literature on Thirsk and its environs, as well as the usual tourist information material.

A plaque on the outside wall will tell you that Thomas Lord was born here – a name famous well outside Thirsk as the man who founded Lord's cricket ground. Born in Thirsk in 1755, he established the first cricket ground at Marylebone, London, in 1787, hence the famous Marylebone Cricket Club (MCC) synonymous with English cricket. The site was moved to Regent's

Park in 1811 and subsequently to St John's Wood in 1814.

Continue, past the famous vet's surgery on the left, to Thirsk Hall, an early Georgian house extended and enlarged between 1771 and 1773, by John Carr the York architect.

The parish church lies ahead. Leave the church by the steps from the porch to the left, crossing the road and following the sign to the car-park but veering off left along a footpath which runs alongside Cod Beck. This is a lovely area with mature willow trees hanging over grassy banks which, in spring, are covered with wild flowers, the church soon vanishing from sight behind leaves.

Ahead is a metal footbridge. Cross, and you find yourself in Old Thirsk. Pass cottages ahead and bear right onto an extended green, known as St James' Green in its central portion, a broad, attractive area of grassland.

Cross the main road out of Thirsk and keep in the same direction, past more cottages, an open section with new development ahead, but keeping past some pleasant, early nineteenth-century cottages on the right. Follow the footpath sign now (Thirsk's town footpaths are singularly well marked) which leads to a lovely riverside path. Turn right as you reach the road at the fine eighteenth-century stone bridge, noting the 1866 Salem Chapel, sadly derelict, ahead. As you wind along Finkle Street back into the market-place, you pass a cluster of rather charming old shops on the corner, and the Old Three Tuns on the right – not to be confused with the handsome Queen Anne coaching-house in the market-place, but a much older, slightly gnarled and characterful country pub.

Back in the market-place take time to explore one or two alleyways and ginnels on the north side, perhaps the one just to the right of the Red Bear Inn which has a little court complete with old pump. These lead into the Gillings Court re-development area, where several of the older and semi-derelict buildings have been demolished, but housing development replacing it is sympathetic in scale, style and materials.

If you've time (another thirty minutes) for a little countryside and riverside walk along the Cod Beck, take the path alongside the Fleece Inn again, this time bearing slightly left to pick up the continuation of the path along Villa Place. This emerges at the town's new swimming-pool, to the left of which are a grassy slope and stile leading to a riverside footpath by the Cod Beck. Follow the riverside path for about half a mile to a concrete bridge, known as Lock Bridge, maybe having some connection with plans to turn Cod Beck into a navigation from the River Swale. Don't turn left back along the river but bear right to cross the white wooden footbridge ahead. Once across, turn sharp left by a thick hedgerow, heading for kissing-gates and a path by arable fields emerging at the stone bridge, by the garage, on Finkle Street. There are lovely views from this walk, westwards to the Pennines, eastwards to the Moors, meadow, hedgerow and riverside.

# Index